C000229836

Medieval Realms

for Common Entrance
and Key Stage 3
Second edition

MARTIN COLLIER
ROSEMARY REES
COLIN SHEPHARD

HODDER
EDUCATION
AN HACHETTE UK COMPANY

Also available: *The Making of the UK for Common Entrance and Key Stage 3* second edition ISBN 9781471808685

The authors and publisher would like to thank Bob Pace of Belmont School, Mill Hill, and Niall Murphy of Radley College, Abingdon, for their valuable feedback.

Note: The wording and structure of some written sources have been adapted and simplified to make them accessible to all pupils, while faithfully preserving the sense of the original.

Words printed in small capitals (first mention only) are defined in the glossary on page 186.

Although every effort has been made to ensure that website addresses are correct at time of going to press, Hodder Education cannot be held responsible for the content of any website mentioned in this book. It is sometimes possible to find a relocated web page by typing in the address of the home page for a website in the URL window of your browser.

Hachette UK's policy is to use papers that are natural, renewable and recyclable products and made from wood grown in sustainable forests. The logging and manufacturing processes are expected to conform to the environmental regulations of the country of origin.

Orders: please contact Bookpoint Ltd, 130 Milton Park, Abingdon, Oxon OX14 4SB. Telephone: +44 (0)1235 827720. Fax: +44 (0)1235 400454. Lines are open 9.00a.m.– 5.00p.m., Monday to Saturday, with a 24-hour message answering service. Visit our website at www.hoddereducation.co.uk

Text acknowledgements

p.13 Rebecca Fraser, *A People's History of Britain*, Chatto and Windus 2003, adapted from p.84; **p.25** Toby Purser, *Medieval England 1042–1228*, Heinemann 2004, adapted from p.39; **p.36** Ben Johnson, *Historic UK*, an internet journal, 2013; **p.43** *B* Roger of Wendover, *Flowers of History,* translated by J.A. Giles (London: Henry G. Born, 1849), Vol. II, pp.308–9, *C* Chris Trueman, www.historylearningsite.co.uk/index.htm; **p.49** Judith Kidd and Linda Richards, *Power and the People 1066–1485*, Heinemann 2002, p.67; **p.64** M H Keen, *England in the Later Middle Ages*, Methuen 1973, p.272; **p.67** Ian Dawson, www.historylearning.co.uk; **p.69** A R Myers, *England in the Late Middle Ages*, Penguin 1976, adapted from p.30; **p.87** Charles Ross, *Richard III*, University of California Press 1981, p.80; **p.88** Michael Hicks, *Richard III*, Tempus Publishing Limited 2000, p.195–6; **p.95** *G* Philip Lindsay, article in *Argosy*, 1972; **p.96** H Paul Kendall *Richard III* Allen and Unwin, 1955; **p.97** *C* Keith Dockray, *Richard III A Source Book*, Sutton Publishing 1997, p.76; **p.103** John Guy, *Thomas Becket*, Viking 2012, adapted from pp.318–21; **p.111** Tony McAleavy, *Life in a Medieval Abbey*, English Heritage 1996, p.14; **p.127** Adapted from J. Sumption, *Pilgrimage: an Image of Medieval Religion*, London in 1975, quoted in Nigel Saul, *A Companion to Medieval England 1066–1485*, Tempus 2005 p.226; **p.131** Terry Jones and Alan Ereira, *Crusades*, Penguin 1996, adapted from pp.52–3; **pp.139 & 144** Frances and Joseph Giles, *Life in a Medieval Village*, Harper and Row 1990 p.206 & p.200; **p.151** Edward Miller and John Hatcher, *Medieval England: Towns, Commerce and Crafts 1086–1348* page 390 published Longman in 1995; **p.155** Judith Kidd and Linda Richards, *Power and the People 1066–1485*, Heinemann 2002, p.229; **p.165** Allan Todd, *Crime, Punishment and Protest*, CUP 2002, p.31; **p.169** Allan Todd and Martyn Whittock, *Crime and Protest*, Pearson 2009, p.4; **p.170** Ian Dawson, *Crime and Punishment through Time*, John Murray 1999, p.52; **p.172** Ian Mortimer, *The Time Traveller's Guide to Medieval England*, The Bodley Head 2009, p.48; **p.173** Adams, Bartley, Bourdillon and Loxton, *From Workshop to Warfare: the lives of medieval women*, CUP 1983, p.5; **p.180** *C* Adapted from Toby Purser, *Medieval England 1042–1228*, Heinemann 2004, p.34; **p.181** *B* Philip Sauvain *Old World*, Stanley Thornes, 1991; **p.182** *B* Adapted from Collier and Rees, *History in Progress 1066–1603*, Heinemann 2008, p.22; **p.183** *C* Hadyn Middleton and Henrietta Leyser, *Invasion and Integration*, OUP 1986; **p.184** *C* Adapted from Collier and Rees, *History in Progress 1066–1603*, Heinemann 2008, p.95; **p.185** *C* Philip Lindsay, article in *Argosy*, 1972.

© Martin Collier, Rosemary Rees, Colin Shephard 2007, 2014

First published in 2007

This second edition published 2014 by

Hodder Education
An Hachette UK Company
Carmelite House, 50 Victoria Embankment
London EC4Y 0DZ

Impression number	10 9 8 7 6 5 4
Year	2018 2017 2016

All rights reserved. Apart from any use permitted under UK copyright law, no part of this publication may be reproduced or transmitted in any form or by any means, electronic or mechanical, including photocopying and recording, or held within any information storage and retrieval system, without permission in writing from the publisher or under licence from the Copyright Licensing Agency Limited. Further details of such licences (for reprographic reproduction) may be obtained from the Copyright Licensing Agency Limited, Saffron House, 6–10 Kirby Street, London EC1N 8TS.

Cover photo © The British Library Board (MS Royal 16 G. VI f.360)

Illustrations by Tony Jones/Art Construction, Janek Matysiak, Edward Ripley, Steve Smith

Typeset in 12pt ITC Officina Book by DC Graphic Design Limited

Printed in Italy

A catalogue record for this title is available from the British Library

ISBN 9781471808715

CONTENTS

HOW TO USE THIS BOOK

This book is divided into three overlapping sections. Each one covers the whole period 1066–1485 but from different perspectives.

SECTION 1 GOOD AND BAD MONARCHS

Section 1 covers political history. It introduces you to the **monarchs** who ruled between 1066 and 1485: the good, the bad and the in-between. It works chronologically through the entire period, beginning with William I and ending with Richard III.

SECTION 2 RELIGION IN THE MIDDLE AGES

Section 2 overlaps with the first, and looks at the importance of **religion** through medieval times.

SECTION 3 HOW DID ORDINARY PEOPLE LIVE?

Section 3 covers social history. It explores the same period as Sections 1 and 2 but through the **lives of ordinary people**.

You could work straight through the book – we have written it to work that way – or you could mix and match by slotting Units from Sections 2 and 3 into the chronological survey in Section 1. The chart on the opposite page shows where Units 9–17 fit into the Section 1 chronology.

Use the tasks!

 The Tasks have been provided specifically to guide your reading of the text. Some of them like this are steps on the way to the **Summary task** which comes at the end of most units.

Examine the sources!

Sources are the raw material of history. Without sources we simply would not be able to find out about the past.

- In the source captions for many sources you will find **questions** labelled like this ❓ that encourage you to look closely at, or think about the sources.
- There are also **Source Investigations** on particular topics.
- **Practice Evidence Questions** on pages 180–185 include sources as on a Common Entrance examination paper.

Monarch	Nickname	Notable events	Dates	Age at death	Cause of death	Pages
Norman						
William I	the Conqueror	Conquered England/Battle of Hastings	1066–87	59	Riding accident	10–31
William II	Rufus	First Crusade	1087–1100	40	Hunting accident (or was it?)	32
Henry I		Brought peace and stability to England	1100–35	67	Natural causes	32
Stephen		Civil War, chaos. Cousin Matilda took over 1141–42 while he was in prison	1135–54	58	Natural causes	33–36
Angevin						
Henry II	Curtmantle	Murder of Thomas Becket	1154–89	56	Hounded to death by son	37
Richard I	the Lionheart	The Third Crusade	1189–99	42	Shot by an arrow (bolt-wound went septic)	37
John	Lackland or Softsword	Magna Carta	1199–1216	49	Dysentery	38–43
Plantagenet						
Henry III		First 'Parliament'	1216–72	65	Natural causes	44–47
Edward I	Longshanks	Conquered Wales. Castle builder	1272–1307	68	Died in battle	48–57
Edward II			1307–27	43	Probably murdered	60
Edward III		Started Hundred Years' War with France	1327–77	65	Natural causes	60–61
Richard II		The Black Death / The Peasants' Revolt	1377–99	32	Probably murdered or may have starved himself to death while in prison	62–69
Lancaster						
Henry IV	Bolingbroke		1399–1413	47	Got leprosy. Son took over before he died of natural causes	68
Henry V		Battle of Agincourt	1413–22	35	Dysentery	70–77
Henry VI			1422–61	50	Went mad. Murdered	78–79
York						
Edward IV			1461–83	40	Died suddenly of natural causes	79
Edward V	One of 'The Princes in the Tower'		April–June 1483	12	Possibly murdered by his uncle	93–96
Richard III		Battle of Bosworth	1483–85	32	Killed in battle by Henry Tudor's army	80–97

▼ Units 9, 10, 11 & 12

▼ Unit 13

▼ Units 14 & 15

▼ Units 16 & 17

If you go to www.hodderplus.co.uk you can get a copy of this chart that you can customise, plus lots of ideas for how to revise the content.

Evaluating sources

Evaluating a source means deciding how far you can trust it. If an historian found a new source that suggested something unusual about a topic they had already studied, they would not take it at face value. They would ask 'Do I trust it?' They would find out more about the source. They would evaluate it.

Evaluating sources is a skill you need to acquire for Common Entrance but it is also a skill you need to acquire in order to become a good historian.

The 5W test

A useful set of questions to help you evaluate a source is the 5W test: Who, Where, When, What, Why? (see below)

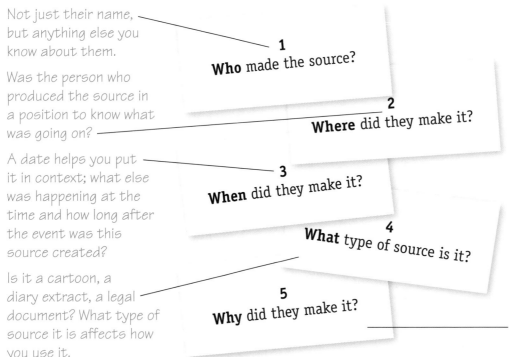

Not just their name, but anything else you know about them.

Was the person who produced the source in a position to know what was going on?

A date helps you put it in context; what else was happening at the time and how long after the event was this source created?

Is it a cartoon, a diary extract, a legal document? What type of source it is affects how you use it.

1 Who made the source?

2 Where did they make it?

3 When did they make it?

4 What type of source is it?

5 Why did they make it?

Some sources, such as a census, usually set out to tell the truth; others, like cartoons, set out to distort it.
Some sources, such as a diary or a letter, were written to be private; others, such as a newspaper, were written to be read by anybody.
Is the author/artist trying to inform or persuade someone?
Is he/she trying to make things look good or bad?

The first place to look for information about a source is in the caption called **the attribution**. Sometimes you will have quite a lot of information about a source, sometimes more sparse. The more information you have about a source, the easier the evaluation.

Behind each question lies **the importance of your background knowledge**. The more you know about a period or an event or a topic the easier you will find it to evaluate sources. What else do you know about this person, this period, this place, this event, this audience? How does the source match up to or challenge what you already know? What other sources have you seen from this period? Does this source agree or disagree with them?

These questions together will help you to decide **whether you trust this source** to tell you the truth. Only when you have worked out how reliable a source is as evidence will you be able to come to any decisions about how useful it is likely to be for the enquiry you are following. But remember:

1 Respect sources. Don't fall into the trap of believing that all sources are one-sided so they can't be trusted. This is silly. Sources are all we have – but we use them thoughtfully.

2 **Even unreliable sources are useful** as evidence of, for example, what a person thought about an event. Their report of the event may be one-sided, but that in itself provides useful evidence of their attitudes.

Example 1: A visual source

Now let's see how the 5Ws work with a source you are going to meet later on – the Bayeux Tapestry. (See Source 5 on page 20.)

1
Who made the source?

Most historians agree that Bishop Odo, the half-brother of William the Conqueror, ordered it to be made. He took part in the Battle of Hastings. Bishop Odo didn't actually make the source himself. He would, however, have told those who did make it what it should show.

2
Where did they make it?

Odo did not make it himself. As to who actually did, we are not sure. Most historians think it was created by English embroiderers, working in the famous embroidery works at Winchester. Some French historians say it was made in Normandy.

3
When did they make it?

It was probably ordered in 1070 and made some time afterwards.

4
What type of source is it?

Although it is called a tapestry, it isn't one. A tapestry is woven. This is an embroidery, made by stitching coloured wools on to linen.

5
Why did they make it?

It was produced to tell the story of the Norman conquest of England. As it was ordered by a Norman and the Normans won at Hastings, it would be reasonable to assume that it tells the story from the Norman viewpoint.

So we have a source telling the story of the Battle of Hastings, which was produced at least four years after the battle on the orders of a close relative of the winner, who was there at the time. Just how reliable, then, would you judge the source to be as evidence of what happened at the battle?

Cross-referencing

It is time to check the source against other sources – which we call **cross-referencing**. It would be sensible to find an English point of view. The main source for English history at this time is the *Anglo-Saxon Chronicle*. Unfortunately there is only one entry in it that actually mentions the Norman invasion:

Source Ⓐ

William the earl landed at Hastings on St Michael's Day; and Harold came from the north, and fought against him before all his army had come up; and there he fell, and his two brothers, Girth and Leofwin; and William subdued this land.

This is no help with the detail of the actual battle. The tapestry is the only source we have about what happened at Hastings.

Unwitting testimony

Although we doubt the reliability of its story of the battle, the Tapestry does give us reliable evidence about other aspects of the time. For example:

- Some Normans fought wearing chain-mail armour and metal helmets with nose-pieces.
- Some Normans fought on horseback.
- Some Saxons fought with spears and swords.
- Some Saxons only had shields for protection and no body armour.
- The materials used give us reliable evidence of the cloth and dyes that were available at the time.

Historians call this **unwitting testimony** because the evidence is unintentional. Such testimony is, therefore, likely to be reliable.

Conclusion

By now you will have realised that the Bayeux Tapestry is reliable evidence in parts. It is reliable if you want to know about Norman and Saxon arms and armour, or about embroidery materials. But it is not very reliable as evidence of the events that led to William's victory at Hastings. But, and this is a very big but, it is the only evidence we have for the battle itself, and so we have to use it, but carefully!

Example 2: a written source

Here is a source you will use on page 94.

Source **B**

After his coronation in July 1483, King Richard decided he must kill his nephews. This was because as long as they were alive, people would not think him the true king. He wrote to Sir Robert Brackenbury, the Constable of the Tower, asking him to put the children to death. Sir Robert refused. Then his page suggested Sir James Tyrell. Tyrell agreed, and Richard sent him to Brackenbury with a letter commanding Sir Robert to deliver up the keys of the Tower to Tyrell for one night. Tyrell decided that the Princes should be murdered in their beds the next night. He chose Miles Forest and John Dighton to do the job. Forest was one of the princes' guards and had murdered others. The two men pressed feather beds and pillows on the children's faces until they stopped breathing.

An extract from *The History of King Richard III* written in 1513 by Thomas More.

This seems to be quite a straightforward story. But is it? Let's try the 5W test.

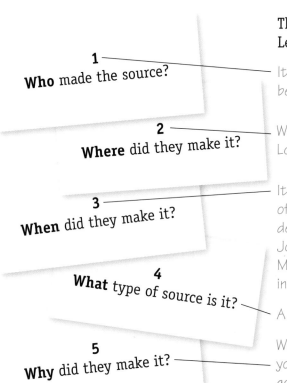

1 Who made the source?

It was written by Sir Thomas More. More was a lawyer who became Henry VIII's chancellor in 1529.

2 Where did they make it?

We don't know where he wrote it but it was published in London.

3 When did they make it?

It was published in about 1513 when More was undersheriff of London. More was five years old when the events he described happened. He got most of his information from John Morton, who was one of King Richard's enemies. Morton was one of the people who invited Henry Tudor to invade England and become king in Richard's place.

4 What type of source is it?

A book.

5 Why did they make it?

We have to do a bit of guess-work here. Reading the extract you can see that More does not show King Richard in a good light. More got his information from an opponent of Richard and was working for Henry VIII, Henry Tudor's son.

Conclusion

Now you will have realised that Thomas More wasn't a **reliable** source of evidence about King Richard III. But the evidence is still **useful** because it tells us a lot about More's attitudes. He was, for example, prepared to attack the reputation of King Richard III by using information he hadn't checked for accuracy. In doing this he was, too, supporting the monarch who was his employer and whose father had killed King Richard III in battle in order to seize the throne of England.

Things are not always what they seem!

NB A source written by a modern historian can be evaluated in the same way.

Writing good history

There is nothing like the 5W test to help you write good history. However, there is one golden rule: **think before you write!** This is as true of a pupil setting out to write a history essay as an historian writing a massive history book.

The most common reason pupils find writing about history difficult is that they have not thought about it enough before they start. Good thinking leads to good writing. So, look closely at the question you are answering, decide on your arguments, then work out what you are going to write before you start:

● the points you wish to make
● the order you are going to make them in
● the evidence and facts you will use to back the points up.

Structure
Good writing needs clear structure.

Write in paragraphs. Each paragraph should deal with one of the points which you wish to make.

Each paragraph needs a structure too. For example:

● **Point** At the start of the paragraph you should make your point.
● **Explain** your point further in a sentence or two.
● **Evidence** Provide evidence (facts) to back up your point.
● **Reiterate** Mention your point one more time.

Link your paragraphs together with phrases such as:

● On the one hand…
● On the other hand…
● An even more important reason…

Every good piece of written work has:

● **an introduction**, in which you summarise the question you are addressing and the argument you will be developing
● **a conclusion** that restates your main argument one last time.

Style
When you are writing history essays, try to write in a **formal style** – imagine you are writing to the Queen rather than to a friend.

Check
Always read your work through. If it is on a tablet or computer it might look OK but be full of mistakes. It helps to read your work out loud to yourself to make sure that it sounds right. Even in an exam you should always aim to check your work for errors.

Argument + Evidence = History
When you are talking to a teacher or a friend, you might make a point that they do not agree with. They might then ask you to prove your point. If you are unable to do so, they might say 'that is just your opinion. You can't back it up with evidence'.

The same applies when you are working as an historian. It is one thing to make a claim, but for other people to accept your point, you have to support your claim with evidence; a fact, a figure or even a quote from another historian.

Here are some statements. On their own, they are just claims or opinions without support.

● King Henry V was a successful warrior king.
● The Crusader seizure of Jerusalem was brutal and bloody.

Here are some facts. On their own they are interesting but do not prove anything.

● His armies won many battles in France including Agincourt in 1415.
● Over 70,000 Muslims were killed in the attack in 1099.

But when you put the sentences together, your claims become arguments supported with evidence.

● King Henry V was a successful warrior king: his armies won many battles in France including Agincourt in 1415.
● The Crusader seizure of Jerusalem was brutal and bloody: over 70,000 Muslims were killed in the attack in 1099.

So back your claims up with evidence!

Good and bad monarchs

Source ❶

A medieval king pictured in the Westminster Psalter

What made a good medieval monarch?

The first part of this book investigates a number of medieval monarchs to see how well they did their job. When you have finished studying them you will be asked to make some decisions about how good these monarchs were. In the Middle Ages the MONARCH was the most important person in the country. He (and it was usually a 'he' in those days) had an enormous amount of power. He was helped by the fact that people believed that he was chosen by God to rule the country. However, being a monarch could also be a dangerous occupation. Monarchs had to keep on good terms with the NOBLES and with the Church. They also had to try to avoid uprisings by the peasants. As you will see, there are several examples of monarchs being killed, murdered or deposed (thrown off the throne)!

What...?

MONARCH
A king or queen who rules a country.

NOBLES
People of high rank in society.

Task

1 On the facing page is a summary of the duties of a medieval king. Now look at the list of characteristics below. Choose the three most important ones for a medieval monarch. Add more qualities if you wish.

handsome cruel brave musical honest

feared healthy lazy fair educated

trustworthy strong greedy male

respected hated clever popular

ruthless

2 Choose one duty and explain how your chosen characteristics would help the king perform that duty.

Did you know?

Of the eighteen kings who reigned between 1066 and 1485, only four died of old age. Four were murdered (one was murdered with a red hot poker), two died of dysentery and two died in battle!

A medieval king had to...

... lead his armies to win new lands and defend his country

... make sure the justice system worked properly and that people were treated fairly

... spend money wisely and not ask for too many taxes

... get on well with the nobles and choose advisers they approved of (he couldn't govern the country without the help of the nobles)

... keep law and order across the country so people could lead their lives in peace

... have leadership qualities so that people would follow and obey him

... have healthy sons who would be his heirs

... work with Church leaders

... have a strong claim to the throne that people recognised

Source **2** *A portrait of William II by a monk in St Albans.*

UNIT 1 How did William and the Normans conquer England?

What is this all about?

In 1066, a huge fleet set sail from Normandy, bound for England. The ships carried the soldiers, horses and armour of William, Duke of Normandy. He was on his way to England to press his claim to be the rightful King of England.

This unit focuses on three issues:
- **1.1** Why did William think he should be the King of England? Was his a good claim?
- **1.2** How did William win the Battle of Hastings? Was it William's skills, his opponents' bad luck, or something else?
- **1.3** There is a difference between winning a battle and gaining control of a country. So how did the Normans gain control of England?

┌─ **Did you know?** ─┐

EDWARD THE CONFESSOR
Edward was called the Confessor because he was very religious. He spent a lot of time praying. He also built the first Westminster Abbey.

┌─ **Did you know?** ─┐

THE ANGLO-SAXONS
Originally came to England from Germany in the fifth century. They cleared the Celts out of England and then defended England against the Viking invasions.

1.1 Did William have a good claim to the throne?

In January 1066 the King of England, Edward the Confessor, died. He and his wife Edith had failed to produce a child to succeed to the throne. Anglo-Saxon customs were not clear about how a successor should be chosen in this situation. The problem was made worse because, over the years, Edward had promised the throne to a number of people. Now the struggle to succeed Edward as King of England had come to a head. The two strongest claims for the English throne in 1066 were:

- Harold Godwinson, who was the most powerful man in England
- William, Duke of Normandy.

There was also a third contender, the Viking king Harald Hardrada of Norway. You will find out more about him later.

Flashback: William visits Edward

By the winter of 1051–52 it was clear to many that Edward was probably not going to have a son. His wife Edith was childless and, in 1052, she had been temporarily sent to a convent because her father, Godwin, was in disgrace. The question was, who was going to succeed Edward?

- In 1052, the Anglo-Saxon Chronicle tells that 'Earl William' of Normandy visited the court of his cousin King Edward. The Chronicle does not mention that William was promised the throne.
- The Normans later suggested that Edward had sent Robert of Jumièges, Archbishop of Canterbury, to Normandy sometime in 1051 or 1052 to offer William the throne.

Whatever the truth, the Normans claimed that from this moment onwards William was the rightful heir to Edward's throne.

10

Did you know?

HAROLD GODWINSON
Harold's father Godwin, Earl of Wessex, had been the most important Anglo-Saxon in England apart from the king. When Godwin died in 1053 his son took over his job as Earl of Wessex. You can see how he got his surname!

What...?

OATH
A formal promise, often sacred in nature.

CRUSADE
A military expedition, often religious in nature.

The rise of Harold Godwinson, 1052–66

The 27-year-old Harold Godwinson was made Earl of Wessex on the death of his father in 1053. For the next twelve years he was to be the most powerful nobleman in England.

- His sister, Edith, was married to Edward the Confessor.
- His brothers were also in powerful positions, for example Tostig was made Earl of Northumbria in 1055.
- The Godwins controlled much of England and had strong armies.

In 1063, when the Welsh decided to invade England, the Godwin family led an army that crushed them.

Did Harold swear an oath of loyalty in Bayeux?

In 1064 or 1065, Harold travelled to France. Why he did so is not known and what happened when he got there has caused considerable debate. It has been suggested that Harold was visiting William as Edward's ambassador. One account suggests that he was captured on his way to see William by the Count of Ponthieu. William then came to Harold's rescue. What happened next is the important part of the story. The Bayeux Tapestry clearly shows Harold swearing an OATH to William. He is touching the relics of a saint. What the oath was about, we are not too sure.

Source ❶

Yet did the wise king entrust his kingdom to a man of high rank, to Harold himself.

The *Anglo-Saxon Chronicle* said this on Edward's death in 1066. ❓▶ *What does this prove?*

- The Norman writer William of Poitiers (writing in the 1070s) insisted that Harold swore to support William's claim to the English throne when Edward died. He also said that Harold swore fealty (loyalty) to William as his lord. But a Norman in 1070 would say that, wouldn't he? There are other possibilities.
- Perhaps Harold swore an oath out of gratitude for being rescued.
- Maybe he was forced to do so as condition of his release.
- Harold might have sworn an oath of friendship (on Edward's behalf) between England and Normandy, not an oath of fealty.

Whatever the truth, the claim that Harold had broken a sacred oath was used by the Normans as the excuse for war. To break such a promise was seen at the time as a terrible crime against the Church and God. William portrayed his invasion of England as a religious CRUSADE to punish Harold. He received the support of Pope Alexander II, which was thought to be very important.

┌── Did you know? ──┐

THE BAYEUX TAPESTRY
Stitched together in the
1070s on the orders of
William's half-brother,
Odo of Bayeux, the
Tapestry is the Normans'
side of the story.
Therefore you can't
necessarily believe all of
it. There are three basic
parts to the tapestry:
- In the middle are the
  main events.
- Above the pictures is a
  description in Latin of
  the story. You may be
  able to work out what
  it says.
- In the top and bottom
  margins there are
  symbolic decorations
  of animals and objects.

Edward's deathbed wishes

As King Edward lay dying in December 1065, the leading nobles of England gathered to discover who he would nominate as the next king. It is interesting that William did not travel to England despite the Norman claim that he had been promised the throne by Edward in 1052 and by Harold in 1064 or 1065. However, all of the sources, whether English or Norman, are clear about what happened next. On his deathbed Edward nominated Harold to be his successor.

On 6 January 1066 Edward was buried in his magnificent new Westminster Abbey and Harold was crowned the same day.

Harold was in a strong position:

- Harold had been chosen by his brother-in-law, King Edward, to be his successor.
- He had the support of the English nobles, including Earl Morcar and Earl Edwin.
- He had been accepted as king by the Witan, the gathering of nobility and clergy.
- Harold had a strong reputation as a military leader. This put him in a good position to resist any invasion attempts.

In the eyes of most English people, this was enough to make him the rightful King of England.

Sources A–C give evidence about the events of 1064 when Harold supposedly visited France.

Source ❷

King Edward's funeral shown in the Bayeux Tapestry. ❓▶ *What do you think is happening at each of the numbered points?*

WHAT IS THE TRUE STORY OF HAROLD'S OATH?

Source Ⓐ

Scene from the Bayeux Tapestry. ❓▶ *Can you find: Harold; William; an altar; the box containing saint's relics?*

Source Ⓑ

Harold, who was a prisoner of a local count after a shipwreck on the French coast, had been forced to swear to be William's liege man, that is his servant. He had sworn this oath of loyalty on a box containing the remains of holy saints.

Written by Rebecca Fraser, *A People's History of Britain* published in 2003.

Task
See page 4 to find out more about these sources using the 5Ws test.

Source Ⓒ

When they met … Harold swore loyalty to William using the sacred ritual recognised among Christian men. In front of other people, he swore without anyone making him do so that he would represent William at the court of his lord, King Edward; secondly that he would make sure that, after the death of King Edward, William would be confirmed as King of England.

Adapted from *The Deeds of William, Duke of the Normans and King of England* by William of Poitiers (1071). He was one of King William's priests.

Summary task

'William had a strong claim to the English throne'.

Using **all** of the sources and the information you have studied in the last four pages, explain how far you agree with this statement.

QUESTIONS

1 Look at **Source A**.
The Bayeux Tapestry was stitched together on the orders of William's half-brother, Odo of Bayeux.

Do you think the tapestry is reliable in telling us what actually happened?

2 Read **Source B**.
What, according to the historian Rebecca Fraser, did Harold swear to do?

3 Read **Source C**.
How far does **Source C** agree with **Source B**?

4 Using **all** the sources and your own knowledge, how far do you think it is true that Harold agreed that William should succeed Edward as the next King of England?

1.2 1066: The year of three battles

A third claimant: Harald Hardrada

Did you know?

After many years of raiding the east coast of England, many Vikings had come to live in England. From 1017 to 1035 a Viking king, Cnut, ruled England. He thought that he was so powerful that a number of stories were made up about him. One was that he had his throne placed next to the sea and commanded that the waves turn back. He got his feet wet.

It might seem complicated enough to have two claimants to the English throne. But there was a third! He was Harald Hardrada, King of Norway. Why did he think he should be king of England? For 36 years, from 1016 to 1042, England had been ruled by Norwegians. The last one, who was called HarthaCnut, had promised that when he died, Magnus, King of Norway, could have England too. But that never happened. When HarthaCnut died, his half-brother Edward (the Confessor) seized the English throne.

Now Magnus' son, Harald Hardrada, decided to resurrect his claim.

It was a complicated time. Hardrada's claim to the throne was not strong but his armies most certainly were. He was one of the most feared Viking warriors in Europe. And to add to King Harold's problem, Hardrada was supported by Tostig, Harold's estranged brother.

So although Harold was now king, he knew his position was not secure. He knew he might have to fight to stay in power. So Harold raised his armies and waited for nine months. His army in the south watched the English Channel for signs of a Norman invasion. His army in the north waited for an attack from Scandinavia.

As September came, Harold was forced to send his armies home. The harvest needed to be brought in and he no longer had the food to keep his army fed. Just as his soldiers started on their way home, his rivals struck.

Hardrada sailed a fleet of 300 ships up the River Humber. He landed at Riccall on the River Ouse and marched towards York. While on his way back to London, Harold heard the news that Hardrada had landed in Northumbria and burnt to the ground Scarborough, Cleveland and Holderness.

Did you know?

Hardrada means 'hard reign'. This is a pretty good nickname for Harald; he had fought in his first battle when only 15 years old. Harald went on to fight in battles across Europe before returning home to Norway. What did he do when he got back to Norway? He raided the Danish coast. Harald was not a man to pick a fight with.

The Battles of Fulford Gate and Stamford Bridge

Hardrada found his way to York barred by Harold's loyal allies, his brothers-in-law: Edwin, Earl of Mercia, and Morcar, Earl of Northumbria.

But at the Battle of Fulford Gate, Hardrada and Tostig defeated this northern Anglo-Saxon army and massacred thousands of experienced troops. They then marched on to York, which surrendered.

In response to this defeat, Harold hurried north with his southern army, covering 190 miles in four days.

On 20 September Harold surprised and defeated the Viking army at the Battle of Stamford Bridge (see Map 1). Hardrada and Tostig were killed. However, despite Harold winning a famous victory, the impact on his army was severe. This is very important when trying to understand what happened next. Thousands of his best troops, including many HOUSECARLS and archers, died in battle. Harold returned south with a much weakened and very tired army.

What...?

HOUSECARL
A member of the king's bodyguard.

Map ❶

One third of the Viking army was miles away at Riccall guarding the Viking ships. The rest of Hardrada's army were relaxing in the fields by the river at Stamford Bridge. They had just won a great victory. They were waiting for hostages to be delivered from the city of York. Most had discarded their mail shirts and helmets in the hot sun. A few were guarding the bridge over the River Derwent.

Harold's arrival caught them completely off guard. Viking guards on the bridge kept Harold's army back for long enough for the rest of Hardrada's army to put on their armour and take up position away from the river. They formed a shield wall.

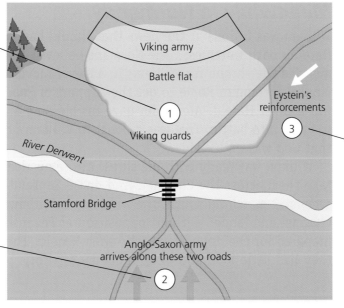

Harold's army battered at the wall in hand-to-hand combat for hours. Reinforcements arrived from Riccall led by Eystein. But when Harald Hardrada was killed the Norwegian army crumbled. The Vikings ran away and were pursued all the way back to their fleet at Riccall. Many were killed including Tostig. Only 24 out of the 300 Norwegian ships sailed back to Norway.

Plan of the Battle of Stamford Bridge.

Map ❷

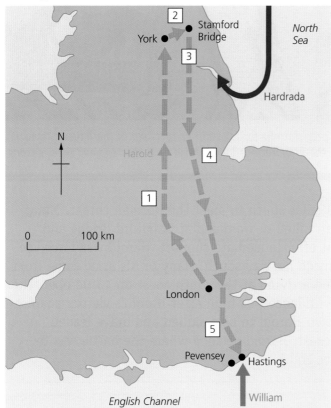

Battles in England, 1066.

> **Did you know?**
>
> Why did Tostig fight against his brother Harold? Tostig was Earl of Northumbria. In 1065 the Northumbrians accused Tostig of murder and misrule and staged a rebellion. Instead of siding with Tostig, Harold supported the rebels, threw Tostig out of England and made Morcar Earl of Northumbria.

Task

Make your own rough copy of Map 2 and add labels at the points numbered 1–3 to explain:
• the movement of Harold's troops
• what happened in each battle.

You can add labels 4 and 5 using the next two pages.

┌─ **Did you know?** ─┐
William was well
informed of Harold's
movements through a
system of scouts and
spies.
└─────────────────┘

Meanwhile in Normandy

William was furious at the news that Harold had been crowned king: was Harold's oath worthless? The Normans believed that Harold should have guarded the throne for William. In a clever move, William sent the Norman monk Lanfranc to Rome to get the support of Pope Alexander II for a holy war against Harold. Alexander gave his blessing and sent William a banner to carry into battle. This was a boost to William's campaign. He could claim that God was on his side.

William was ready with his ships. All he needed was a favourable wind to take them across the Channel. And on 28 September, with Harold's weary army still marching south, the wind came. William crossed the English Channel and landed without opposition at Pevensey. His army immediately prepared for the hoped-for battle with Harold. They wanted a quick battle; they had little food and were in enemy territory.

Source ③

William's preparations for invasion as recorded in the Bayeux Tapestry.
❓ *Do the preparations look careful or rushed to you? Give reasons.*

Harold arrives

Harold's army marched 260 miles south to meet the Norman threat. Many of his best soldiers had been killed or wounded at Stamford Bridge and Edwin and Morcar could not offer immediate support. Harold was forced to recruit new soldiers as he made his way south. Many of his army came from Kent and Essex. They started arriving at the south coast on 13 October. The men were tired but their confidence was high after Harold's victory against Hardrada's army. It had shown Harold to be a skilled and brave leader.

On arrival at the south coast, Harold decided where the battle was to take place. He chose Caldbec Hill.

Task

Study the five features of Caldbec Hill listed here. Do you think Harold chose a good site? Why? Give reasons.

1   It was quite heavily forested and not suited for open battle.
2   The hill was steep and difficult to attack.
3   The hill gave Harold a clear view of the countryside around.
4   To the south of Caldbec Hill was open ground known as Senlac Ridge. The ground sloped down to the position held by the Normans (Senlac Hill).
5   The low land surrounding Caldbec Hill and Senlac Ridge was marshy while Harold's army was on the high, dry land.

When should he fight? This was a hard decision. There were three good reasons to wait.

● Not all of Harold's army had arrived, some were still marching south. On the night of 13 October he only had an army of around 7,500 men. This was the same as the Normans but if he waited, he would have a much larger army.
● William had already been in England for two weeks. His army was rested and well fed – they had taken as much as they could from the surrounding area. However their food might soon run out.
● William's army consisted of three groups: Bretons led by Alan Fergant, Flemish troops led by Eustace of Boulogne, and Normans. If they were forced to wait for action, divisions might appear.

But Harold did not wait; he ordered that his troops be ready for battle the next day. Why did he do this?

● Maybe he thought the Normans would not wait so he wanted to be ready.
● It might be that Harold knew William's troops were spreading terror amongst the local people with their looting and that he wanted to do something about it straight away.
● It is possible that Harold thought, if he waited, some of his own troops might lose heart or desert.
● Harold might have been very confident that, after defeating Hardrada's army, he could defeat William's forces with some ease.

Night fell. The Normans were camped 16 miles away near Hastings, with Harold's army camped on Caldbec Hill. The meeting point for Harold's troops was the Old Hoare Apple Tree. Few soldiers slept much. Instead they spent their time preparing themselves for the battle ahead. Prayers were said and weapons sharpened.

Before dawn, William's troops began marching towards the battlefield. William's army was well disciplined. The march from Hastings to the battlefield would not have taken more than a few hours. However, the approach to Caldbec Hill was quite tricky: there were two streams and plenty of marshy ground to cross. For soldiers weighed down by armour and weapons, these were not easy obstacles to overcome. However, they managed it with little fuss and approached the battlefield in good order.

Did you know?

William liked a good battle. He was just 19 when he took part in his first battle at Val-es-Dunes in 1047. According to one chronicler of the time he 'hurled himself at his enemies and terrified them with slaughter'.

Map **3**

The battle line-up

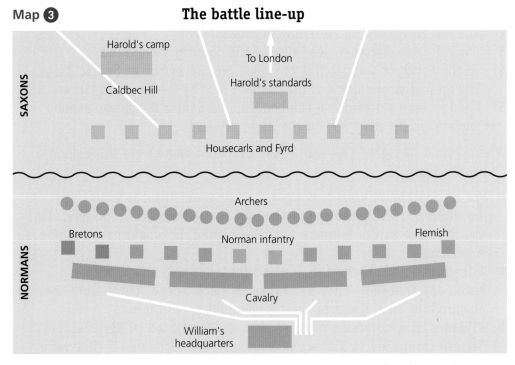

Plan of the Battle of Hastings.

As the sun rose on the battlefield, the armies moved into position (see Map 3). William placed his Norman foot soldiers in the middle of his army. There were archers at the front and CAVALRY to the rear.

As the Normans came into view, Harold moved his troops down Caldbec Hill and settled about 250 yards away from William's army. Harold put his best troops, the housecarls, in the front row of the Saxon army. They were responsible for forming a shield wall to give protection against the Norman arrows. Behind them were the foot soldiers known as the fyrd. Harold took up his position to the rear. The Saxons did not use archers.

The troops stared at each other across the battlefield. They shouted rude things at each other and chanted like a crowd at a football match. The Saxons shouted 'ut, ut, ut' which meant 'out, out, out'. The battle was about to begin.

The Normans attack

Suddenly a young man called Taillefer broke from the French ranks. He charged up the hill to the Saxon lines. The Saxon housecarls chopped him down. The battle had begun. The Normans fired their arrows into the Saxon ranks but the housecarls used their shields effectively and few were killed. Soon the Normans ran out of arrows and their archers were not equipped to fight hand to hand with the Saxon housecarls. First advantage was with Harold.

The Saxons have the upper hand

The Saxons now attacked. Harold's soldiers threw anything that they could find including rocks and stones on the soldiers below. William ordered his cavalry to counter-attack. The Norman cavalry charged up the hill towards the shield wall. As they neared the Saxon lines they threw their spears then turned and returned to their lines.

What...?

CAVALRY
Troops who fight on horseback.

Did you know?

Taillefer was a minstrel. He led the Norman troops in songs such as the popular Song Of Roland.

Did you know?

William is known to history as William the Conqueror because he conquered England. Because his mother wasn't married to his father when he was born he was known at the time by the less appealing name of William the Bastard.

However, they too failed to make much of an impression:

- Many housecarls used heavy axes with which they cut down the Norman horses and their riders.
- The Norman cavalry had to ride up the steep hill which slowed them down.

There was no doubt about it; the Saxons really did have the upper hand. By midday, the Bretons on the right of William's line were in retreat and some of his soldiers began to panic. As the Saxons chased the Bretons down the hill the rumour spread that William had been killed. William had to do something – quickly.

William is alive!

William took off his helmet and rode along the Norman lines to prove that he was still alive. This calmed the nerves of many of his troops. At around that time, some of the Norman cavalry led by Odo went to the aid of the Bretons. The Saxon troops who had chased the Bretons down the hill were now stranded. It was too muddy for them to return to their ranks and they were cut down by the Normans on horseback. Harold could have ordered a full attack but he did not do so. At this point in the battle, Harold's brothers Gyrth and Leofwine were killed, possibly by Odo's cavalry.

'Half time'

The Norman attacks had not succeeded but nor had the Saxons pressed home their advantage. Around 2 p.m. the battle paused. Both sides reviewed their situation.

- To win a battle like this you had to kill the enemy's leader. This was a battle about who should be king. If you got rid of the other claimant you had won.
- Some Saxons from Harold's right flank had been lost but otherwise his troops were in good shape. They had a strong position. They could hold out until the end of the day.
- William's archers had run out of arrows, the hill had proved too steep for his cavalry. He needed the Saxons to come and fight in his ground. What should William or Harold do next?

A cunning plan

William came up with a cunning plan. He thought about what had happened in the morning when the Bretons ran away. The Saxons had lost their discipline and had chased the Bretons down the hill. Stranded, they became an easy target for the Norman cavalry. William's plan was to trick the Saxons into thinking that the Normans were running away, thereby drawing them into battle at the bottom of the hill. He issued a new set of orders to the cavalry telling them of the plan.

> **Did you know?**
>
> William had a terrible temper. During the siege of the French town of Alençon, the defenders were very rude about the fact that William's mother had been born a peasant. He was not happy. When he took the town he ordered 32 of the leading citizens to have their hands chopped off.

Did you know?

The Bayeux Tapestry was probably made in Winchester. Therefore it could be called the Winchester Tapestry! It is called the Bayeux Tapestry after the Bishop of Bayeux, who ordered it to be made.

The Norman foot soldiers and cavalry were ordered forward. The cavalry charged up the hill, fought with the Saxons and then turned, pretending that they were running away. The Saxon army fell for the trick; housecarls and fyrd breaking ranks to chase the Normans down the hill. A number of reports from the battle suggested that this happened twice. It is not certain whether Harold gave an order for his soldiers to chase the French or if they acted against his orders. Whether he ordered it or not, Harold now had good reason to be very worried.

Source ④

The Bayeux Tapestry shows Harold's death. The Latin inscription says 'King Harold is killed'. Which of the two soldiers do you think is supposed to be Harold? The one on the left, the one on the right, or both?

Harold dies

The battle was now opening up. The Norman archers were able to pick up a number of their used arrows and began firing them into the Saxon lines. With the housecarls engaged in hand-to-hand fighting, the shield wall had gone. The arrows now caused many more casualties. This was the crucial turning point of the battle. Harold had remained at the top of the hill, surrounded by his housecarl bodyguard. However, even they were unable to prevent a stray arrow hitting the king. The Bayeux Tapestry appears to show Harold being hit in the eye but that is not definitely what happened. What is sure is that news of Harold's death spread quickly amongst the ranks of the Saxon army.

Source ⑤

From the Bayeux Tapestry. From what you know about the battle, write a caption to explain what you think it shows here. If you can read Latin, try to translate the inscription.

Did you know?

To show his thanks to God, William ordered that an abbey, Battle Abbey, be built where the last line of Saxon resistance had stood.

William wins

Sensing victory, William ordered his foot soldiers forward. Many Saxon soldiers bravely fought on but some began to flee into the forests that surrounded the battlefield. A number of the Norman cavalry chased the Saxons into the forest although this was a dangerous thing to do. Some were ambushed by the Saxons and were killed. But this would not change the course of the battle. The housecarls fought to the end but were killed to the last man. A Norman knight rode up to Harold's body and drove his sword into his heart. Harold had been killed. His banner showing a red dragon was in William's possession. The Normans had won.

Task

Why do you think that Sources 6 and 7 give different accounts of the battle?

Source ❻

King Harold assembled a large army but he was taken by surprise by William and the Normans before he was fully ready. But the King nevertheless fought hard against William, with the men who were willing to support him, and there were heavy casualties on both sides. There King Harold was killed and Earl Leofwine his brother, and Earl Gyrth his brother, and many good men, and the French were masters of the battlefield.

Adapted from the *Anglo-Saxon Chronicle* of 1066.
❓▶ *Why did William have an advantage in the battle?*

Exam practice

See page 180 for a practice evidence question on the Norman Conquest.

Source ❼

Harold's large army were ready and lined up in close formation. Realising that they could not attack such an army without taking big losses, the Normans and their allies pretended to run away. The barbarians … thinking that they were winning, shouted with triumph ... and chased the Normans who they thought were running away. But the Normans suddenly turned their horses round, surrounded Harold's men and cut them all down so that not one was left alive. The Normans played this trick twice with great success.

Adapted from *Gesta Willelmi* by William of Poitiers. He was one of King William's priests.
❓▶ *What words show that the writer did not think much of the Anglo-Saxons?*

Summary task

1   Using all the information in the last four pages, copy and complete a diagram like this. Add at least one point to each arm.

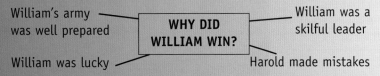

William's army was well prepared — **WHY DID WILLIAM WIN?** — William was a skilful leader

William was lucky — Harold made mistakes

2   Once you have completed your diagram, highlight what you think is the most important reason that William won and write some sentences to explain why this was so important.

1.3 How did William gain control of England, 1066–87?

Did you know?

William's coronation was a tense occasion. When the crowd inside Westminster Abbey shouted that they accepted William as king, the crowd outside got excited and started making a lot of noise. At this point the Norman soldiers guarding the Abbey lost their nerve and burned down a number of houses around the Abbey. Not a good start to the reign!

William was crowned King of England on Christmas Day 1066 in Westminster Abbey. London and the south east of England had surrendered to the new king but much of the rest of England lay out of his control. William's main problems were how to **keep** control of what he had and how to **gain** control of the rest of England.

1 Castles

Castles were William's main weapon in seizing control of England. They had an obvious function – to house Norman soldiers and knights – but castles were also meant to frighten the local population. They became a symbol of Norman military power and control. They reminded people that the Normans were in England to stay.

William ordered that castles be built in London, Hereford and Winchester to remind the 'rich, untrustworthy and bold' Saxon citizens that the Normans were now in charge. The Norman writer William of Poitiers wrote that castles in London were built 'against the fickleness of the vast and fierce populace'.

The Normans usually built their castles in important places, for example on high ground dominating a town, at the mouth or crossing point of a river, or at an important road junction. Although the first castles were made out of wood and earth, they towered over other buildings around them.

Did you know?

The White Tower by the River Thames was built of white Caen stone from Normandy. It dominated the city around it, standing at a towering 30 metres tall. The Tower contained everything that was needed to resist a siege including a fresh water supply, stores and kitchens. It was never successfully stormed but this is not surprising considering that the walls of the Tower are 5 metres thick!

Source **8**

A modern photo of the White Tower at the Tower of London.

What...?

MOTTE
A mound or hill.

KEEP
A strong and central tower of a castle.

BAILEY
A compound.

- The MOTTE of the castle was a hill on which was placed a fort known as a KEEP. The keep also served as living quarters. Initially the Normans built the keep out of wood but soon changed to using stone, which was easier to defend. The most famous Norman stone keep is the White Tower at the Tower of London (Source 8).
- Below the motte was a compound called a BAILEY, with living quarters, animals and even a church. The bailey was often surrounded by a moat or ditch and was also difficult to attack.
- All around both motte and bailey was a strong wall with lookout towers. Again, stone quickly replaced wood.
- Within the motte and bailey could be found all that was needed to survive a siege including a water supply and food reserves.

Diagram ❶

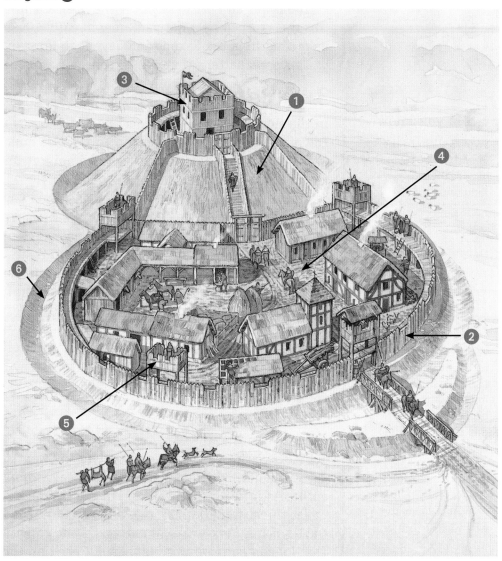

An artist's impression of a motte and bailey castle.

Task
Use the text on this page to name correctly the features numbered 1–6 on Diagram 1

Source ❾

The King [William] rode into all the remote parts of his kingdom and fortified strategic sites against enemy attacks. For the fortifications, called castles by the Normans, were scarcely known in the English provinces, so the English, despite their courage and love of fighting, could put up only a weak resistance to their enemies.

A writer of the time, Orderic Vitalis, reflected on the impact of castle building.

2 Land

William knew that Norman rule would be fully more secure when the vast majority of land was in Norman hands. Many Normans had supported William's campaign in 1066 and expected to be rewarded with land.

William immediately gave to his closest friends and followers the land taken from the families of the Saxon leaders who had died at Hastings.

● In 1067 William handed Harold's land to one of his closest and most loyal friends, William fitz Osbern.
● The lands of Harold's brothers Gyrth and Leofwine were given to Ralph the Staller and William's own brother Bishop Odo.

However, at this stage at least, William did not want to upset the remaining living Saxon earls and he did not take the lands of Edwin, Morcar and Waltheof. William was aware that rebellion might break out at any point.

There was an uprising against the Normans in Devon and Cornwall but this was crushed by a Norman army in early 1068. In response William took more land from the Saxons and gave it to Norman families.

This set a pattern that was to continue throughout William's reign.

3 Violent suppression

In the summer of 1068, William and a large army went north. Saxon lords Edwin, Earl of Mercia and Morcar, Earl of Northumbria were resisting the Normans. William ordered castles to be built at Warwick, Nottingham and then at York. As he returned to London for the winter, William ordered more castles to be built in Lincoln, Huntingdon and Cambridge. The arrival of William at York and the construction of castles was a clear sign to the Saxon nobles in the north that Norman rule was permanent. They had a choice, to fight against it or accept it; many chose to fight.

William had left a small army, led by Robert Comin, in the north. In January 1069 this Norman army was attacked in Durham and massacred.

The Saxons were becoming more confident. Very soon after, one of the recently built Norman castles at York was destroyed. Although York was soon brought back under Norman control, a far greater danger than a few rebellious Saxons loomed into view. A large army led by King Swein of Denmark had set sail, aiming to conquer England.

Rebellions

Once the Danish army had landed in the north of England in September 1069, the last great Saxon earls rallied to Swein's cause: Waltheof of the East Midlands, Edwin of Mercia and Morcar of Northumbria. They were not enthusiastic about Swein's claim to the throne but felt that their power was under threat from Norman rule and saw Swein as their chance to drive back the Normans. York was again attacked and this time burned to the ground. The Norman garrison was butchered. Rebellion then broke out in the west.

> ⌐ **Did you know?** ¬
>
> Swein's claim to the English throne was that he was the nephew of King Cnut.

> ⌐ **Did you know?** ¬
>
> Waltheof was one of the most powerful Saxon earls. His support was important to William because his lands guarded the route to the north. Despite promising William his loyalty in 1066, he was always ready to plot against William and was eventually executed in 1076.

Map 4

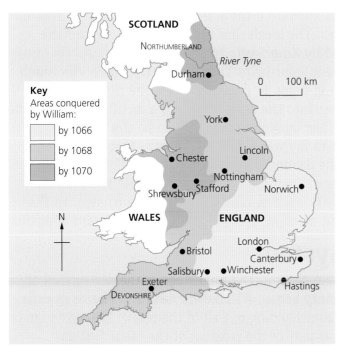

A map showing the Norman conquest of England.
❓▶ *Find where you live, or where your school is, on this map. When, if ever, was your area conquered by William?*

Source 10

And there came to meet them Prince Edgar and Earl Waltheof and Maerleswegen and Gospatric with the Northumbrians and all the people riding and marching with an immense army rejoicing exceedingly and so they all went resolutely to York and stormed and razed the castle and captured an incalculable treasure in it and killed many hundreds of Frenchmen and took many with them to the ships … When the King found out about this he went northwards with all his army … and utterly ravaged and laid waste that shire.

An account from the *Anglo-Saxon Chronicle* of the 'Harrying of the North'.

Source 11

A Viking army landed and marched on York. The Vikings found much support amongst the people. Together, they seized York. William now faced a Viking or Saxon kingdom in the north of England. He reacted with brutality. His army marched north, devastating the countryside and killing all adult males.

Historian Toby Purser writing in *Medieval England 1042–1228* published in 2004.

A Saxon army invaded from the English/Welsh border area known as the Marches. William's rule was seriously threatened. His response was rapid and ruthless.

- William fitz Osbern led a Norman army down to the West Country where it crushed the Saxon rebels outside Exeter.
- Another Saxon force from the west was defeated at Stafford by an army led by William himself.
- The King then successfully bribed Swein's brother to withdraw from York, and recaptured the burned city. Straight away, in December 1069, William repaired York's two castles and sent his soldiers out into the countryside to ensure that all resistance was crushed.

The Harrying of the North, 1069

William was determined that he would not have to face such an uprising again. It was time to teach the Saxons a lesson. What followed, the so-called 'HARRYING of the North', was to prove to be a turning point in the Norman conquest of England. Across the north of England, property and land was burned or destroyed and all food seized. As a result, thousands of Saxons died of starvation. The cruel plan worked; Saxon resistance was all but crushed. Opponents such as Waltheof surrendered and begged for mercy.

> **What…?**
> **HARRYING**
> The act of raiding or attacking.

Task
Discuss:
a) Which side – Saxons or Normans – does the author of Source 10 favour?
b) To what extent is Source 10 biased?
c) What are the differences between Source 10 and Source 11?

What...?

FENS
Wet marshlands in the east of England. They have now been drained but in the eleventh century you needed a boat and local knowledge to get around.

FEUDAL
Relating to the social system whereby poorer people held land belonging to a richer person in exchange for allegiance and service.

HOMAGE
Honour and allegiance shown to a lord/king.

The Saxons' last stand

At the end of 1069, William appointed the warrior priest Thurold of Fecamp to be Abbot of Peterborough. The locals, led by the Saxon Hereward the Wake, invited the Danes led by King Swein to protect them.

They asked the wrong people for help! The Danes stripped Peterborough of its wealth before returning home to Denmark much the richer.

Hereward led his followers into the FENS and set up a fortified camp on the Isle of Ely. There he was joined by Morcar. This was to be the Saxons' last stand. The only way to get to Ely was using secret paths through the fens that were only known to the Saxons. Whilst the people of Ely supported Hereward, the monks in the cathedral did not and they told the Normans how to cross the fens. In 1071 the Saxons were forced to surrender to the Normans although Hereward managed to escape, never to be heard of again.

4 The Feudal System

William was now very much in control. The final stage in the destruction of the power of the Saxon nobility began. With Edwin dead and Morcar in exile in Normandy, William set about handing out all of the rest of the Saxon lands. He completed this exercise as part of the creation of the FEUDAL System.

The aim behind the Feudal System was that every group in society owed military service. In that way the King could quickly raise an army to crush any revolts.

- **The King** In theory, all of England belonged to the King. In practice, William kept about a sixth of the land.
- **Barons** The great Saxon earldoms such as Wessex, Mercia and Northumbria were broken up, because the holders of these positions had proved to be too powerful. Instead, much of England was divided among around 170 Norman barons who gave an oath of military service and paid HOMAGE to the King.
- **Knights** The barons gave smaller amounts of lands to knights in return or a promise of military service.
- **Villeins** The knights' lands were farmed by peasants called villeins who could also be called up for military service if need be.
- **Serfs** At the bottom of the pile were the serfs who were owned by the knights.

More castles

A network of more castles was built to support the Feudal System. As William appointed new regional rulers, so castles such as Durham Castle were built. Such castles acted as places to rule from, as well as serving a military purpose. Castles were also built to protect the borders of William's lands in places such as Chester, to prevent attacks from Wales, and Newcastle-upon-Tyne, to prevent attacks from Scotland.

THE KING

THE BARONS
(NOBLES)

THE KNIGHTS

THE VILLEINS

THE SERFS

The Feudal System. There were many more people on the bottom rung than this picture can show.
The vast majority of people in England were villeins or serfs.

5 The Church

For a couple of years after 1066, William allowed the Saxon leaders of the English Church to continue their work. Stigand, who had been a friend of the Godwin family, was allowed to remain as Archbishop of Canterbury.

But after the events of 1069 William mistrusted all Saxon leaders. William realised that his control of the Church was crucial if he was to maintain control of the country.

● In 1070 he sacked Stigand, replacing him with the Norman bishop Lanfranc (see page 104).
● The leading Saxon monks and abbots were thrown out of their jobs and the monasteries were looted of their Saxon treasure.
● Norman bishops were appointed to York, Rochester and Winchester.

With Lanfranc in charge, the Church in England was brought under closer control of the King. During the reigns of Edward and Harold, it had been very much under the control of the Pope. Under Lanfranc:

● New monasteries and church schools were set up.
● The King's courts developed independently of Church control.

William and Pope Gregory

In 1066 William had fought under the banner of Pope Alexander II but he was not prepared to allow any Pope great influence in the running of England. In particular he did not want the Pope to appoint bishops. In 1073 a new Pope, Gregory VII, was chosen. Gregory was a great reformer who hated the way important jobs in the Church were given out by political leaders to people who did not have the best interests of the Church at heart.

In 1075 Gregory demanded that William swear him an oath of fealty (loyalty) as King of England but William refused.

Instead William insisted that he, not the Pope, appointed bishops and abbots. He also insisted that no letters from the Pope could be read out in English churches without his permission.

> **Did you know?**
>
> A letter from the Pope was called a Papal Bull.

Source **12**

Pope Gregory VII in 1073. He was probably the single most powerful person in Europe. **?** *Explain how the engraver has made him look important.*

> **Did you know?**
>
> The Normans also built many new churches and cathedrals. You will find out more about these in Section 2 (Unit 10).

6 Local administration

Some of William's measures to control England were new ones. Castles were new. The Feudal System was new. Some of his measures were not new. He simply took over control of the structures that already existed. How he dealt with the Church is one example; another is local administration. William kept the main features of Anglo-Saxon government and administration but used them to his own advantage.

Did you know?

DANEGELD

A tax originally raised by Alfred the Great to pay off Danish invaders. The problem was that, because the Danes were being given money for going away, they kept on coming back in order to get more money for going away! King Cnut was Danish himself so he did not need to raise taxes to pay himself to go away. He raised Danegeld but used the money for improving defences.

- England continued to be governed in districts known as 'hundreds'.
- England was an important source of income for William. He needed money to pay his large armies in Normandy and England. The Saxon taxation and coinage system worked well. An example was the raising of a tax known as Danegeld which had been raised in England for a number of years. William continued this method of raising money.
- The system of sheriffs stayed as the important link between local and national government.
- The great city of London, so important to the wealth of England, was granted a Charter by William that allowed it to keep all of its old privileges.
- The Anglo-Saxon kings had consulted their nobles at a meeting of the Witan. William set up the equivalent Great Council, which the barons had to attend. All the important archbishops and bishops were required to sit on the Great Council.

Minor problems!

It will be clear that England was, by the early 1070s, very much under William's control. He spent less and less time in England – only a quarter of his time in the end – although there were still threats to his control. Here are some examples.

Scotland: 1072

By the 1070s, the only remaining serious claimant to the English throne was a great nephew of Edward the Confessor, Edgar the Atheling. In 1072, King Malcolm of Scotland married Edgar's sister Margaret. William realised that Malcolm might use his forces to back Edgar's claim to the throne. He led his armies north in a show of strength. The two kings met at Abernethy and, amongst other things, Malcolm agreed to expel Edgar from Scotland.

Roger of Hereford: 1075

The greatest threat to William's control of England in the later years of his reign came not from the Saxons but from the next generation of Normans. In 1075, one of William fitz Osbern's sons, Earl Roger of Hereford, rebelled in protest about the loss of rights he felt were due to him as a leading noble in the country. In particular, he felt that he did not have the same power as his father. Roger was supported in his rebellion by Saxon Earl Waltheof amongst others. William had little difficulty putting down the rebellion. Roger was tried for treason under Norman law and imprisoned; Waltheof was tried for treason under English law and beheaded in 1076.

Did you know?

Robert was not very tall. His nicknames were 'Gambaron' which meant 'Little Fat Legs' or 'Curthose' which meant 'Short Trousers'.

What...?

CORRUPT
Using dishonest means to achieve power or financial advantage.

Family problems

William also had trouble from his family.

- One of his sons, Robert Curthose, felt that he had not enough power. Their quarrel ended in battle in Normandy in 1079 which Robert won (with the help of King Philip of France).
- Another member of William's family to cause him trouble was his half-brother Odo. As Earl of Kent and Bishop of Bayeux, Odo had become a very wealthy man, partly because he was very CORRUPT. Odo had ambitions to become the next Pope and, by 1082, had spent a fortune on a palace in Rome. Most of the money had been raised in England. William disapproved of Odo's corruption and had him arrested.

Domesday Book

The never-ending warfare was very expensive. In 1085 the Vikings led by a new King Cnut (son of Swein) again threatened invasion. This was a more serious threat than William had faced for at least ten years. He returned to England determined to find out how much military service and how much taxation money he could raise. The survey on military service is lost but the survey on landowning, property and tax, later known as the Domesday Book, survived.

Source

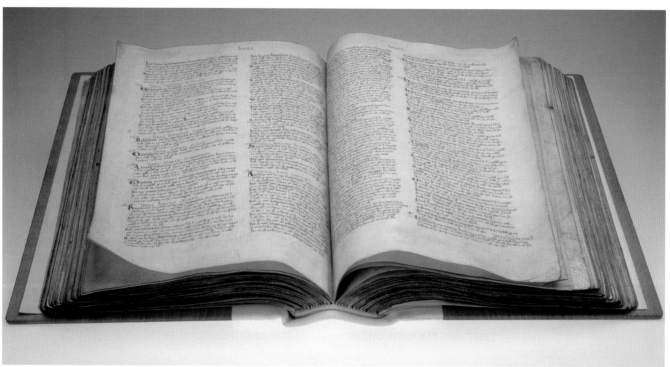

A copy of the Domesday Book, which is now kept in the British Library. Domesday is a nickname. William never called it that. ❓ *Can you think of reasons why this survey might have got the name Domesday? If you are stuck, look at www.domesdaybook.co.uk and go to the FAQ page.*

Did you know?

William had grown fat in middle age. Indeed he was so fat that he did not fit into his coffin. When his servants tried to squeeze his body into the coffin at the funeral, the corpse burst open. The smell was so terrible that the priests who were conducting the funeral ran off. Not a good ending.

What...?

HIDE
A measure of land area.

The idea of undertaking such a survey was not new. What was different was its size. Royal officials travelled the land collecting information on the size, resources and present and past ownership of every HIDE of land. London was not included because of its complexity.

The book, arranged by county, was presented to William at Salisbury on 1 August 1086. It was an excellent example of William's efficiency as a ruler, as well as one of the most useful sources for historians studying the Middle Ages.

However William is never likely to be remembered primarily as an efficient administrator. His fame is as a powerful and ruthless conqueror.

William died in 1087. He was on yet another military campaign in France and was riding through a burning town. His horse was startled by a falling timber and reared up. William was thrown forward onto the pommel of his saddle which ruptured his kidney. He died several days later of internal bleeding. It was a violent end to a violent life.

Summary task

How did William maintain control?

1 Here are a number of reasons why William was able to maintain control of England 1066–87.

He built castles.	He controlled the Church.	The Saxon opposition was weak.	He used extreme force.
He did the Domesday survey.	He kept some Saxon customs.	He introduced the Feudal System.	

For each one, give an example and explain in your own words **how** this helped William maintain control.

2 Working in a small group, choose three reasons from question 1 that you think are more important than the others. Write down your three choices and explain why you chose them.

Filling in the gaps: William II and Henry I

Common Entrance History includes all the monarchs from 1066 to 1500 but, as you can choose which one to write about, you don't need to know about all of them in the same depth. We have chosen eight kings for the depth studies. That will provide you with all you need to answer Common Entrance questions. Then between the units, this feature – Filling in the gaps – summarises key information about what happened between the depth study kings. You don't need to learn this. But it should help you understand the next unit better if you read it.

William Rufus (1087–1100)

When William the Conqueror died his eldest son Robert was away on a Crusade, so his second son William, known as Rufus, became King of England. William II was a bad-tempered and violent man. He faced rebellions from his barons and even his own brother Robert tried to oust him when he came back from the Crusade. William had no respect for the Church and in 1097 the Archbishop of Canterbury, Anselm of Bec, was so fed up with William's bullying that he went to France. William Rufus was killed in an apparent hunting accident by a man called Walter Tirel who aimed an arrow at a stag, missed the stag, and pierced the king in the chest. Whether this was an accident or murder is unknown to this day.

Source 1

... thickset and muscular with a protruding belly; a dandy dressed in the height of fashion, however outrageous, he wore his blond hair long, parted in the centre and off the face so that his forehead was bare; and in his red, choleric face were eyes of changeable colour, speckled with flecks of light.

Description of William Rufus according to William of Malmesbury, *c*.1128

Henry I (1100–35)

William Rufus was succeeded by his younger brother Henry, who was better educated and cleverer. Straight away he made peace with the Church, invited Anselm back to England and issued a Charter of Liberties that promised fair rule. When threatened by his elder brother Robert, Henry invaded Normandy, defeated his brother's army in 1106 and kept him in prison until he died. Henry became Duke of Normandy as well as King of England.

By the summer of 1120, Henry I had every reason to be pleased with himself. He had been ruling England for twenty years. No one questioned his rule. He had worked with the powerful barons and with the Church to govern sternly but well. During his reign, England stayed peaceful and prospered.

What is more he had an heir, a son called William, who would be king when he died. Henry knew that nothing weakened a country more than disputes about who should be king.

Everything in England seemed safe and secure. What could possibly go wrong? And then disaster struck.

UNIT 2 Matilda or Stephen: who should reign?

What is this all about?

Civil War – a bloody one! Between 1139 and 1153, according to the chroniclers, 'All England was in flames' and 'Christ and his angels slept'. It was a dark and desperate time. In this short unit you will examine the reasons for this civil war. Was it all because the barons would not accept a woman to rule England?

Did you know?

Chroniclers wrote that, after hearing about the death of his son, Henry I did not laugh again for the rest of his life.

Source ①

Medieval manuscript showing the sinking of the White Ship and Henry above it, looking sad.

How a shipwreck changed history

In November 1120 the White Ship was making a routine crossing from Normandy to England. In 1106 Henry I had conquered Normandy and there was a lot of traffic between the two countries. There was nothing special about this particular trip, except that on board was William, Henry's only legitimate son. He was part of a large group of about 300 nobles, their wives and sons. CHRONICLERS say that, because the trip to Normandy had been successful, most people on board were very drunk and persuaded the captain to race the White Ship against some smaller ships to see who would reach England first. The sea was calm and the moon was bright. There was no reason to suppose that disaster lay minutes away. No one knows why (maybe the crew were drunk, too) but the White Ship hit rocks and sank very quickly. Everyone on board was drowned except one man. And that man was not Henry's son!

What...?

CHRONICLER

Someone, usually a monk, who wrote down what he thought were the most important events. The accounts were called chronicles. Some, like the Anglo-Saxon Chronicle, were written over hundreds of years by many different monks. Others were shorter and written by just one person.

Task

Write a longer caption for Source 1 explaining why the sinking of the White Ship was such a disaster for Henry I and how the artist has represented this. Read the information on page 32 before you start.

What...?

LEGITIMATE

Means 'legal'. A king's legitimate children were his children by the woman he was married to. Illegitimate children were his children born to someone he was not married to. Only legitimate children were allowable as heirs.

Henry's problem

Henry was left with a huge problem. He needed to be certain that, when he died, there would be a peaceful handover to his successor. But who was this to be? He had more than 20 illegitimate children but now his only LEGITIMATE heir was his daughter Matilda. In 1120 she was a young woman of eighteen, married to the Holy Roman Emperor who was a powerful European ruler. Matilda was a stranger to England, as she had been sent abroad when she was eight years old so that she could be trained in the language and customs of her new home. In 1120 it looked as though Matilda and her German husband would rule England and Normandy after Henry's death. Henry didn't really believe that the powerful English barons would accept a woman as monarch, especially a woman who was thought of as a foreigner.

Why wouldn't the barons accept a woman?

Legally, there was no reason why a woman couldn't rule medieval England as its queen. The problem lay in what medieval people expected of a monarch and in what a monarch had to do to keep the kingdom secure and prosperous. A medieval monarch had to be physically strong enough to travel around the kingdom on horseback, administering justice and quelling rebellions; a monarch had to lead armies into battle; a monarch had to be strong enough to control and gain the respect of powerful barons. For all these reasons, most medieval people believed women could not be monarchs.

Henry's solutions

Desperate for an heir, Henry tried three approaches to the problem:

- His first idea was to produce more sons himself. His wife had died in 1118 and so, three months after William's death in 1120, Henry married again. His second wife was a young woman, Adela of Louvain. But no child was born to them.
- His second idea was to persuade the barons to accept Matilda. In 1125, Matilda's husband died. So she came back to her father's court. Time was running out for Henry. In 1127 he made all his barons swear they would support Matilda as their queen when he died.
- His third idea was to get some grandsons. In 1128, Henry married Matilda to Geoffrey Plantagenet, Count of Anjou. They had three sons (Henry, Geoffrey and William) and so the SUCCESSION seemed secure.

However, everything was not as happy as it might have been. Although Henry regarded Matilda, her husband and their children as his heirs, he refused to allow them any sort of power base in England or Normandy. This led to furious quarrels between Matilda and her father. Those barons who were completely loyal to Henry felt they had to oppose Matilda. This was not good news for her, and built up trouble for the years ahead.

Task

Read about Henry's solutions. Why was Henry so worried about the succession?

What...?

SUCCESSION

The process by which the Crown passes from one person to the next.

Did you know?

Henry I is said to have died from eating 'a surfeit of lampreys': too many eels, his favourite food.

What...?

CIVIL WAR

A war between citizens of the same country. It might be a war between barons and monarch, between two powerful families fighting for power or, as happened in England in the seventeenth century, between supporters of the King and supporters of Parliament.

Civil war!

King Henry I died on 1 December 1135. Would all the barons keep their promises to Henry and support Matilda as queen? Certainly not! Stephen, who was Matilda's cousin and the richest baron in England, was on the spot and moved quickly. On 22 December he had himself crowned King of England and then recognised as Duke of Normandy. Many great barons rallied round him. A furious Matilda, stuck hundreds of miles away in Anjou, decided to fight. She concentrated first on Normandy, which her armies invaded in 1136, 1137 and 1138. By 1139 she was ready to take on England.

A bloody CIVIL WAR broke out. Law and order collapsed. Barons swapped sides and built castles to defend their lands. A chronicler wrote that 'All England was in flames'.

Matilda had plenty of support in the West Country and made her base in Gloucester. But Stephen controlled London and the wealthier part of what he thought of as his kingdom. Even so, Matilda and her armies advanced steadily eastwards. They gained a tremendous advantage when they defeated Stephen's forces at the Battle of Lincoln in 1141 and captured Stephen himself.

Source **3**

Source **2**

King Stephen is supposed to have been cross-eyed.

This picture of the Empress Matilda comes from a medieval manuscript. ❓▶ *What do you think she is holding in her hand?*

Did you know?

Did you know?

King Henry II, who reigned after King Stephen, was the first of a long line of **Plantagenet** kings of England. Their name comes from the yellow broom flower (in Latin, **planta genista**) which was the badge of Henry II's father (Matilda's second husband), Geoffrey of Anjou.

Source 4
An historian writes

Matilda had an unfortunate personality. She was proud and overbearing, arranging everything as she thought fit. She did not get the crown as she had hoped, not because she was lacking in courage, but more because she had an arrogant and haughty manner and was heartily disliked.

Written by Ben Johnson, editor of the journal *Historic UK* in 2013.

Source 6

When some people saw that King Stephen was a good-humoured, kindly and easy-going man they committed all manner of horrible crimes. And so it lasted for nineteen years while Stephen was King, till the land was all undone and darkened with such deeds, and men said openly that Christ and his angels slept.

From the *Anglo-Saxon Chronicle*.

At this point many of Stephen's supporters, including his brother, were prepared to abandon him and support Matilda as Lady of England and Normandy. Much encouraged, Matilda advanced on London. A splendid welcome with feasting and the ringing of church bells, to be followed by her coronation, was waiting for her. She then made a major mistake. She angrily turned down the citizens' request to have their taxes reduced, and at a stroke turned the Londoners against her. On 24 June as she prepared to enter the city in triumph, the bells rang out to call the citizens to arms and London's gates were slammed shut against her. The civil war broke out all over again.

In 1153, both sides finally reached a settlement. The deaths of his wife and his eldest son had depressed Stephen so much that he was prepared to give up. Matilda realised that she really could only ever hope to control the West Country and that she would never be accepted as Queen of England, and was ready to make peace too. So by the Treaty of Winchester (1153) Stephen and Matilda agreed that Stephen should stay on as King of England for the rest of his life. But when he died, Matilda's eldest son Henry would succeed to the throne.

Matilda retired to Normandy. Stephen lived for eleven more months. After fourteen years of civil war, no one was going to argue about Henry's right to succeed. In December 1154, aged 21, he was crowned King Henry II in Westminster Abbey and began his rule in peace.

Source 5
An historian writes

Matilda sent for the richest men in the kingdom and demanded from them a huge sum of money. She demanded, not with gentleness, but with an air of authority. The men complained that they had no money left because of the war. At this, Matilda, with a grim look, her forehead wrinkled into a frown, every trace of a woman's gentleness removed from her face, blazed into unbearable fury.

Written by Rosemary Rees, in a school textbook published in 1997.

Summary task

Sources 4 and 5 are modern historians' assessment of Matilda.

1 Read Source 4. Why does the historian Ben Johnson think that Matilda didn't get the crown of England?

2 How far does Source 5 support his view?

3 How far does what you have read in this unit support his view?

4 Many kings of England had an 'arrogant and haughty manner'! Write a paragraph saying whether or not you agree that the only reason Matilda did not become Queen of England was because she was a woman.

Hint: You will need to use the information in this unit and the sources to support your argument. You should also refer to the good and bad qualities of a monarch that you considered on page 8 and refer to these in your answer.

Filling in the gaps: Henry II and Richard I

Source ❶

King Henry II, 1133–89.

Henry II

Henry II reigned from 1154 to 1189. He married Eleanor of Aquitaine, which brought him plenty of French territory to add to his empire.

Henry II was a thick-built man, highly educated but with a fierce temper as you will see in his dealings with Thomas Becket (see pages 100–103). He had a number of sons, his favourite being John. However, his sons rebelled against him towards the end of his reign which made him even angrier. But to remember Henry purely as a monarch with a very bad temper is unfair on him.

- He set up a Great Council and governed England well. Especially important were the improvements he made in the running of the legal system and taxation.
- Trade with Germany and Italy flourished, especially the wool trade.
- There was only one revolt – in 1173–74 – and that was easily crushed.
- He introduced strong English rule in Ireland in 1172 and made the Welsh recognise the power of the English Crown.

Source ❷

This statue of Richard I stands outside the Houses of Parliament in London. It was installed in 1899.

Richard I (Richard the Lionheart)

When Henry died he was succeeded by his son Richard. King Richard was a great soldier who was heavily involved in the religious wars between Christians and Muslims known as the Crusades. Indeed Richard led the Third Crusade. You can find out more on pages 132–33. He was away from England for most of his reign, in fact he only visited England twice. Both times he came simply to raise more money for his wars abroad, especially the Crusades and wars against Philip II of France.

When Richard was away, the country was run well by Hubert Walter who was, amongst other things, Archbishop of Canterbury. Knights living in the country were given greater responsibly in day-to-day government.

In 1192 Richard was returning from the Crusades when he was taken prisoner by one of his enemies, Duke Leopold of Austria. For two years he was kept prisoner until he bought his release in 1194 using £100,000 of tax money raised in England. He died in 1199 leaving England a much poorer country.

His brother John succeeded him. You are going to examine John's reign in detail in the next unit.

UNIT 3 Who made the biggest mistakes: John or Henry III?

What is this all about?

From Units 1 and 2 it will be clear to you that for a king to control England he needed the support of his barons. That is how William I got control – he gave them land in return for their armies and loyalty. From then on being a strong king meant having a good relationship with your barons. They ran the country for you. They even raised money for you.

In this unit you will study two kings who quarrelled with the barons – John in 3.1 and Henry III in 3.2. They both ended up waging civil war against them. But they also made some other mistakes. Your job will be to work out what they got wrong and why. At the end you will decide which of the two made the biggest mistakes.

Map **❶**

Key
- Lands held by Henry as King
- Lands held from the King of France
- Lands held by marriage (belonged to the King's wife)
- Lands claimed but others controlled

0   250 km

The Angevin Empire. **?** *If you were a king trying to control all the empire, where would be the best place to live?*

3.1 King John

What did John inherit from Richard I?

When John became king he inherited a large empire. His power stretched all the way from the edge of Scotland to the south of France – see Map 1. It included all of England and much of France. It was known as the Angevin Empire. It had fine farming land, important ports and trade routes, flourishing towns and a growing population.

However, it was not automatically his. To take possession of the French part of the Empire lands he had to promise to serve the King of France. And the current King of France and the French barons did not want John as king. They wanted his nephew Arthur.

Back in England, John was better placed. He had the goodwill of the barons. They all agreed he was the right person to be the next king. However, John's brother Richard had left some big problems for John to sort out. Richard had spent much of his reign fighting Crusades in the Holy Land. This meant he more or less ignored England – leaving the barons and the Church leaders to run the country for him. He ran up big debts paying for these wars.

Did you know?

ELEANOR OF AQUITAINE
She was queen in two countries: France between 1137 and 1152 because she was married to Louis VII, and England between 1154 and 1189 as wife of Henry II. See pages 174–175 for more detail.

What did King John do?

John's first need was to get himself accepted as king by Philip II of France. Luckily his mother, Eleanor of Aquitaine, helped him. She was French and she persuaded Philip that John should be king, not Arthur. In return John pledged loyalty to Philip and agreed to be his vassal – that is, to serve Philip. So in 1200 John took control of his lands in France and the reign had got off to a good start.

 Task

Over the next four pages you are going to examine King John's reign in outline. You are going to find out what he did (and why we think he did it) and you are going to examine the results of each of his actions. As you read each section prepare an 'action' card like this:

John **ACTION**

Action: He agreed to be Philip's vassal

Reason: So the French king would accept him as king

Result: + He got his land in France
− He was under Philip's control

ACTION

He married Isabella of Angoulême

In 1200 John married Isabella of Angoulême. This was a useful move because control of Angoulême would help John to keep a firm grip on his Angevin empire. But it did not work out well.

Did you know?

In the Middle Ages noble families promised their daughters in marriage when they were very young. It is possible that Isabella was only eight years old when she was promised in marriage. She could be properly married when she was twelve years old.

- A powerful baron called Hugh, Lord of Lusignan, had already been promised that Isabella would be his wife when she came of age. When Hugh heard that John had married her, he was furious.
- Hugh demanded compensation from John. John refused so Hugh complained about John's behaviour to King Philip of France.
- Philip ordered John to appear before a French court to answer for his actions. He had the power to do this because John was his vassal.
- John refused to appear before the court and, in 1202, Philip ordered that John should lose his lands in France.

ACTION

He murdered his nephew Arthur

Philip made John's nephew Arthur Lord of Aquitaine, Maine and Anjou and declared war against John. At first John was the more successful. He even took Arthur prisoner. What happened next did great damage to John's reputation. In 1203 John ordered that Arthur be murdered. Arthur was stabbed to death, a stone was tied to his body and he was thrown into the River Seine. This murder caused widespread disgust among the barons in both France and England. Many French barons became supporters of Philip in his war against John.

ACTION ➡

┌─ Did you know? ─┐

John did not trust the barons. To force them to do what he wanted he took as hostage the sons of the barons that he thought might rebel against him. He treated the family of one baron, William de Braose, particularly badly. John demanded that de Braose pay a very large fine and when he couldn't do so, John sent him into exile and starved his wife and son to death.

He increased taxes on the barons

Things now went from bad to worse for John. His mother Eleanor of Aquitaine died so he lost control of Aquitaine. King Philip conquered Norway so he lost that region too. John spent most of his reign trying (and mostly failing) to win back these French lands. He had two big problems:

- Normally the barons could be relied on to provide a king with an army but in this case they refused because they did not trust John and the English barons did not think that the French lands were important. Their land was in England. Normandy was nothing to do with them. It was the king's problem.
- If John could not get an army from the barons then he needed to recruit whoever would fight for him. So he recruited mercenaries (soldiers who fight for anyone who pays them). These mercenaries were expensive and they were not really loyal to John. His armies also needed modern weapons.

To pay these mercenaries, and to pay for these weapons, he decided to tax the barons very heavily.

- He used all the feudal powers at his disposal. For example, any baron who did not provide an army had to pay a tax called scutage instead. John demanded scutage from the barons.
- He also increased inheritance tax and tax on the property of widows.
- He imposed huge fines for crimes committed by barons.
- He sold important positions at court to the highest bidder. Many barons had to borrow money to pay King John. They resented these taxes greatly and they did not trust John to use the money well.

ACTION ➡

┌─ Did you know? ─┐

King John had a number of nicknames given to him by people at the time. One was 'Lackland' because he was not given land by his father (unlike his brothers). The other was 'Softsword' because his armies were occasionally defeated in battle. The second nickname is a bit harsh because John was really quite a good general.

He tried to run the country without the barons

The feudal barons were the 165 most powerful barons who owned much of the land in England. They had supported John when he came to the throne in 1199. Instead of appointing these barons to important jobs John chose to ignore their advice and do things his way. He took a personal interest in running the country. Unlike his brother and father (who were hardly ever in England), after he lost Normandy in 1204, John stayed most of the time in England. He was serious about running England well. The problem was that he was held personally responsible for any mistakes.

ACTION ➡ ## He quarrelled with the Pope

Kings had to work with Church leaders, not against them. In 1207 the job of Archbishop of Canterbury was vacant. The usual pattern was for the king to propose someone and the Pope to approve them. But Pope Innocent III did not like John's candidate and instead appointed Simon Langton. What happened next?

Source ❶

This medieval painting shows a monk offering John a poisoned chalice, a drink laced with deadly poison.

? *There is no other evidence this ever happened but what does it tell you about the relationship between John and the Church?*

- John was not pleased with the Pope's choice. He confiscated the land of the Archbishop of Canterbury and banished the monks attached to the Cathedral.
- The Pope retaliated in 1208 by imposing an interdict on England. This meant that all the churches had to shut.
- John responded in fury by confiscating the property of any priest who carried out the interdict.
- In 1209 John was EXCOMMUNICATED from the Catholic Church.

What...?

EXCOMMUNICATION

This was the most serious punishment that any Pope could hand out. If someone was excommunicated it meant that he or she could not go to church and take part in any church services. This would mean that if you died while you were excommunicated, you would go to hell.

ACTION  *He tried to recapture Normandy*

One of John's driving ambitions was to regain land in France. In 1206 he had one success – he won back Gascony. He was determined to get Normandy as well. In 1214 he gambled. He allied with the Count of Boulogne and Otto of Brunswick to launch an attack on Poitou to try to win back Normandy. His armies were totally defeated at Bouvines. The result was he lost credibility as an army leader, and most of the taxes he had raised had been wasted.

🔼 Task

You should have made at least six action cards by now. There should be one on:

- marrying Isabella
- choosing officials
- murdering Arthur
- quarrels with the Pope
- raising taxes
- attacking Normandy.

Now do some work with them.

a) Lay them out on a sheet in front of you and discuss with a partner how they are connected with each other.

b) Which of these do you think were mistakes? They would be mistakes if they damaged John or damaged England.

c) Of these mistakes, which do you think did the most serious damage to John? Why?

Keep the cards. You will need them later.

What...?

MAGNA CARTA
Translated into English
means Great Charter.

Magna Carta

John was in a weak position. To him each of his actions so far might have seemed sensible and fair. To others in England they looked like mistakes. They thought that John was either dangerous or incompetent.

Some of the leading barons met to discuss their grievances against John. They were told of a charter dating from the time of Henry I that spelled out the rights and liberties of the barons. They decided they needed something similar – a new charter, agreed by the king – that would secure their rights and would control the king. Some were prepared if necessary to fight against the king to force him to sign it. In 1215 around 40 barons, mainly from the north and west of England and East Anglia, met in Bury St Edmunds. They chose Robert fitz Walter to lead them.

They sent soldiers to occupy London and John was forced to negotiate. On 19 June 1215, at Runnymede near Windsor, MAGNA CARTA was signed. The rebel barons promised to serve John and it seemed that a peaceful solution to the problem had been found.

Source ❷

No freeman shall be arrested and imprisoned, or disposed, or outlawed, or banished, or in any way molested … unless by the lawful judgement of his peers and by the law of the land.

Chapter 39 of the charter.

What did the charter say?

Magna Carta outlined the feudal rights and liberties of the barons and other groups including merchants, knights and clergy.

- It put limits on the taxes such as scutage that the King could raise from the barons.
- Chapter 14 defined the powers of the Great Council. It said that a monarch had to ask the advice of the barons before he could raise taxes. He did not have to get their approval but he had to discuss it.
- The rights of the Church were made clear.
- The liberties enjoyed by London and other towns were guaranteed.
- The courts were to be improved so that everyone had the right to a fair trial.

How did John react?

Magna Carta did not stay in force for long. John had signed the charter but he did not accept it. He especially hated Chapter 14. After two months John got Pope Innocent III to declare that Magna Carta was against God's will – nothing could limit the power of a monarch appointed by God. Civil war broke out again. John's experience and skill as a soldier allowed him quickly to defeat the rebels in all parts of the country except London. It looked as if John might be able to crush the rebels entirely.

In desperation, the London rebels offered the throne of England to Louis of France (son of King Philip) in return for help. Louis landed with his armies in England in 1216. Many barons flocked to join him. The tide of the civil war had turned back in favour of the rebel barons.

At this cliff-hanger moment, John died (of natural causes, probably dysentery). One of the most tempestuous and controversial reigns was over.

Did you know?

After John's death in 1216, Isabella of Angoulême returned to France and married Hugh of Lusignan. So he got the promised wife in the end!

WHY DID JOHN SIGN THE MAGNA CARTA?

SOURCE INVESTIGATION

Did you know?

Four copies of the Magna Carta have survived. Two of the copies are on display at the British Library in London. One copy is in the archives at Lincoln Cathedral and the other at Salisbury Cathedral. You can read a full translation of the charter on the British Library website at www.bl.uk.

The signing of the Magna Carta was a key point in history; when the power of the monarch was brought under control and the liberties of the people were recognised for the first time. Read and study the sources carefully and then answer the following question.

Source A

An early twentieth-century painting of King John signing the Magna Carta that now hangs in the House of Lords in the British Parliament. The original is enormous – about 5 metres across.

Source B

Seeing that he had the support of only seven knights, King John tried to deceive the barons into making peace by promising them the laws and liberties they required. But the king's messengers told the barons that John was trying to deceive them. So the barons chose the fifteenth of June for the king to meet them at Runneymede. When the two sides met they began a long discussion about terms of peace. King John, seeing that he was inferior in strength to the barons granted the Magna Carta.

Roger of Wendover, *Flowers of History*, 1215.

Source C

1214 was a disastrous year for John. Once again, he suffered military defeat in an attempt to get back his territory in northern France. He returned to London demanding more money from taxes. This time the barons were not willing to listen. They rebelled against his power. The barons captured London. However, they did not defeat John entirely and by the Spring of 1215, both sides were willing to discuss matters. The result was the Magna Carta.

Chris Trueman, historylearningsite (2000–2013).

QUESTIONS

1 What are the differences between **Sources B** and **C** in their attitude to King John?
2 Which of **Sources A, B** or **C** do you think is the most reliable in telling us about the signing of the Magna Carta? Explain your choice of source.
3 Using **all** of the sources and your own knowledge, how far do you agree that the barons forced John to sign the Magna Carta?

3.2 Henry III

Source ❸

A portrait of Henry III painted in 1250.

Imagine someone suggesting to a younger pupil at your school that they become your monarch. It may sound silly for someone so young to become a country's ruler but it happened in the Middle Ages. In 1216, John's son Henry became king of England at the age of nine, although for the first eleven years that he was Henry III, he was told what to do by his guardians William Marshal and then Hubert de Burgh. All the problems left over from John's reign needed solving:

● Their first task was to end the Civil War. They used the iron fist! The rebel barons were (ruthlessly) defeated at Lincoln and a French fleet was destroyed. Louis returned to France.

● The second task was to solve the problems that had led to the Civil War. Here they used the velvet glove! William Marshal reissued Magna Carta. He was lucky in that one of its biggest opponents, Pope Innocent III, had died. Now the charter was discussed and agreed with the barons and approved by the new Pope. It was finally sealed in 1225 at a public ceremony in front of a crowd made up of both former rebel and loyal barons. It was accepted into English law. It was binding on king and barons alike.

Henry III was still only eighteen. Things had started well. This did not last.

 Task

As you study Henry's reign you will prepare action cards just as you did for John's reign. Make one card for each of these actions:
• building impressive churches and cathedrals
• appointing Poitevins to top jobs
• trying to win back French lands
• trying to buy the throne of Sicily
• ignoring the Provisions of Oxford.

Henry takes charge

From 1227 Henry began to rule in his own right. Like his father he believed that a king's power had been given to him by God. He distrusted the barons and they distrusted him.

Cathedrals

Henry ordered the building of a large number of churches and cathedrals. The most famous work undertaken during his reign was the rebuilding of Westminster Abbey and the Palace of Westminster. The problem was that such building was very expensive and the money for these projects had to be raised through taxes.

Did you know?

Henry III was a very religious man. He admired Edward the Confessor and took to dressing like him, wearing simple robes instead of grand expensive ones. Even when on his travels he still insisted on hearing Mass three times each day.

Did you know?

At one point in 1250 there were over 800 people working at the Westminster Abbey building site. Henry insisted that the tomb of Edward the Confessor be moved to the centre of the Abbey. In doing so he created the tradition for England's monarchs to be buried in the Abbey.

┌─ **What...?** ─┐

JUSTICIAR
One of the most important officials at court in the Middle Ages. He looked after all of the king's business.

POITEVINS
People from Poitou in west central France. In the fourteenth century the Poitevins were disliked in the rest of France just as much as they were in England. Peter des Rivaux thought so much of himself that he appointed himself sheriff of 21 counties!

MARK
A weight of gold or silver equal to 8 ounces or 226.8 grams. Now you can work out how many kilograms of gold and silver that Henry paid to the Pope and you can understand why the barons were so annoyed!

Foreign influence

Henry appointed a number of non-English advisers and gave top jobs in the Church to foreigners such as the Frenchman Peter des Roches (who was made Bishop of Winchester). In the winter of 1231–32, foreign church tax collectors started to receive anonymous threatening letters. Henry blamed his English JUSTICIAR, Hubert de Burgh, for having something to do with the letters and he sacked him.

Henry replaced Hubert with an Englishman, Stephen of Seagrave. But he was just about the only Englishman in a position of real power. At the Exchequer, a POITEVIN, Peter de Rivaux, made a number of changes that gave Henry more power. Sheriffs were given greater power in the regions at the expense of the barons. To make matters worse, most of the English sheriffs were sacked.

In response to this foreign influence some barons, led by Richard the Marshal, attempted a rebellion in 1233. They were easily defeated. Richard was killed in Ireland in 1234.

The rebellion did persuade Henry to sack des Roches and des Rivaux in 1234 but he gave the latter a new job in 1236. Henry's marriage to Eleanor in 1236 brought a fresh wave of foreigners to court.

French wars

Henry was as unsuccessful as his father in his foreign policy.

● In 1229 Henry tried and failed to re-conquer Aquitaine.
● In 1230 his expedition to recover Brittany also failed.
● He was defeated again in 1242 when he tried to win Poitou from the French king, Louis IX.

Henry's wars cost too much money and the barons were not very pleased because taxes were too high.

King of Sicily

In 1254 Henry promised to give the Pope money to fight a war in Sicily in return for choosing his son Edmund as king of Sicily and Apulia. The fee was a huge 135,541 MARKS plus an annual sum to be paid to the Pope. Henry's idea to make Edmund king of Sicily was not just about prestige. In the fourteenth century Sicily was a rich island. It was also well placed to control the Mediterranean and had been part of the Norman Empire. But this was too much for the barons. Simon de Montfort had been one of Henry's foreign favourites. However, they had fallen out over money, family and Simon's behaviour when ruling Gascony on Henry's behalf. Simon now emerged as the leader of the disgruntled barons. They met in Oxford in 1258 and drew up the Provisions of Oxford, which limited Henry's power.

Provisions of Oxford, 1258

- A Council was to be set up to advise the King. The majority of its members were to be nobles. The King could not make decisions without the Council's agreement.
- The Council was to choose the King's important officials including the Chancellor.
- A regular Parliament would be held every three years. Fifteen members of the Council would meet with a further twelve barons to discuss the issues of the day.
- Henry swore an oath promising to rule according to the points set out by the Provisions.

Did you know?

PARLIAMENT
The word parliament comes from the French *parlemenz* meaning discussion.

At the time Henry had little choice but to accept these proposals. But three years later he decided that he would ignore them. He did not want a regular Parliament. Civil war loomed. King Louis IX of France was asked by both sides and in the Mise of Amiens, 1264, he decided in Henry's favour.

Civil war (again)

The barons were not happy with Louis' decision and civil war broke out. For a couple of years the barons had the upper hand. The King's army was defeated at the Battle of Lewes in 1264 and Henry himself and his son Edward were taken prisoner.

In 1265 the barons' leader, Simon de Montfort, called a Parliament. Two knights from each shire and two burgesses from each town were asked to attend. The Parliament met to discuss such issues as tax. This was a much more ambitious Parliament than had originally been proposed under the Provisions of Oxford. Most importantly, for the first time, 'commoners' were invited. Up to now Parliament had only ever included barons. But this Parliament included knights and BURGESSES. With the King and his son still prisoners, and the decisions taken by the barons, this was a radically different form of government from that of the last 200 years. Some of de Montfort's supporters began to feel he had gone too far. When Edward escaped from captivity in 1265 he led Henry's loyal barons to defeat de Montfort at the Battle of Evesham. De Montfort was killed and the other rebels were savagely pursued and executed. By 1267 the civil war was over and Henry had won.

What...?

BURGESS
An important person in a town.

Parliament did not meet again in Henry's reign. However, the idea that the barons, knights and important townspeople were to be consulted about the issues of the day was here to stay.

Henry's death

Henry had a long reign – nearly 60 years. He survived civil war and rebellion. Yet he gets much less attention than most other kings of England. He died in 1272 and his body was laid alongside that of his hero Edward the Confessor.

Summary task

1 Who made the biggest mistakes?
You have been gathering together action cards for John and Henry. Use these cards to compare their performance. Draw a scale from –5 (big mistake) to +5 (great success). Put John above the line and Henry below the line. Then place each action on the scale.
Now use this plan to help you to compare John and Henry's performance.
a) Did they have any successes?
b) What was John's most damaging mistake?
c) What was Henry's most damaging mistake?
d) Did John and Henry make similar mistakes?

2 Here are two pairs of pictures (right) of John and Henry III, drawn by the same person at different times. In each pair, John is on the left. What impression do you get of each king from the pictures? How is the second pair different from the first?

3 Essay question.
Describe the main events that led to the signing of Magna Carta.
Hint: Make sure you look at both the longer term and the shorter term causes. You should mention all the events on your John action cards in your essay. NB See page 183 for a practice evidence question on King John.

John   Henry

Pulling it all together

For each king you have studied so far, fill out a card like this. You might not be able to fill out every row.

King:		
Top tasks for a king	**Score out of 5**	**Reason for score**
Win wars		
Gain territory/keep what you've got		
Get on well with barons		
Get on well with church leaders		
Keep law and order and peace in the country		
Spend money wisely		
Have healthy sons		
Be a good leader		
Have a good claim to the throne		
Average score		

UNIT 4 Edward I: why was he such a success?

What is this all about?

Edward I was King of England from 1272 to 1307. He learned from his father's mistakes. He surrounded himself with intelligent advisers and made sure that he consulted his leading barons, churchmen, knights and townsmen. Edward also had great success as a war leader – he brought both Wales and (for a short while) Scotland under English control. Edward sounds like a successful king all round!

Through the first part of this unit, 4.1, you will find out how he achieved this reputation. In 4.2 you will examine Edward's impact on the story of castles which you began on page 22.

4.1 How did Edward deal with Wales and Scotland?

Source ❶

A statue of Edward I in York Minster

When Edward I became king in 1272 he was 33. He was already an experienced soldier. He had been on Crusade. He had led his father's armies to victory against rebel barons in the civil war. He had a reputation as an ambitious, impatient and ruthless leader. He had ferociously hunted down and punished the king's enemies.

His first big challenge as a king was how to deal with Wales.

Task

Make your own copy of this simple diagram. As you work through the unit add notes to it to make your own concept map about Edward's reputation. You can use a different colour for each branch and use pictures as well as words. You could add other main 'branches' if you wish.

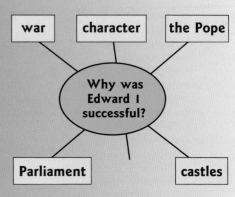

war | character | the Pope

Why was Edward I successful?

Parliament | castles

Did you know?

On 25 April 1284 Edward's wife, Eleanor of Castile, gave birth to a son at Caernarfon Castle. He was christened Edward. In 1301 he was made Prince of Wales. Ever since then the eldest son of an English monarch has been given the title.

Wales

None of the English kings had ever conquered Wales. They had not really tried. It was a country of dense forests, high mountains and poor roads. And as long as the Welsh did not trouble England there was no particular reason to conquer it.

In the 1250s the border areas (see Map 2 on page 56) were run by the Marcher lords who were loyal to the king – but the rest of Wales was under the control of a Welsh prince, Llywelyn the Great of Gwynedd. He paid homage to Edward's father Henry. The relationship between Wales and England remained stable.

Llywelyn the Last

Llywelyn the Last was Llywelyn the Great's grandson. He had inherited one third of Wales from his grandfather. The other two thirds had gone to his brothers Owain and Dafydd. He believed that these lands should be united and he fought against his brothers and won. By 1267 he was in control of all Wales. But even this did not change the relationship with English. He promised homage to Henry III and Henry recognised Llywelyn's right to be Prince of Wales. So far the pattern was much the same as in earlier years.

However the situation was about to change. Despite his promise, Llywelyn was not very loyal to Henry. He joined Simon de Montfort's opposition to Henry III (see page 46) and then when Henry died Llywelyn went out of his way to show Edward that he did not think much of him.

- He refused to give homage to Edward I.
- In 1273 he married the daughter of the leader of the rebel barons.
- He started to build a castle at Dolforwyn to resist any English invasion.

It won't surprise you, given Edward's reputation, that he decided to take action. But notice how he did it.

- He summoned Parliament – all the leading knights, citizens and burgesses. They agreed to raise the tax on selling wool and leather. Wool was Britain's most important product at that time.
- He asked Llywelyn once again to pay him homage.
- He raised a strong army of 15,000 men and marched on Wales. This was the largest army ever raised by an English king.

Llywelyn saw that he had no chance and decided to talk not fight. The resulting treaty was not a success for Llywelyn but neither was it a total disaster.

- Llywelyn promised to give homage to Edward but Edward no longer recognised that he was OVERLORD of Wales.
- However, Edward allowed Llywelyn to keep the title of Prince of Wales.
- Edward also realised that it made good sense to be kind and he allowed Llywelyn to keep some of his land around Snowdon.

Wales conquered

However, the Welsh prince was not content. In 1282 Llywelyn and his brother Dafydd attacked Edward's castles at Flint and Rhuddlan. Edward sent another army into Wales. This time the result was decisive. Llywelyn was killed in battle at Irfon Bridge in December 1282. Dafydd was captured and executed. Edward stripped Llywelyn's family of their lands and, by the Statute of Rhuddlan of 1284, Wales was divided up into English-style counties. English laws were applied to Wales.

Edward was determined that the Welsh would not rebel again. In 1283 he ordered the building of three great castles of Conwy, Harlech and Caernarfon. Wales was fully under English control.

Did you know?

Wool was by far the most important commodity produced by farmers in the Middle Ages. English wool was sold across Europe, especially in Antwerp which is now in Belgium. Wool was so important to the English economy that the king's ministers in Parliament sat on woolsacks.

Did you know?

Edward I's nickname was Longshanks, meaning long legs. He was very tall.

What...?

OVERLORD
A powerful feudal ruler.

Source 2
An historian writes

After the death of Llywelyn ap Gruffydd, Dafydd was captured and executed by hanging, drawing and quartering – a public and cruel death. Edward enforced English law and language and divided Wales into seven counties enforcing the feudal system. Llywelyn's dream of a united Wales had been ruined.

Judith Kidd and Linda Richards in *Power and the People 1066–1485*, published 2002.

Did you know?

The Scots and the French were often friends and ALLIES against the English. Their friendship has been known in Scotland as the Auld Alliance.

Did you know?

There are different stories of how Wallace became an OUTLAW. Some say he killed the son of the governor of Dundee who was bullying him. Others that he killed two English soldiers who accused him of stealing fish. Either way he fled to the woods and joined other outlaws.

What...?

ABDICATE
Give up the throne.

What about Scotland?

Even more of a potential thorn in any king of England's side was Scotland. Scottish kings had, in the past, given homage to the English kings. However, in 1189 King William the Lion of Scotland bought freedom from homage from Richard I of England. After his success in Wales Edward wanted to have greater control over Scotland. First he tried the marriage route. In 1286 King Alexander II of Scotland died and was succeeded by his four-year-old granddaughter Margaret, Maid of Norway. Edward spotted his chance and arranged the marriage of Margaret to his (then six-year-old) son Edward. Unfortunately, Margaret died on her journey to England in 1290.

'Lord Paramount'

There was no clear successor, so the Scottish nobles, who feared a civil war between the rival claimants, asked Edward to help them judge who had the best claim. This was Edward's great opportunity. He agreed to do this but only on condition that the nobles recognise him as 'Lord Paramount' of Scotland. Caught between the prospect of a civil war in their own country and giving homage to Edward they reluctantly chose the latter.

In 1292 Edward chose John Balliol as King of Scotland. Edward now used his new power to interfere in the running of Scottish affairs. He ordered John Balliol to London and demanded he provide an army for him to pursue a separate war against France. John Balliol's position was impossible and the Scottish nobles jointly renounced their homage to Edward and asked the French for help in fighting a war against Edward!
Edward's response was speedy and ferocious. He sent an army to capture Berwick-on-Tweed who slaughtered everyone in the town. He captured John Balliol and forced him to ABDICATE. Then his army continued north and totally defeated the Scottish army at Dunbar in 1296.

Map ❶

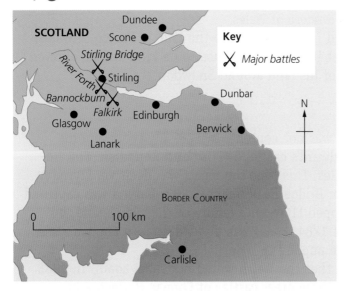

A map showing the battles between England and Scotland.

Enter William Wallace!

William Wallace was the leader of a group of outlaws. Following the humiliation at Dunbar, Wallace decided it was a time for the Scots to rise up in full-scale revolt against the English. Through 1297 he led his men as they swept across Scotland attacking the English wherever they could find them. Wallace's gang of outlaws had turned into a successful guerrilla army. They killed the sheriff of Lanark, supposedly because he had killed Wallace's sweetheart. Although totally outnumbered they seized Lanark, Glasgow and Scone. More Scots flocked to join Wallace's army including the future king of Scotland, Robert Bruce.

<table><tr><td>

Did you know?

During the wars in Wales, Edward I became aware of the efficiency of the Welsh longbow – a deadly weapon up to six feet long. It was probably the decisive weapon at the Battle of Falkirk and was later used with great success against the French cavalry at battles such as Crécy in 1345 and Agincourt in 1415.
</td></tr></table>

The Battle of Stirling Bridge

Edward was alarmed by the news of Wallace's success and sent an army of 40,000 foot soldiers and 300 horsemen north to deal with the threat. However, an approaching English army was not the only problem facing Wallace in the late summer of 1297. Many Scottish lords who had joined up with Wallace were uneasy and changed sides. Despite this setback, Wallace managed to push the English armies south of the River Forth and his armies laid siege to Dundee. In early September 1297, Wallace's spies informed him that an English army led by the Earl of Surrey was advancing on the Abbey of Cambuskenneth. Wallace called off the siege of Dundee and rushed to face the English. His army caught the English soldiers attempting to cross the river at Stirling Bridge on 11 September. The battle was a disaster for the English and a triumph for Wallace.

'Hero of Scotland'

The English were utterly defeated and Wallace was now the hero of Scotland. He was made regent (which means he took charge) while the real king John Balliol was a prisoner in England. He did not wait for a very angry Edward to get another army together; instead he decided to invade England. Wallace's army got as far south as Newcastle before hearing of an English army of 100,000 foot soldiers and 8,000 cavalry coming his way.

The Battle of Falkirk

Wallace did not want a fixed battle. He knew he was outnumbered and that was not how he had succeeded in the past. He tried to organise a surprise attack more in the style of the Battle of Stirling Bridge but he was betrayed by two Scottish nobles and Edward found out about his plans. Instead Wallace retreated from the English forces, operating a 'scorched-earth' policy – destroying all food and supplies that Edward's army could use. Edward's army did begin to suffer – food was short and morale was low.

Finally the two armies met face to face at the Battle of Falkirk, 22 July 1298. The battle was a disaster for Wallace. His army was outnumbered three to one and one of his most important allies, Comyn, Lord of Badenoch, led his men off the battlefield halfway through the fight. Wallace's army was beaten but he managed to escape capture by fleeing to Stirling and then to France.

Conclusion

Edward ordered that Scotland come under English rule although it could keep its own laws. Scottish nobles and knights could sit in the English parliament but had to give up their forts and castles. This was not the end of the story. English control did not last (see page 60) but for now it was another resounding success for Edward.

Source ③

A statue of William Wallace in Dryburgh in the Scottish Borders.

What happened to William Wallace?

Wallace tried to get Philip, King of France, to support the Scottish cause. He failed and returned to Scotland in 1303 to carry on fighting the English. Edward offered a reward of 300 marks for the capture of Wallace. This was a very large sum of money for the time. Eventually, one of Wallace's servants, Jack Short, betrayed Wallace to the Scottish baron John Monteith, who captured him and took him to Dumbarton Castle, and then to London. On 23 August 1305 Wallace was tried in Westminster Hall, accused of treason against Edward. Wallace denied the charges. He argued that he could not be guilty of treason against Edward because Edward was not King of Scotland and had no right to send an army there.

Wallace was found guilty and condemned to death. He was dragged through the streets of London to Smithfield. He was then hanged, drawn and quartered. His head was put on a pole on London Bridge, his right arm was sent to Newcastle, his left arm to Berwick, his right leg to Perth and his left leg to Aberdeen. It was a horrible death.

Task

Work in pairs to write two plaques to go with the statue in Source 3 explaining what Wallace achieved. One of you be positive: emphasise Wallace's heroism and successes; the other be negative: emphasise his criminal past and his failures. Discuss which of these plaques gets closest to the truth.

Source ④

Edward I presiding over Parliament. ❓▶ *Use the internet to find a picture of Parliament today. What similarities and differences do you see?*

Edward and Parliament

There was more to Edward's success than his war record. He was only able to win his wars against the Welsh and the Scots because he kept the support of people in England. In particular, he knew how to work with the barons in Parliament. Edward's wars and castles cost a lot of money. Magna Carta had stated that no monarch could raise taxes without 'the common consent of the people'. This did not mean that the king had to ask everyone's consent and it certainly did not mean that he had to ask the poorer people what they thought. But it was a check on the king's power and Edward was the first king to know how to handle it. He used his Great Council (selected group of advisers) well. You have already seen how he summoned Parliament before he started his conquest of Wales. In 1295 he called another Parliament known as 'The Model Parliament' with the aim of seeking advice before he embarked on his Scottish campaigns.

Did you know?

As part of his money raising, Edward I taxed Jewish moneylenders. When they could no longer pay, they were accused of disloyalty and Edward abolished their right to lend money at interest. He decreed that every Jew over seven years old had to wear a yellow badge. Later he arrested all the heads of Jewish households: 300 were taken to the Tower of London and executed. Others were killed in their own homes. In 1290 the King banished all Jews from the country.

Did you know?

When Edward's wife Eleanor died in 1290 Edward was devastated. She had born him 16 children – most of whom had died as babies. Her body was taken from Lincoln to London. The journey took 12 days. Edward ordered that a stone cross be built at each point that her funeral procession stopped for the night. The final stop was at Charing Cross in London and a replica of the Eleanor Cross still stands outside Charing Cross station today.

This was a very different attitude from his father's. Even so things were not all plain sailing for Edward. When the barons and many merchants did not like his plans for high taxes in 1297, they made Edward agree to the Confirmation of the Charters. This said that Edward could not raise taxes without Parliament's approval. This was a change. Before they had given advice; now they had to approve. Edward agreed to the Confirmation because he was, at the time, at war with both France and Scotland. Edward's strength was that he understood that, if he was going to govern effectively and have the money he needed, then he would have to give ground occasionally. For example, in 1303 Edward I gave merchants the right to trade freely in return for accepting a new taxation system.

Edward and the Pope

Edward dealt with the Church far better than most of the previous kings. Again, he learned from the mistakes of others. In 1296, Pope Boniface VIII thought that he would try and impose his authority on Edward I. In a letter called *Clericis laicos* he told all of the priests in England that they should not pay tax to Edward without his permission. Edward was not pleased and threatened to take the lands of any clergy who did not pay tax. Importantly, he got the support of the people through the Great Council and Parliament for his stand. The Pope backed down and Edward had won the day.

Edward died as he had lived – fighting a war. In 1306 there was a new Scottish rebellion and despite ill health Edward joined the campaign. But he died en route to Scotland in 1307. On his tombstone it reads: 'Here lies Edward I, Hammer of the Scots.' This is how they chose to remember at the time. Do you think that is how Edward should be remembered?

Summary task

You should have now compiled a diagram summarising the different elements of Edward's achievements. Add to it as you study Unit 4.2 with details about castles. Then use it to help you write an essay:

'Why was Edward successful in extending royal control in England and beyond?'

In your essay you will first need to **describe how** Edward extended royal control. You will need to mention Wales, Scotland, the relationship with the barons and the Pope.

Then you will need to use your own judgement to **explain why** he was able to do this. Your chart will give you many ideas to work with but make sure you consider how each of the following helped him succeed:

- his skills as a military leader
- his character
- the way he worked with Parliament.

4.2 How and why did castles change?

What is this all about?
Through the previous units there have been many references to castles. In Unit 1 they were vitally important to the Normans in their conquest of England. In this unit they were equally important to Edward in conquering Wales more than 200 years later. However, Edward's castles were very different from William's. Between 1066 and 1300 castles had changed significantly. Find out how and why.

Stage 1: Motte and bailey

The Normans used castles to establish their authority in England. The first motte and bailey castles were built in strategically important locations such as river crossings or crossroads. They were constructed mainly of wood, were very easily burned down and could not be built very tall. Their purpose was to act as a base for groups of soldiers who were controlling a region. The more troublesome a region, the more castles were built.

Stage 2: Stone keep castles

After the 1069 rebellion, William decided that he needed to build more permanent reminders of Norman power. Stone keep castles were built to last. The most famous of these castles were the White Tower at the Tower of London (page 22) and Rochester Castle in Kent (Source 5). With a stone keep, there was no need for a mound of earth. Instead a keep was built with strong foundations and could be built high. The defenders could spot attackers several kilometres away which gave time to prepare their defences.

There was still a bailey but it too was surrounded by a stone wall. The front door of the keep was on the first floor so if attackers penetrated the outer walls the defenders could lift the wooden steps inside, making it near impossible for the attackers to get into the keep.

As attackers found ways to damage a stone keep the design evolved. Rochester originally had square towers with sharp corners. Miners were able to undermine these corners and the edges could be damaged by rocks fired from a trebuchet. You can see from Source 5 that one tower has been rebuilt as a round tower. This was much stronger. They still served the same purpose as motte and bailey castles to house a garrison but they were also able to withstand a long siege.

Source **5**

Rochester Castle. In the foreground is the curtain wall. In the background is the tall stone keep. Building this castle cost one third of the king's annual income.

Stage 3: Concentric castles

Castle building reached its peak with the CONCENTRIC castles built in Wales on the orders of Edward I. The most famous are at Harlech, Beaumaris (below), Caernarfon and Conwy. They are called concentric because of the way the heart of the castle was defended by a series of curtain walls. But Edward's castles had many other improvements.

- **Gatehouse** A concentric castle had a very heavily defended entrance. Guarding the gatehouse was a **drawbridge** that could be raised when attacked. The entrance was also defended by a series of **doors** and huge iron gates called **portcullises**.
- **Curtain walls** The outside curtain walls were lower to allow archers to see an approaching enemy. The curtain wall nearest the castle was higher to give the defenders the best possible opportunity to defend their castle.
- **Towers** Towers were a variety of shapes. For example, at Caernarfon, there were towers within towers. The greatest of Caernarfon's towers is the Eagle Tower, which has walls 5.4 metres thick.
- **Double walls** The walls were made from two walls with the hollow between them filled in with rubble. This was to give them extra strength.
- **Arrowslits** Slits were built into the walls so that archers could fire at attackers from different angles.
- **The sea** Most castles were built by the sea which allowed large boats to supply the castle and made a siege virtually impossible.
- **The town wall** Outside the castle the town was also surrounded by a strong wall.

What...?

CONCENTRIC
Of circles, sharing the same centre.

Did you know?

At the bottom of the keep's wall was a slope called a batter, which helped objects or liquids dropped by the defenders to bounce or splash onto the attackers.

Did you know?

The portcullis became the symbol of the Royal Exchequer (where they kept the royal money). If you look at a modern one-penny piece you will see a picture of a portcullis on the tails side.

Source 6

An aerial view of Beaumaris Castle.

Map 2

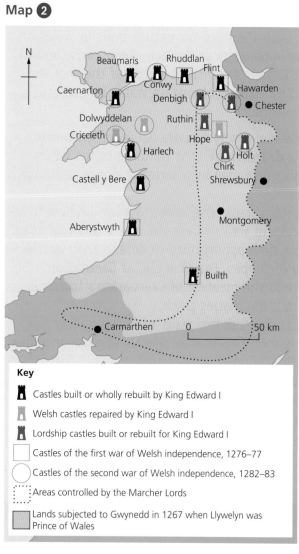

Castles in Wales

Key

🏰 Castles built or wholly rebuilt by King Edward I

🏰 Welsh castles repaired by King Edward I

🏰 Lordship castles built or rebuilt for King Edward I

▢ Castles of the first war of Welsh independence, 1276–77

◯ Castles of the second war of Welsh independence, 1282–83

⦙ Areas controlled by the Marcher Lords

▨ Lands subjected to Gwynedd in 1267 when Llywelyn was Prince of Wales

Source 7

A medieval illustration showing castle building.

Task

Study Source 7.

1 What job is being done at A, B, C and D?

2 What tools are being used? Make a list.

3 Which of these tools are still used today?

4 For each tool not still in use, how would this job be done today?

How was a castle built?

First the site of the castle would be completely cleared and the ground plan was marked out. The foundations were dug down to bedrock and filled with rubble so the ground could take the weight of the castle walls. Most castles were built of high quality blocks of limestone, sandstone, granite or marble. Rubble was used to fill in the thickness of the walls between facings of stone blocks. Much of the stone was cut to size at the quarries rather than at the building site, although any intricate carving would be done at the site. The stones were lifted into place in baskets, in wheelbarrows, on shoulders or by crane. Plumblines were used to make sure the walls were level and straight. In winter, the tops of unfinished walls were covered in thatch for protection. The higher the castles went, the more scaffolding was needed. Holes were left in the walls for poles to hold the scaffolding.

Source 8

An artist's reconstruction of Caernarfon Castle and the walled town.

Case study: Caernarfon Castle

Edward I employed Master James of St George to build Caernarfon. He probably met him in Savoy (which is on the borders of Italy and France) on his way back from the Crusades. Master James had huge experience building castles across Europe.

Edward had seen at first hand how useful the castles built by Crusaders in the Holy Land had been. He asked Master James to copy some of their best features. Master James brought a small but highly skilled staff of STONEMASONS and engineers with him from Europe, backed up with labour from across England. Master James needed carpenters, diggers and woodcutters as well as labourers. Building a castle in hostile territory meant that he also needed a large group of soldiers to protect his workforce.

Building was often disrupted by events elsewhere. The craftsmen who built Caernarfon were also needed to help Edward fight his wars in Scotland and France. Their skills were much in demand in sieges, battles and when putting up forts to secure a conquest. In 1293 work came to a stop on the castle as workmen travelled to Gascony; in 1302–3 little work was done because of the war in Scotland.

Because the castle was not finished for so long it was open to attack. In 1294 rebels led by Madog ap Llywelyn stormed the castle walls and burned whatever they could find. Caernarfon Castle was virtually finished by the time that Edward I died in 1307 but it had cost £27,000 to build, the equivalent to a king's normal revenue for a year. It is no wonder he needed to raise all those taxes.

Edward I was the last great castle-building king. From this time on castles were less important.

- England became more settled. In the troubled border areas people still needed castles to protect them but through much of England there was no need.
- Kings and nobles wanted to live in comfortable palaces or manor houses not austere castles.
- The development of gunpowder meant that not even the strongest castles could withstand attack.

What...?

STONEMASON
Someone who carries or carves stones.

Did you know?

Edward's castles in Wales were not just built for conquest. They were designed so that English families could come and settle there, with the full protection of the castle walls. They were also built as home and office for Edward's officials in Wales such as Sir Otto de Grandison who became constable of Caernarfon in late 1285.

Life in a castle

Castles were also homes. Inside the castle, the people could eat, garden, work, pray, play or be entertained. These pictures show some of the activities that might be going on in a normal day.

Morning

Task A
Look closely.

First work with a partner to identify all the activities taking place in each picture. Notice who is involved: lords, ladies, servants or soldiers. Notice where it is happening.

Task B
Write a story.

Your story should include at least three of the characters that you see in the illustrations. It should take place in a single day. And it should all take place inside the castle walls. If you like, you could try to illustrate your story like a medieval manuscript.

Evening

Filling in the gaps: Edward II and Edward III

A mezzotint engraving of Edward II, created centuries after his death.

Edward II 1307–27

Edward II was not like his father. He did not like wars and when he did have to lead his army he was a very poor general. He also made mistakes in choosing his advisers. He had favourites to whom he gave too much power and influence. Put the two together and you have a recipe for disaster, or at least a bad reign.

As you have already read, Edward II's father put a huge amount of effort into conquering Scotland although he was never securely in control. Edward managed to undo all of his father's work in a relatively short time. In 1313 the Scots again rose against English rule, led by Robert Bruce. Edward's response was to send an army to Scotland but it was defeated by Bruce in 1314 at Bannockburn and the Scots declared their independence from England. By the end of his reign, Gascony had also been lost to the King of France.

Edward's choice of advisers did not go down well with the barons. He gave top jobs to his favourite people whether they were well-suited to them or not. His first favourite was Piers Gaveston. Edward made him regent when he had to leave the country. Gaveston was bold and witty but he was an incompetent ruler.

Later in Edward's reign his favourite was Hugh Despenser, who was arrogant, cruel and treacherous and who made many enemies. In 1321 Parliament tried to exile Despenser. Edward's response was to raise an army, and capture and kill the leader of the anti-Despenser group.

In the end it was Edward's wife Isabella who brought him down. In 1325 she went to France, supposedly to arrange the marriage of their son Edward (they were not original when it came to naming him). She then returned to England but with an army! She quickly captured London, arrested and hanged Despenser, forced her husband to abdicate and had him thrown into prison. Eight months later he was brutally murdered, reportedly impaled on a red-hot poker.

An effigy of Edward III in Westminster Abbey.

Edward III 1327–77

Edward III was different again. Unlike his father he was a brilliant soldier and an excellent king. Edward allowed and encouraged Parliament to develop. The House of Lords and House of Commons emerged as distinct Houses of Parliament. In the country, the Justices of the Peace were given greater powers to run their local regions.

He was king for 50 years and a couple of other important things happened in his reign that we deal with in other units. In 1337 a series of wars that were later to be called the Hundred Years' War broke out between England and France. Some events of the wars are covered in Unit 6. In 1348 the most terrible plague, known as the Black Death, killed almost half the people in England. It is covered in detail on pages 158–163.

Source

What...?

LOLLARDS
The name 'Lollard' comes from the middle Dutch word 'lollaerd', which means mumbler.

PILGRIM
A person who makes a journey to a holy place.

A drawing of Geoffrey Chaucer in a medieval manuscript.

Task
Tabloid newspapers did not exist in the Middle Ages but if they had, what headlines might they have written for the events on pages 60–61? Choose two 'stories' from the reign of Edward II or Edward III and write headlines to accompany them.

Edward's reign is also famous for developments in literature and religion.

● **John Wycliffe** A professor at Oxford University, Wycliffe produced the first Bible to be written in English (up until then they had been written in Latin or Greek). He also criticised some of the ideas of the Catholic Church. His ideas were popular and he soon had a following of people known as LOLLARDS.

● **Geoffrey Chaucer** One of the most famous writers in the history of the English language, Chaucer wrote the Canterbury Tales about a group of PILGRIMS on their way to visit the tomb of Thomas Becket at Canterbury Cathedral. The story is about much more than the pilgrims; it paints a vivid picture of life in medieval England.

However, Edward's reign did not end happily. In 1376 his son Edward, the Black Prince, who was a great soldier, died. He had lost his heir. And on a warm summer night in June 1377, Edward III himself died. He was alone, having been deserted by his friends. His mistress, Alice Perrers, fled, first slipping the rings from his fingers and pocketing them. The crown of England now passed into the hands of his ten-year-old grandson Richard.

UNIT 5 Richard II and the Peasants' Revolt: was he brave or devious?

What is this all about?

In 1377 Richard II became King of England. He was only ten years old. He inherited a kingdom that was outwardly successful, but serious problems were festering beneath the surface. For four years he was king in name only. Others made decisions for him – sometimes very bad ones. Then suddenly, faced by a new challenge – thousands of angry peasants and villagers were marching to London to see him – the boy-king took control. How well did he do? You decide.

Task

On the next two pages the text describes the different problems that were brewing in England in the fourteenth century.

1 Work in pairs. One of you make a list of the concerns of the peasants. The other make a list of the concerns of the king and his advisers.

2 Compare your lists. Which is longer? Is there anything that comes on both lists?

In 1381 the peasants were angry for many different reasons. Some were long-term – problems that had built up over many years. Others were short-term and had occurred, more or less, during the reign of Richard II.

The Black Death

The Black Death hit England in the 1340s. Between one third and one half of the population of England died. As well as personal tragedy, the Black Death caused big changes in English villages. Peasants formed the bulk of the population and so, inevitably, most of the people who died were peasants.

This led to a serious labour shortage. The peasants who survived were in great demand. Those who were free got higher wages from landowners. Some even started leaving their lords to look for higher wages elsewhere. Serfs, who were not free, wanted to buy their freedom and worked for the landowners for cash. Or they simply ran away to another place. The feudal structure that had held English villages together for hundreds of years appeared to be collapsing.

Source 1

This portrait of the young King Richard II was painted by an anonymous contemporary artist.
? *How old do you think Richard is in this painting?*

The Statute of Labourers 1351

The government stepped in to try to stop the huge increase in wage bills and the changing relationship between peasant and lord. The Statute:

● set the maximum wage payable at the 1346–47 rates,
● arranged for runaway peasants to be returned to their lords,
● reaffirmed the right of lords to claim certain services from their peasants.

For a while this worked. But by the time Richard II came to the throne, the peasants were becoming restless again and many were refusing to serve their lords, demanding an end to what they saw as slavery.

Did you know?

JOHN BALL
In 1366, the Church banned him from preaching, but he clearly never stopped because the Archbishop of Canterbury had him imprisoned three times. His sermon made to the rebels at Blackheath on 13 June 1381 inspired them to continue their rebellion.

Source ❷

'When Adam delved [dug] and Eve span, Who was then the gentleman?'

This was part of a poem written in the early 1300s by Richard Rolle de Hampole. 'Gentleman' refers to the upper class. Its message was that all people were equal. John Ball used it as the basis of much of his preaching.

Religious ideas

Some priests within the medieval Christian Church began criticising accepted beliefs. Travelling preachers, in particular a priest called John Ball, taught that everyone was equal before God. To the peasants, this was an extremely attractive idea. It linked in with their growing resentment that they had to give up to two days a week unpaid labour to the Church. Abbots and bishops claimed that, because their estates belonged to the Church, they should not rent them out or give the peasants their freedom. Old customs, they said, should not be interfered with in any way. The peasants, on the other hand, wanted to be free of a burden they believed made the Church rich and themselves poor. Priests like John Ball gave them a religious argument for wanting this freedom.

War with France

The Hundred Years War with France started in 1337. Initially, England was very successful with tremendous victories at Crécy in 1346 and Poitiers ten years later. Money seized from the war was invested in building splendid manor houses and churches and the peasants could see the positive side of war. But by 1377 a series of military disasters resulted in French raids on the English coast. People began to fear for their homes, their jobs and their lives.

The Poll Taxes

For the peasants, this was the final straw. Money had to be found to pay for the war with France.

- In 1377, the year Richard II came to the throne, the first Poll Tax was imposed. Everyone over fourteen years old, rich and poor, had to pay four pence to the government. This clearly hit the poor far harder than the rich.
- In 1379 another Poll Tax was introduced but this time an attempt was made to link the tax to income. The poor still paid four pence while barons paid £2 (120 times as much). This didn't raise enough money.
- In 1380 a third Poll Tax was imposed. The rate was three times that of 1377 – 12 pence – and the same for everyone! This was both unfair and an intolerable burden on the peasants.

Poor government

Richard II himself cannot be blamed for all these problems but his council can. The boy king did not rule alone. He was too young. Instead, he was 'guided' by a council of nine of the greatest barons in the country, led by his uncle, John of Gaunt. The council didn't rule particularly well; they spent a lot of time arguing amongst themselves as they struggled to control the king in their own interests. This lack of a strong king certainly allowed these social and political problems to fester.

Source 3
An historian writes

What united all, peasants, poor priests, skilled workers and wealthy townsmen of Bury and Cambridge, was the common burden of the poll tax and a common surge of discontent with authorities who had achieved nothing but the oppression of the people.

M H Keen, *England in The Later Middle Ages*, published 1973.

Did you know?

WAT TYLER
The leader of the Kent section of the Peasants' Revolt. Everything we know about him was written by his enemies – the ruling classes – and in particular by a French chronicler called Jean Froissart. But even they are all agreed about his intelligence, eloquence and charisma.

It's quite clear that young King Richard and his advisers were sitting on a powder keg of trouble. The Peasants' Revolt, when it broke out in 1381, challenged medieval ideas and concepts about society and people's position within it. As such, it was a serious and concerted attempt by thousands of peasants to limit the power of the Crown. It, too, reflected dangerous new ideas about the ways in which society should be organised and the Church structured. How well did Richard II, then aged 14, cope with the crisis?

What follows is the story of the Peasants' Revolt. Although the revolt affected areas as far apart as Hampshire, the Wirral and the Scottish Borders, most of the action came from peasants in Kent, Essex, Suffolk and Norfolk.

In May 1381, a tax collector arrived in the Essex village of Fobbing to find out why villagers there hadn't paid their poll tax. He was thrown out. So were the soldiers who were sent to restore law and order. The Essex villagers organised themselves. Rebellion spread and riots and demonstrations became common. Men sharpened scythes and sickles and dusted down the longbows they had fought with in France.

The peasants march to London

In early June 1381, rebels from Kent, led by Wat Tyler, captured Canterbury, seized the sheriff and made a bonfire of all his records. They opened up Maidstone prison and released John Ball, who had been imprisoned for preaching that all men were equal. Joined by the Essex rebels, they marched on London. Their aim was to put their demands before the King. They claimed they had no quarrel with him; in fact, they seemed to look on Richard II as their only true leader. Their quarrel was with the council of nobles, Church leaders and tax collectors. Thousands of peasants from all over the country downed tools and joined the rebels from Kent and Essex. Many tradesmen, priests and outlaws joined, too. As they marched, they destroyed tax records and tax registers, and burned buildings that housed government records. They attacked manor houses and destroyed documents that gave details of labour services that the peasants owed to their lord or to the Church. By 12 June around 60,000 rebels were camped outside the walls of the City of London; the Essex contingent at Mile End and those from Kent at Blackheath.

King Richard and his advisers took refuge in the Tower of London, which was a royal palace as well as a fortress. Soldiers guarded them, but the troops were not used. The rebel forces, massed in two huge groups, were too great to be challenged. Then the rebels sent word that they wished to talk with the King.

It's quite clear that young King Richard and his advisers were sitting on a powder keg of trouble. The Revolt challenged medieval ideas about society and people's position within it. It challenged the power of the king and his council. It reflected dangerous new ideas. How would Richard II cope with the crisis?

Did you know?

SERFS
A serf was virtually a slave. Serfs were owned by their masters and unable to leave the lord's manor, or do ordinary things like get married, without his permission.

The crisis deepens

Richard decided to meet with the rebels. The very next day, accompanied by his closest advisers, he was rowed down the Thames towards Blackheath. Unfortunately the two advisers Richard had chosen to accompany him were Simon Sudbury (his Chancellor and also the Archbishop of Canterbury) and Robert Hales, his Treasurer. These two were, of all Richard's advisers, the men the rebels hated the most, as they were linked with the Poll Tax and the imprisonment of John Ball. As soon as they saw who was on the barge, the rebels began chanting 'Traitor, traitor' and 'Kill them, kill them'. Fearing the worst, Richard's attendants refused to moor the barge to let him land, and rowed smartly away to loud jeers and insults from the rebels.

Source ④

… savage hordes approached the city like waves of the sea and entered it by violence. At their head a peasant captain urged the madmen on. With cruel eagerness for slaughter, he shouted in the ears of the rabble, 'Burn! Kill!'

In June 1381, the English poet John Gower watched the rebels pouring into London.

Map ①

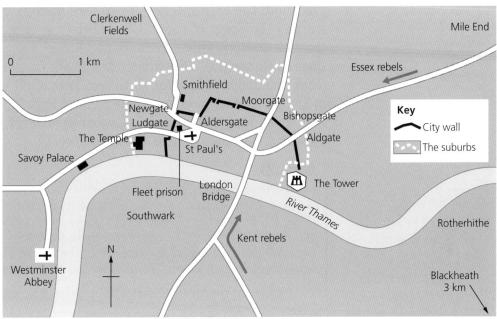

The routes taken by the rebels into the City of London.

That night, Richard watched from the windows of the Tower as flames leapt from the Savoy Palace, the London home of his uncle, John of Gaunt. Chanting rebels surrounded the Tower, demanding to meet the King. How had the rebels got into the City? The answer was simple: the people of London had opened the city gates to the rebels. Once in, they went on the rampage. As well as ransacking and firing the Savoy Palace, they broke open the Fleet prison, attacked lawyers and burnt down the Temple where the legal records were kept. London was in the hands of the rebels and they seemed to be out of control.

Meeting at Mile End

It was clear to Richard that he had to meet face-to-face with the rebels. The following day he rode out, with an escort of nobles and soldiers, to Mile End. There, he faced Wat Tyler. Allowing Tyler to kiss his hand, Richard listened to the rebels' demands. They wanted an end to serfdom, the abolition of all labour services, the death of all 'traitors' (defined as the King's advisers) and pardons for all those taking part in the rebellion.

Richard immediately agreed to all these demands, except the one concerning 'traitors', saying that only the law courts could decide who was a traitor. To show he meant business, Richard had 30 clerks ready to write out charters of freedom so that the rebels could take them back to their lords as proof of Richard's promises.

So far, so good. However, some of the rebels, not liking what Richard had said about the 'traitors', decided to take matters into their own hands. They stormed the Tower of London, found the two men they considered to be the arch-traitors, Simon Sudbury and Robert Hales, and promptly beheaded them on Tower Hill. They stuck their heads on poles and mounted the poles on London Bridge for all to see. That night there were terrible riots in London and more killings. But Richard kept his promises. The peasants were given their charters and many of them went home. But a sizeable body remained, demanding more from the King.

Task

Read Source 5.
1 Who, or what, does Thomas Walsingham blame for the Peasants' Revolt?
2 The 5Ws test (see page 4) will help you evaluate this source. Use internet research to find out more about Thomas Walsingham. Do you think Thomas Walsingham's account is likely to be accurate?

Source ❺

Many believed that the thoughtlessness of the Archbishop and his provincial bishops was responsible, because in their care lies the faith and stability of the Christian religion. Certainly they allowed John Wycliffe and his followers to behave shamefully, and preach throughout the whole country to corrupt the people. It seems to me that these evil times are the result of the sins of the people of the earth, especially the friars. Nowadays there is a saying 'This is a friar and therefore a liar.'

Written at the time by Thomas Walsingham, a Benedictine monk at St Albans Abbey.

Meeting at Smithfield

A further meeting was arranged. On the evening of 15 June King Richard met again with Wat Tyler, this time at Smithfield, a market and fairground outside the city walls. The choice of meeting place was the idea of the Lord Mayor of London, Sir William Walworth. He wanted to get the rebels as far away from the city as possible, fearful that any attempt by the troops to attack the rebels in the city would result in either the city burning to the ground or the rebels vanishing into its alleyways, courtyards and twisting back streets.

Once at Smithfield, the King and Tyler greeted each other politely. This time, Wat Tyler's demands were even more extreme. He asked for all lords' estates to be reduced in size and for all Church lands to be divided among the peasants. Once again, Richard agreed. Suddenly there was a scuffle between Wat Tyler and Sir William Walworth. Tyler fell from his horse, a dying man. No one knows whether this assassination was planned or was the result of a misunderstanding. But as soon as the peasants realised what had happened, they raised their bows. The royal party were within seconds of being massacred.

Source 6
An historian writes

Richard did not keep any of his promises, claiming they were made under threat and were therefore not valid in law. The poll tax was withdrawn but the peasants were forced back into their old way of life – under the control of the lord of the manor.

Ian Dawson www. historylearningsite.co.uk

What...?

VILLEIN
A peasant who was entirely subject to his lord and kept on the lord's manor.

It was the boy-king Richard who saved the day. He rode toward the peasant army shouting 'Sirs, would you shoot your king? I will be your chief and captain. Follow me and you will have what you seek!' Confused but by nature loyal, the peasants followed their king, who led them away from the city, towards open farmland at Clerkenwell. There, Richard repeated the promises he had made to Wat Tyler at Mile End. The peasants believed him. Leaderless, but with their main demands met, they set off for home.

Broken promises

Once the peasants had dispersed, Richard broke all his promises. Any peasants remaining in London were rounded up and killed. All London householders had to swear loyalty to the King. Wat Tyler's head was cut off and stuck on a pole on London Bridge. With London secure, royal troops then had to subdue the countryside. They moved through Essex and Suffolk, putting down minor rebellions and hanging peasants who were involved. In Chelmsford and Colchester, batches of rebel leaders were hanged on the roadsides as a dreadful warning to others. A royal army restored the abbot of St Albans, who had been forced to grant a borough charter and they hanged John Ball, who had been taken to St Albans from the Midlands for trial. Troops restored order in Cambridge, where a college that owned land had been burned and a judge beheaded. Everywhere peasants were fined or imprisoned, and there was much work for the hangman. The charters granted by the King were shown to be worthless. Perhaps Richard II showed his true colours at Waltham, where he told the peasants 'VILLEINS you are and villeins you shall remain'.

Who won?

By the autumn of 1381 the Peasants' Revolt was over. Hundreds of peasants had been killed or injured in the fighting or had been hanged as a punishment. Their leaders were gone – hanged or in hiding. The royal promises had been broken; the charters granted to them by Richard II had been withdrawn; and the peasants were forced back into their old ways of life.

In the short term it looked very like a defeat for the peasants. But there is a different way of seeing it. Richard and his council had been given a big scare.

- Just months later the Poll Tax was withdrawn.
- Within ten years Parliament abandoned all attempts to control wages.
- Eighty years later, artists were interpreting the revolt in the style of Source 7.
- Just over a century later all peasants were free.

Task

1 King Richard II had one attempted meeting with the peasants and two actual meetings with them. It seems that these meetings were his own idea and against the wishes of his advisers. Do you think this makes him:

brave stupid stubborn foolish sensible?

Choose the words that you think best describe Richard's actions and explain why.

2 Use what you know about medieval kings to explain how likely it was that the meeting at Smithfield was a trap and Wat Tyler was deliberately killed.

Source **7**

This picture, painted in about 1460, shows John Ball (on the horse), Wat Tyler (wearing a black hat on the left) and their peasant supporters. **?** *What moment in the Revolt do you think this is supposed to show?* **?** *How likely is it that this is a true record of what happened?*

Postscript: what happened to Richard?

Richard II survived the Peasants' Revolt but his reign did not end well. He was inconsistent – first working with Parliament but then trying to rule without. In the end, Richard's reign turned nasty, taxes went up and his enemies were thrown into prison. A group of barons, led by Henry of Bolingbroke, forced Richard to abdicate and threw him into the Tower of London where he was murdered. In 1399 Henry Bolingbroke became Henry IV.

Summary task
Overall, and bearing in mind what you know about medieval kings, how well do you think King Richard II handled the Peasants' Revolt? Score Richard on a scale of −5 to +5 and write some paragraphs to explain your score.

Task
You fill in the gaps
The only medieval English king we have not told you anything about in this book is Henry IV. Do some research of your own to write a 'Filling in the gaps' feature. You have a maximum of 200 words to sum up his whole reign, which was 1399–1413. If you are stuck for ideas you can start with en.wikipedia.org.

THE PEASANTS' REVOLT OF 1381: WHY DID IT HAPPEN?

Source A

A foolish priest called John Ball used to preach to the people as they came away from Mass on Sundays:

'My friends, the state of England cannot be right until everything is held in common and there is no difference between nobleman and peasant and we are all as one. Why do nobles lord it over us? We are all descended from our first parents, Adam and Eve, so how can they be better men than us?'

Written at the time by the French historian Jean Froissart. He worked in England for the wife of Edward III. He wrote Froissart's *Chronicles* which told the history of Europe 1326–1400. He interviewed people who were present.

Source C

The Peasants' Revolt had many causes: resentment of the government's weakness, hatred of the land-owner's policy of repression after the Black Death and dissatisfaction at the wealth and greed of the higher clergy. The poll tax was the last of many grievances.

A R Myers, *England in The Late Middle Ages*, published Penguin 1976.

Source B

This is a fifteenth-century painting of the murder of Simon Sudbury, the Archbishop of Canterbury, and Robert Hales, the Treasurer.

QUESTIONS

1   Read **Source A**.
    a) Who does, the author, Jean Froissant, blame for the Peasants' Revolt?
    b) Is he likely to be biased in what he says?

2   Look at **Source B**.
    It was painted sometime between 1460 and 1480, nearly 100 years after the murder of Simon Sudbury and Robert Hales. Can this source still be useful to someone studying the causes of the Peasant's Revolt?

3   Read **Source C**.
    How far is **Source C** backed by **Sources A** and **B**?

4   Using **all** the sources and your own knowledge, how far do you agree that the main reason for the Peasants' Revolt in 1381 was the Poll Tax?

UNIT 6 Who was the real Henry V?

What is this all about?
Henry V was king from 1413 to 1422. He has been described as 'the greatest man ever to rule England'. This reputation rests largely on his famous victory over the French at the Battle of Agincourt in 1415. You are going to study this battle first and ask some difficult questions: was it really a great victory? Was Henry responsible for the victory? Have writers like William Shakespeare made him look better than he really was? Then you are going to look at some other information about him before finally deciding whether or not he was a good king.

┌─ **Did you know?** ─┐

The Hundred Years' War lasted longer than 100 years: from 1337 to 1453.

Background: England v. France

The Battle of Agincourt took place during The Hundred Years' War between England and France. See if you can work out why this war started. William the Conqueror already owned lands in France when he won the Battle of Hastings in 1066 and became King of England. This meant that later English kings controlled large areas of France – more in fact than the French king!

However, in 1204 King John managed to lose much of this territory. This was a blow to England's prestige and meant that England now had a powerful rival on its doorstep. It soon caused other problems as well. Trade was important to England. Wine was imported from France but this trade was now under threat from French pirates. The French also stopped the cloth merchants of Flanders from buying English wool. Nothing much was done about this until Edward III became King of England in 1327.

In 1328 the King of France, Charles IV, died. He had no sons, and all his brothers were dead. He did have a cousin, Philip, and a sister, Isabella.

Philip quickly seized the throne. This greatly annoyed Edward because he was Isabella's son – she and his father, Edward II, were married. Edward thought this gave him the right to be King of France.

The situation got worse in 1337 when Philip announced he was going to conquer Guyenne, a part of France still under English control. Edward decided to invade France. The Hundred Years' War had started.

The Hundred Years' War before Henry V

Edward III had much success in France. In 1346 he had a great victory at the Battle of Crécy where the English archers played a crucial role. His son the Black Prince became a living legend – a brilliant general, brave and heroic. In 1356 he won an equally brilliant victory against the French at Poitiers. Edward and the Black Prince died within a year of each other in 1376–77 and the French won back some land. In 1396 peace was agreed and that is how it stayed until Henry V started the fighting again in 1415.

He was determined to win back the lands in France that he thought were rightfully his.

Task
1 List as many reasons as you can why Edward III decided to invade France. Remember, some of these reasons might go back a long time before Edward.
2 Number your reasons, starting with 1 for the most important.

Map ①

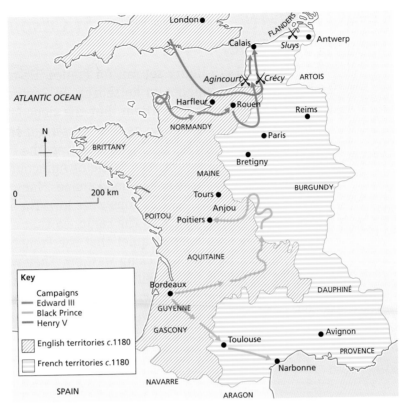

France at the start of the Hundred Years' War.

Map ②

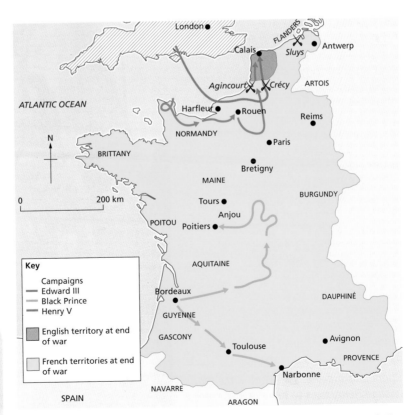

Task

Compare maps 1 and 2.

Describe the main changes.

France at the end of the Hundred Years' War.

What...?

DAUPHIN
The eldest son of the King of France.

DYSENTERY
Severe infection and inflammation of the intestines.

Task

Source 1 is a good source to try out the 5Ws test (see page 4). You should also look at Source 4 on page 76. How far do you trust Source 1 to give you a reliable impression of Henry V's character?

The Battle of Agincourt, St Crispin's Day (25 October) 1415

On 11 August 1415 Henry set sail for France. He took with him 6,000 archers and 2,500 knights on horseback. In September, after a month's siege he captured the town of Harfleur. But the siege left his army weakened by disease and hunger. He knew he was not strong enough to fight the French army and tried to retreat to Calais. However, the French army, led by the DAUPHIN, barred his way near the castle of Agincourt.

The English army was not in good shape. Many of the soldiers were suffering from DYSENTERY and rations were low. The night before the battle Henry ordered total silence in the camp, so that everybody could get a good night's sleep. It was so quiet that the French thought they had crept away! Morale in the English camp was low. They were worn out, hungry and outnumbered by the many-skilled, heavily armoured French knights. In Shakespeare's play *Henry V*, written nearly 200 years later, Henry makes a speech to his troops on the evening before the battle.

Shakespeare shows Henry rallying his troops, lifting their spirits, and showing great leadership qualities. This speech has become famous.

Source ❶

He that shall live this day, and see old age,
Will yearly on the vigil feast his neighbours,
And say 'To-morrow is Saint Crispian.'
Then will he strip his sleeve and show his scars,
And say 'These wounds I had on Crispian's day.'
Old men forget; yet all shall be forgot,
But he'll remember, with advantages,
What feats he did that day: then shall our names,
Familiar in his mouth as household words
Harry the King, Bedford and Exeter,
Warwick and Talbot, Salisbury and Gloucester,
Be in their flowing cups freshly remember'd.
This story shall the good man teach his son;
And Crispin Crispian shall ne'er go by,
From this day to the ending of the world,
But we in it shall be remember'd;
We few, we happy few, we band of brothers;
For he to-day that sheds his blood with me
Shall be my brother; be he ne'er so vile,
This day shall gentle his condition;
And gentlemen in England now a-bed
Shall think themselves accurs'd they were not here,
And hold their manhoods cheap whiles any speaks
That fought with us upon Saint Crispin's day.

Henry V, *William Shakespeare.* *What is the main message Henry uses to motivate his troops*

Source ❷

Kenneth Branagh as Henry V in a film from 1989.

What...?

MEN-AT-ARMS
Servants who are also bodyguards.

The two sides face each other!

It rained for most of that night, just as it had for the previous two weeks, turning the ground sodden with ankle-deep mud. Both armies rose before dawn and assembled for battle. The English had 5,000 archers and 900 MEN-AT-ARMS. The French army was about 25,000-strong.

The English

The English formed a single line to the south. There were no reserves. The line was divided into three groups of men-at-arms. Each of these groups was made up of the advance, the main body and the rearguard, each about four men deep. Between each of these groups of men-at-arms and on each flank (side) were the archers with longbows. They were protected by large pointed stakes.

The French

The French formed three lines to the north. The front two lines were made up of dismounted men-at-arms. In the third line the men were on horseback. Cavalry was placed on each flank. Between the first and second lines were archers and crossbowmen.

The site

The armies were about 800 metres apart, separated by a gently rolling recently ploughed field crossed by two roads. A slight dip in the field meant that they could clearly see each other. Either side of the field was a forest. The field narrowed to only 800 metres where the armies would meet.

Did you know?

The longbow was made of wood from either the yew or ash tree and was six feet high. The bow-string was made of linen and the arrows were made from birch.

Each archer carried about two dozen arrows under his belt and a variety of points for different purposes, such as penetrating armour. The arrows were deadly at up to 350 metres.

The French crossbow required less skill to use but was very powerful. However, a longbow could shoot twelve arrows in the time it took to fire one crossbow bolt.

Task

This is a simple plan of the battle site.
1 Draw your own copy then use the information above to complete and label it to show how the two sides lined up.

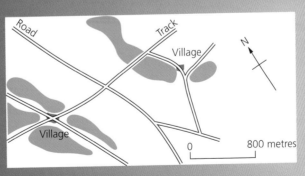

2 Once you have read the information on pages 74–75, draw a second plan to show the main events of the battle.

THE BATTLE OF AGINCOURT

THE ENGLISH ADVANCE

For four hours the two armies stared at each other. The English did not want a battle and the French did not fancy wading through the mud! It was sensible for them to wait for the English to attack as this would put them, with their inferior numbers, at a great disadvantage. Or perhaps they were just going to wait until the English starved and they would win without having to fight.

Henry knew that without food his troops would get weaker, so at about 11 a.m. he ordered his men to advance. They moved forward steadily until the French were just within the range of their longbows. If the French had attacked while the English were advancing and before they had reset their positions the English would have been in trouble. Henry then ordered the archers to drive their stakes into the ground at an angle that would ensure the French horses were impaled by the stakes.

Henry planned to provoke the French into attacking. He ordered the archers to fire. The English archers could fire ten flights a minute and the air was thick with arrows which poured down on the French like rain. Henry's plan worked and the French cavalry on the flanks attacked the English archers on the flanks. It was a disaster.

THE FRENCH ATTACK

The cavalry charged at about 12 miles an hour and flight after flight of arrows hit them. The arrows were not strong enough to penetrate the knights' armour but the horses were not so well protected. Wounded horses threw their riders into the mud. Others crashed into the English stakes.

As the survivors retreated they crashed into their own men-at-arms who were advancing. Everything was now going wrong for the French! Their horses had churned the mud up making it harder for later attacks. The forest narrowed the field, squeezing the French against each other and preventing them from outflanking the English.

The attack was chaotic. The French noblemen all rushed like an undisciplined mob to be in the front line. They were jostling with each other and they had no room to lift their weapons! And all the time the English archers were firing at them. The French had so little room that they even failed to fire their bombards (artillery), which because of the chaos would have probably killed as many French as English.

By the time the French reached the English lines they were exhausted by the mud, the crowding and the arrows. Soon the English lines were protected by a solid wall of French bodies! The French men-at-arms were pushed out towards the English archers. These archers finished the French off: two of them would attack a French knight from the front while a third archer slashed at the unprotected parts behind the knee. They would kill the knight by thrusting their sword through the grille of his faceplate. Many of the French knights were simply stuck in the mud and were trampled on.

THE END

After only half an hour the first two French lines had been destroyed. The English soldiers started to take prisoners for ransom and strip valuables from the dead. This was a normal thing to do in those days. Henry, however, wanted all his men ready for a French counter-attack; there were still more soldiers in the surviving French third line than in the whole of the English army. He ordered that all prisoners be killed. More French soldiers were killed in this way than were killed in the fighting. The French counter-attack failed and the Battle of Agincourt was over. Six thousand French soldiers had been killed and many more were taken prisoner.

Source 3

A fifteenth-century French painting of the battle.
 This is clearly not a very accurate picture. What has the artist got wrong?

Task

Write an essay to answer the question: 'Why did the English win the Battle of Agincourt?'

Make sure you do not simply tell the story of the battle – this has already been done for you. You have to explain why they won.

Planning

In planning your essay you need to organise the reasons for the English victory into the following groups:

• reasons that show **Henry was a good leader**
• reasons that show the **English were good fighters**
• reasons that show the **French made mistakes**
• reasons that show the **English were lucky** and the **French were unlucky**.

Writing

You could start your essay by briefly explaining why, before the battle, the French were favourites. Then you need to write about the different kinds of reasons for the English victory. Use a separate paragraph for each type of reason. You should finish your essay with a conclusion explaining which you think was the most important type of reason for the English victory.

What...?

SEDITION
Activity or speech encouraging people to rebel.

USURP
To take power illegally or unlawfully seize another person's position or authority.

Was Henry V a great king?

The historian Holinshed wrote in 1577:

Source 4

This Henry was a king, of life without spot, a prince whom all men loved, and none disdained, a captain against whom fortune never frowned, nor mischance once spurned, whose people him so severe a justicer both loved and obeyed (and so humane as well) that he left no offence unpunished, nor friendship unrewarded; a terror to rebels, and suppressor of SEDITION, his virtues notable, his qualities most praiseworthy.

Shakespeare used Holinshed's book when he wrote his play *Henry V*. You can see the similarities between Holinshed's and Shakespeare's Henry V.

Was Henry so perfect? On these two pages you will find some more information about Henry. You also need to look at the pictures of Henry carefully.

HENRY THE LAD

When he was about twenty years old Henry chose some unsuitable friends and spent much time in taverns and brothels. He was involved in drunken brawls and generally enjoyed himself.

HENRY THE SOLDIER

He was fighting against the Welsh when he was only 14 years old. He successfully led his father's army in the Battle of Shrewsbury, 1403, against the Percys who wanted to overthrow Henry IV. He won many victories over the French and many people see him as a military genius, a patient and brilliant strategist.

SON OF A USURPER

Henry's father, the Duke of Lancaster, USURPED the throne from Richard II in 1399 and became Henry IV. Not everyone accepted him as king and there were several risings by Richard's supporters. There was disorder in England for the rest of Henry IV's reign leaving questions about Henry V's right to the throne in 1413.

A STRONG KING

When Henry V became king he dealt with the dangers he faced. He put down a rebellion by the Lollards and had one of the leaders, his old friend Sir John Oldcastle, executed.

Source 5

Henry V – a portrait painted almost 200 years after his death.

STRATEGIC THINKING

His decision to invade France was a way of exporting the violence of the nobles to another country. (Having a foreign war is always a good way of diverting people's attention away from problems at home!) After Henry's victory at the Battle of Agincourt he was a national hero and no one dared to challenge him.

HENRY COULD NOT BE TRUSTED

There are many examples of Henry deserting his friends. He turned on Harry and Thomas Percy at the Battle of Shrewsbury in 1403 and had his old battlefield and drinking partner Sir John Oldcastle burned to death.

Source 6

Henry V's marriage to Catherine of France in 1420, painted by an anonymous artist some time in the fifteenth century.

FRANCE WON AT LAST?

In 1417 Henry led another expedition to France and won more victories. In 1420 in the Treaty of Troyes he agreed to marry Catherine of Valois, the daughter of the French king, Charles VI, who recognised Henry as his heir as King of France. However, worn out by the fighting, Henry died of dysentery during a third expedition to France in 1422. Charles VI died soon after him. If Henry had lived for a couple more months he would have been King of France.

LEFT PROBLEMS FOR HIS SON, HENRY VI

Perhaps Henry spent too long in France. He was certainly obsessed with winning the French lands. But the wars put him and England into greater and greater debt. There were discontented rumblings back in England. Many people had opposed Henry's third expedition to France and there was always the danger of other noble families claiming the throne. This is exactly what happened after Henry died.

THE WAR AFTER HENRY: HAD HE REALLY ACHIEVED ANYTHING?

The war went disastrously for England after Henry's death. Henry VI was only a baby and the Duke of Bedford took over command. Helped by Joan of Arc, the Dauphin gradually pushed the English back and by 1450 all that England had left was the port of Calais. The war was over; English dreams of conquering France were at an end.

Summary task

Work in pairs. Turn back to pages 8–9.
1 Using the information about what qualities a medieval monarch needed, design an application form for the job of being a medieval king.
2 Imagine you are Henry V and complete the form.

Filling in the gaps: The Wars of the Roses

Task

1 The information on this page suggests several causes of the Wars of the Roses. Can you add to the list below?
   - More than one person was descended from Edward III and could therefore claim the throne.
   - Margaret of Anjou's treatment of Richard of York.
   - Groups of nobles had grown more powerful during Henry VI's reign.
2 Draw a diagram to show all the causes are linked.
3 Circle the most important cause, that is, if you took this away the Wars of the Roses would not have happened.

The Wars of the Roses is the name given to the civil war between the supporters of the two powerful families, the House of Lancaster and the House of York. It was not called this at the time. We use this name because of the badges of the two sides – the Red Rose of Lancaster and the White Rose of York.

Both families were descended from Edward III and so they both had claims to the throne. The struggle for power between them eventually led to more than 20 years of civil war.

A baby king!

When Henry V died the throne passed to his baby son Henry. Henry VI's reign was not a success. While he was a child, unpopular nobles ran the country for him. They lost nearly all the land won by Henry V in France. You can't blame Henry VI for that. But when he did grow up, Henry VI was a weak king. He did little to stop people breaking the law and he allowed powerful nobles to build up private armies. Henry was religious, generous, peace-loving and liked to live simply. While these can be seen as very good things, it was not what was expected from a king at the time. In 1450 around 30,000 people marched on London to protest about Henry's government. This was known as Jack Cade's rebellion. The marchers fought a pitched battle with the King's soldiers on London Bridge. They were beaten but it was a sign of how unhappy many people were.

Henry VI's advisers

One of Henry VI's greatest failings was his choice of advisers. He relied on a small group of favourite advisers and did not consult his ambitious cousin Richard Duke of York, probably the most powerful man in the country. Richard himself had two claims to the throne! Both his father and mother were descended from Edward III. Henry's lack of consulation led to resentment from Richard and his allies. Through this period, the nobles were gradually dividing into two groups: the Lancastrians who supported Henry VI, and the Yorkists led by Richard.

Richard's opportunity

In 1453 Henry suffered from the first of a series of periods of mental illness. A Council of Regency was set up to run the country, led by Richard.

The war starts

In 1455 Henry was well enough to rule again although it was his wife Margaret of Anjou who was really in charge. She exiled Richard from the royal court. So Richard raised an army, fought against the King's supporters and took the King prisoner at the Battle of St Albans. Richard claimed he only wanted to remove 'poor advisers' from Henry's side. The Wars of the Roses had started.

Task

1 Draw a simple timeline from 1455 to 1487.
   a) Write on your timeline what you think are the five most important events of the Wars of the Roses.
   b) Highlight red the times when the Lancastrians were on top. Leave white those periods when the Yorkists were on top.

2 During the Wars of the Roses there were some weak monarchs and some strong ones. Who do you think was the weakest monarch? Who was the strongest? Write a few sentences explaining your choice.

3 Towards the end of the timeline (right) there are some clues about why the Wars of the Roses ended. Write two paragraphs explaining why the Wars of the Roses came to an end.

Dates	Battles	Developments
1455	Battle of St Albans	Defeat for the Lancastrians, Somerset is killed.
1455–59		When Henry VI has another period of mental illness, Richard is appointed Protector and Margaret is side-lined.
		Arguments erupt about who should succeed Henry: Richard, or Henry's son, Edward.
		Disorder spreads across the country while the nobles quarrel. Margaret persuades Henry to send Richard to Ireland. One of Richard's allies, the Earl of Warwick, nicknamed 'the Kingmaker', becomes more powerful.
1459	Battle of Ludford Bridge	Lancastrian victory. Richard's son, Edward, and Warwick flee to Calais. Lancastrians back in control.
1460	Battle of Northampton	Warwick invades southern England, marches north and defeats Henry at Northampton. Warwick captures Henry.
1460		The Act of Accord: the two sides agree that Henry should remain king and Richard is recognised as next in line to the throne. Richard is made Protector to govern in Henry's name. However, Richard is killed in battle later in the year.
1461		Edward of York (Richard's son) declares himself as King Edward IV.
	Battle of Towton	The biggest battle of the war so far. Edward wins and Henry VI and Margaret flee to Scotland.
1464		Edward IV marries Elizabeth Woodville without Warwick knowing. Warwick's influence over Edward begins to wane.
1469		Warwick turns against Edward.
1470		Warwick invades England and Edward has to flee the country. Warwick announces that Henry is king again.
1471	Battle of Barnet / Battle of Tewkesbury	Edward invades England and defeats Warwick and the Lancastrians in both battles. Henry is murdered shortly afterwards and Edward becomes king again!
1483		Edward IV dies. His heir is the 12-year-old Edward V. Edward IV's brother Richard Plantagenet puts the boy Edward and his younger brother in the Tower of London 'for protection'. Richard declares the boys are illegitimate and announces himself as King Richard III.
1485	Battle of Bosworth	Henry Tudor invades England and defeats Richard who is killed in the battle. Henry becomes Henry VII. He marries Elizabeth of York, the daughter of Edward IV. She is the surviving Yorkist with the strongest claim to the throne. The Houses of Lancaster and York are united.
1487	Battle of Stoke	Henry executes all possible other claimants whenever he can. In 1487 he defeats Lambert Simnel who is claiming to be the young Earl of Warwick with a claim to the throne. Henry VII is a very strong king. He controls the nobles and brings peace to England.

In Unit 7 you will investigate the last part of the story, 1483–87. in greater detail.

UNIT 7 Richard III: wicked uncle or loyal brother?

What is this all about?

King Richard III, the last Plantagenet king of England, reigned for only a little over two years. Yet more books, articles, novels and plays have been written about him than just about any other English monarch. He is probably the most controversial ruler England has had.

- Some see him as a ruthless murderer of his young nephews and as a wicked ruler.
- Others see him as a loyal brother (to King Edward IV), who would have made an excellent monarch, but whose reputation has fallen victim to relentless Tudor PROPAGANDA.

Even today, historians argue about which interpretation is correct. In this unit you will decide what you think.

What's the problem?

What...?

PROPAGANDA
The spreading of selected information and rumour in order to support a particular idea or viewpoint.

PHYSICIAN
Doctor.

The problem in reaching any agreement about the sort of man, and the sort of king, Richard was lies with the evidence. There are hardly any sources from Richard III's time that give us reliable insights into his character and motives. We have to rely heavily on chronicles written in early Tudor times – during the years when anyone with any sense would support the new king, Henry VII, and criticise the king he had defeated in battle, Richard III.

The two men writing nearest to Richard's time are both critical of Richard but their evidence is problematic.

Dominic Mancini was an Italian cleric who came to England in the summer or autumn of 1482, probably as part of a diplomatic mission. He should, therefore, have been in an excellent position to know what was going on. But he spoke no English, never travelled anywhere outside London and his writing is full of factual mistakes. Indeed, he left England shortly after Richard's coronation in July 1483. Much of what he was writing about from then on did not come from first-hand knowledge, but gossip. He names just one person, Dr John Argentine, who was PHYSICIAN to the boy-king Edward V, as one of his informants. He does not give us any clues as to where he got the rest of his information, either while he was in London, or later.

The anonymous author of the continuation of the *Croyland Chronicle* wrote between 1459 and 1486. Because we

This portrait of King Richard III was painted by an unknown artist in the sixteenth century. It was almost certainly copied from a portrait painted of Richard while he was still alive. ❓ *What impression does it give you of Richard? Choose some adjectives.*

don't know who the person was who continued the *Chronicle*, we can't reach a judgement on how likely he was to have been objective about Richard. He suggests that, in southern England at least, Richard was disliked and mistrusted. But perhaps the author was a southerner. Richard's power base was in Yorkshire. Maybe a chronicler in the north would have written differently. We shall never know unless an as yet unsuspected chronicle is discovered. There is an additional complication in that much of the original *Chronicle*, as written down during Richard's life, was destroyed by fire in 1731 and historians are forced to use a much later 1684 copy. So, with all these reservations, let's get on with the story.

┌─ Did you know? ─┐

Richard Plantagenet, Richard Duke of Gloucester and King Richard III are all the same person! Don't get confused.

Richard's background

Stage 1: the baby of the family

At the time of his birth at Fotheringhay, Northamptonshire on 2 October 1452, no one could have predicted that some 30 years later, Richard Plantagenet would have the crown of England within his grasp. True, his father (the Duke of York) may well have had ambitions for one of his sons to be king but Richard was the seventh son and was hardly likely to succeed to the dukedom, let alone the crown. Although three of Richard's elder brothers died in infancy, this still left him the youngest of four boys.

When Richard was born, his brother Edward was ten, Edmund was nine and George was three. There were girls too. Anne was thirteen years old, Elizabeth eight and Margaret six. The last child, Ursula, was born when Richard was three years old. It was in this sprawling family that Richard grew up. His two elder brothers, Edward, Duke of March and Edmund, Duke of Rutland had household governors and tutors at Ludlow Castle in the Yorkist heartland of the Welsh Marches. They were the important sons. As a small boy Richard was probably brought up with George and the girls at Fotheringhay under the watchful eye of Cecily, their mother.

 Task

The story of Richard III is quite complicated. We will be telling it in detail. To help you keep track of events and to help prepare you for your final task:
1 Draw your own timeline of Richard's life 1452–85. Add information as you work through the chapter.
2 a) Above the line note evidence that shows Richard was loyal, kind, good or brave.
   b) Below the line note evidence that shows Richard was treacherous, ruthless, evil or cowardly.

Stage 2: childhood influences

Disaster, however, was to strike the Yorkist family. Richard, Duke of York was killed at the Battle of Wakefield in 1460 along with his second son, Edmund, who was then seventeen years old. Cecily thought it sensible to send the two younger boys, George and Richard, abroad into the care of Philip the Good of Burgundy. Only her eldest son Edward remained to fight for the Yorkist cause against the Lancastrians. But George and Richard's stay abroad was a short one. Political fortunes in England changed. The Lancastrian King Henry VI was deposed and Parliament declared the last three Lancastrian kings to have been usurpers. Edward was proclaimed King of England as Edward IV. Richard returned to England with George so that they could take part in their brother's coronation on 28 June 1461. Edward was just eighteen years old, George was eleven and Richard eight. As the nearest KINSMEN to the king, they played important parts in the elaborate ceremony of the coronation. George was made Duke of Clarence on that day and in the autumn, a month after his ninth birthday, Richard was made Duke of Gloucester.

In common with all young boys of his standing, Richard was sent away from home to live in another great lord's household. Nothing much is known of his whereabouts during his early adolescence. It is possible that Richard, along with George and Margaret, were in Greenwich under the general care of the royal household. What is certain is that in 1465 he was formally placed in the care of Richard Neville, the powerful Earl of Warwick (see box). The young Richard of Gloucester would have spent his time in the great Warwick castles of Middleham and Sheriff Hutton.

┌─ **What...?** ─┐

KINSMAN
A person related by blood or marriage, a relation.

┌─ **Did you know?** ─┐

Richard Neville, Earl of Warwick, was known as 'Warwick the Kingmaker'. His wealth and power meant that whenever he switched sides during the Wars of the Roses, the side he backed (Lancastrian or Yorkist) was the side that produced the king.

Source ❷

A modern photograph of Middleham Castle, North Yorkshire, childhood home of Richard III

These years Richard spent in the north of England were influential. Here he met Anne, the younger daughter of the Earl of Warwick; here he made friends with the young Francis, Lord Lovell, who was brought up by the Earl of Warwick and who was to become one of Richard's most loyal supporters. Most importantly, he was accepted into the close-knit circle of rich and powerful northern noblemen and gentry who were to provide him with his power base in later life.

Early in 1469, Richard was recalled to his brother's court. Although he was just sixteen, he was created Constable of England and given important responsibilities in Wales. All in all, just the sort of progress you would expect to see in the younger brother of a fifteenth-century English monarch. But, as you would also expect in these turbulent times, yet more disaster was about to strike the Yorkists.

Did you know?

What happened to Richard's other brother, George, Duke of Clarence? He wanted to be king too! He first supported Edward, then plotted against him. After a rigged trial in Parliament, George died in mysterious circumstances in the Tower of London, probably being drowned in a barrel of malmsey wine.

Stage 3: a loyal brother to the king?

The years 1469–71 were years of crisis. The Earl of Warwick changed sides and challenged the authority of the Yorkist king, Edward IV. Edward was forced to flee to Burgundy. Richard went with him and, unlike the shifty middle brother George (see box above), shared Edward's months of exile. They returned to England together in the spring of 1471 and set about re-establishing Edward's position.

The official Yorkist account of what happened, *Historie of the Arrivall of Edward IV*, shows Richard in full support of his brother:

Did you know?

For much of his reign Henry VI was mentally ill. The stress of kingship added to his condition. For the final years of his reign he was a pawn, controlled by others. Whoever held the King as prisoner was in charge. Henry was king only in name.

Source 3

The King landed within Humber, on Holderness side, at a place called Ravenspur. The King's brother Richard, Duke of Gloucester, and, in his company, 300 men, landed at another place four miles from thence.

The King, full manly, set upon the Lancastrians at Tewkesbury and so also the King's vanguard, being in the rule of the Duke of Gloucester.

Task

Use these last two pages to add further events and evidence to your timeline.

Richard of Gloucester, as Constable of England, presided over the trial and execution of a number of leading Lancastrians. Some said that he was involved in the murder of Prince Edward of Lancaster (King Henry VI's son) although it seems pretty certain that the prince was killed during the Battle of Tewkesbury. It is far more likely that Richard was involved in the murder of the Lancastrian Henry VI (who had been held prisoner in the Tower of London since the Battle of Tewkesbury), either on the direct orders of his brother Edward or on his own initiative.

Stage 4: a northern lord

Richard was well rewarded for his loyalty. Edward IV gave him tremendous power in the North, a sign of his absolute trust in his younger brother. Edward made Richard:

- Warden of the West March against Scotland (1470)
- Chief steward of the northern estates of the Duchy of Lancaster (1471)
- Keeper of the forests beyond the Trent (1472)
- Steward of Ripon (1472)
- Sheriff of Cumberland (1475)
- Lieutenant of the North (1480)

Not everything Richard had came from royal PATRONAGE. Richard worked hard to get hold of the former Earl of Warwick's lands, and he succeeded. Gradually Richard acquired the lordships of Middleham, Sheriff Sutton, Penrith, Barnard Castle, Durham, Scarborough, Skipton, Richmond and Helmsley. But Richard wasn't just acquiring land and castles, he was acquiring power and support. He controlled an area greater than that previously controlled by Warwick the Kingmaker. And he ruled it well, providing sound government, peace and stability. Even Dominic Mancini, Richard's main critic, had to admit that Richard did a good job (see Source 4).

Then came unexpected and horrifying news. On 9 April 1483, Richard's brother, King Edward IV, died aged 41, after an illness lasting ten days. He left a wife, Elizabeth Woodville, and seven legitimate children. Two of these were boys; Edward, aged twelve and Richard, aged nine. So twelve-year-old Edward was the heir to the throne and would soon be crowned Edward V. What was Richard, Duke of Gloucester, uncle of his brother's orphaned sons and daughters to do? This was his situation:

- He was the most powerful man in the kingdom; he had a huge power base in the North and he was the only surviving brother of a dead king and the uncle of a boy king.
- Edward, his nephew, would need a Council or an individual – a PROTECTOR – to rule for him for at least four years until he was old enough to rule by himself. In his will, Edward IV had asked for Richard to do that job.

However, there was a rival for the job of Protector.

- Anthony Woodville, the Earl Rivers, was also uncle to the boy king Edward. The Woodville family had become very powerful. Edward IV had given them good jobs. To keep their power base they also needed to control Edward V.

Richard had no time for the Woodvilles. He owed them no loyalty and certainly did not want them to challenge his power in England. But if Woodville became Protector it would definitely reduce Richard's power.

- Edward IV and his sons enjoyed a great deal of support from the nobility and the people in general. There was no faction pushing for an alternative claimant. The succession looked clear.

What...?

PATRONAGE
Giving support or protection to someone, usually by putting them into positions of influence.

Source ④

Richard kept himself within his own lands and set out to acquire the loyalty of his people through favours and justice. The good reputation of his private life and public activities powerfully attracted the ESTEEM of strangers. Such was his renown in warfare that, whenever a difficult and dangerous policy had to be undertaken, it would be entrusted to his discretion and his generalship. By these skills Richard acquired the favour of the people

Written by Dominic Mancini, probably between 1483 and 1485.

What...?

ESTEEM
High regard.

PROTECTOR
Someone who rules for a monarch when he/she is too young to rule by him/herself.

Task

What should Richard do now?

Richard has the biggest opportunity of his life. Power beckons. But there are threats. The boxes below summarise the situation at this time.

Sort through the information in the boxes then discuss, in the light of this information:

1   What do you think that Richard is **most likely** to do?
   a) take the job of Lord Protector, or
   b) seize this opportunity and try to become king himself?
2   What would you advise Richard to do and why?

a) Richard was ambitious.

b) Richard's brother Edward IV had successfully seized the throne by force although his claim was weak.

c) Richard did not like or trust the Woodvilles.

d) Richard was the most powerful person in England.

e) Richard was the dead king's younger brother.

f) The King's Council might appoint Woodville Protector instead of Richard.

g) Richard's brother wished him to be Edward's Protector until Edward was older.

h) Earl Rivers wanted to become Lord Protector.

i) Richard's guardian the Earl of Warwick had murdered his political rivals and never been charged with any crime.

j) Richard liked to be in control. Rather than let others do things to him he liked to do things to them. That was how he had become powerful.

k) Whenever he had been weak it had ended in trouble for Richard – for example he and Edward IV had been twice exiled from England by their rivals.

l) Edward IV had been a strong king and the powerful nobles were quite happy that the young Edward should become king now.

Source ❺

This stained glass window in the church of St Matthew, Coldridge, Devon, shows the boy-king Edward V.

The short 'reign' of King Edward V

In a time of such chaos and rivalry the chances of twelve-year-old Edward establishing himself as king depended on what all the other players in the game of power decided to do.

- The Royal Council started to organise a coronation for Edward V.
- William, Lord Hastings, who had been one of Edward IV's closest and most loyal supporters, gave firm backing to Richard of Gloucester as the best way of establishing Edward V on the throne.
- Richard dispatched letters to Elizabeth Woodville, Edward IV's queen, and to the royal council, expressing sorrow at his brother's death and expressing loyalty to Edward V.
- Richard presided over a commemoration service to Edward IV held in York, attended by all the northern nobility and gentry, at which he publicly swore loyalty to the new king.

Events then moved swiftly.

When Edward IV died, Richard, Duke of Gloucester, was in Yorkshire. The boy-king Edward V was in Ludlow with his other uncle, Anthony Woodville, the Earl Rivers. Both men immediately left for London. Earl Rivers took Edward with him, plus a small RETINUE. Richard marched south with a large retinue, including armed guards. The two groups met at Stony Stratford, where Richard lavishly entertained the Woodville contingent. The following morning he then had Anthony Woodville arrested and sent to the northern stronghold of Pontefract. Richard took the young Edward V into his care and together they proceeded to London. This wasn't such a rash move as it might at first seem. He had some powerful people on his side. The anonymous author of the *Croyland Chronicle* tells us:

What...?

RETINUE
People in the service of an important person who usually accompanied that person on his or her travels.

Source ❻

The more far-sighted members of the Council thought that the uncles and brothers of Edward V on his mother's side should be absolutely forbidden to have control of the person of the young man until he came of age.

The barons met to decide what should happen. It was agreed that government should be in the hands of a group of nobles including Richard. Dominic Mancini, who did not admire Richard, tells us what happened next:

Source ❼

[Richard] wrote to the Council declaring that he had been loyal to his brother Edward at home and abroad, in peace and war, and would be, if only permitted, equally loyal to his brother's children. This letter had great effect on the minds of the people who now began to support him openly and aloud; so that it was commonly said by all that the Duke [Richard] deserved the government.

On 10 May, Richard Plantagenet, Duke of Gloucester, was formally appointed Protector of the Realm.

Richard of Gloucester, Lord Protector

Richard lost no time in rewarding his supporters. Lord Howard, Viscount Lovell, the Earl of Northumberland and the Duke of Buckingham were the four who received most, as a reward for past services and a guarantee of future support. This was entirely normal. But he also made sure that there was continuity with Edward IV's reign. John Russell, Bishop of Lincoln (who was passionately loyal to Edward IV and possibly the author of the *Croyland Chronicle*), became chancellor. Most of Edward's household remained in their jobs and there were very few changes made to those who actually governed at local and national level. This included William, Lord Hastings, the sensible, steady and staunch supporter of Edward V and his brother. There was nothing here to surprise or alarm anyone.

Then things got nasty.

On 10 June, Richard wrote to the city of York asking for military assistance to root out a Woodville plot to murder himself and the Duke of Buckingham. This was readily given. On 13 June at a council meeting, Richard had Lord Hastings arrested and, without any trial, summarily beheaded on Tower Hill. Also removed were two other staunch supporters of Edward V: Thomas Rotherham, Archbishop of York and John Morton, Bishop of Ely. Elizabeth Woodville (Edward V's mother) was persuaded to allow her second son, Richard, to go to the Tower of London for his own safety and to be company for his brother, Edward V.

By 21 June, London was flooded with northern supporters of Richard of Gloucester.

Did Richard of Gloucester really suspect a Woodville plot against him? Or was he simply inventing it as an excuse to get rid of the most powerful of Edward V's supporters, so he could make his own bid for the crown? We don't know! However, the sources agree about what happened next.

- On Sunday 22 June, Dr Ralph Shaw preached in St Paul's Cathedral, London. In the congregation were the Dukes of Gloucester and Buckingham. What Dr Shaw had to say was startling indeed. He questioned the dead King Edward IV's right to have ruled, on the grounds that he was illegitimate. He was not, so Dr Shaw said, the legitimate son of Richard of York. The only legitimate son of Richard of York who was still alive was Richard, Duke of Gloucester. It was Richard of Gloucester who should be king.
- On Tuesday 24 June the Duke of Buckingham addressed the leading men of London in the Guildhall. He said that Edward IV, when he was a very young man, had married a woman called Lady Eleanor Butler. He had never divorced her. This meant that his marriage to Elizabeth Woodville was invalid and that the boy-king Edward V and his younger brother Richard of York were both illegitimate (as were their sisters) and so could not rule.

Source 8
An historian writes

The main stumbling block in Richard's path to the throne at the end of May was the continued and stubborn refusal of Elizabeth Woodville to emerge from sanctuary or to release Richard, Duke of York into his custody. It was clearly unsuitable to stage the coronation of Edward V while his younger brother, and heir apparent, was so blatantly withheld from public view. If by now Richard planned to make himself king, it was essential that he should control the persons of both Edward IV's sons. Actions to remove the young king Edward V could not succeed for long if the next legitimate heir was not already in his grasp.

Charles Ross, *Richard III*, published 1981.

 Task

Use these last four pages to add further evidence to your timeline.

In this climate of uncertainty, more soldiers from the north, supporters of Richard, began to march to London under the command of Sir Richard Ratcliffe. On their way they killed Woodville and his two main supporters, Lord Grey and Lord Vaughan, where they were in prison in Pontefract Castle.

Meanwhile, in London, a group of influential nobles hastily presented Richard of Gloucester, Protector of the Realm, with a petition, begging him to accept the Crown. He accepted and a magnificent coronation was held on 6 July 1483 for King Richard III and his wife, Queen Anne.

And if you are wondering what happened to Edward V, turn to page 93. He'd never even been crowned king and, after Richard's coronation, he was never seen again!

Source 9

A contemporary picture of King Richard and Queen Anne, dressed for their coronation. ❓▶ *What do you make of their expressions? Are they devious, cunning, noble or innocent?*

Source 10
An historian writes

Great care was taken to see that Richard's coronation and anointing with holy oil by the Archbishop of Canterbury in Westminster Abbey conformed to normal practice and that it was fully recorded. Those present were drawn from a cross-section of English nobility and gentry. They acclaimed Richard as king and the peerage gave him their oaths of allegiance. Whatever private doubts may have been expressed, Richard was king and God's lieutenant, and was entitled to the allegiance of everybody. All had accepted him as king.

Michael Hicks, *Richard III*, published 2000.

Task

Time to take stock again. Using all the information you have so far, do you think Richard III had planned to seize the Crown all along? Or had he just exploited opportunities as they arose?

Jot down your ideas and discuss them with a partner.

Remember that we do not know the 'right' answer. It all depends on how you interpret events and how you use the information to back up your ideas.

— Did you know? —

William Shakespeare put Richard III in his play *Henry VI Part Three* and even wrote a whole play about him called, of course, *Richard III*. In these plays, Shakespeare variously describes Richard III as a 'bottled toad', 'a rooted hog', a 'hell-hound' and a 'lump of foul deformity'. We can guess that he didn't like him much!

King Richard III of England

After his coronation, Richard III and his court began a major tour of the country – a royal progress – to show himself to the people as their king and so gain their support. Richard III, as was normal and to be expected, richly rewarded his supporters. Most of these were northern lords. Indeed, when Richard got to York on 29 August, he was entertained on a grand scale. His son Edward was invested as Prince of Wales in York Minster and he told the city of York that they needed only to pay half the taxes they owed to him. Richard was consolidating his power base in the north.

Meanwhile in the south, a different story was emerging.

Buckingham's rebellion, October 1483

In October 1483 word reached Richard that many powerful people, including some whom he thought were his supporters, had turned against him. They had raised an army and were plotting to depose him.

Most alarmingly for Richard the rebellion involved Henry Stafford, the Duke of Buckingham, his most loyal supporter. Although he was a Lancastrian he had backed Richard. Together the two men had swept to power. When Richard became king, Buckingham had been richly rewarded. Yet within four months, he had betrayed Richard.

This rebellion was serious. It spread throughout the southern counties of England, the south west and Wales. It was backed by large numbers of the gentry who would usually be expected to support the monarchy and who had initially supported Richard. Something had gone very wrong for Richard.

The rebels' objective was to free Edward V and make him king. Then when they discovered that Edward was missing and probably dead, they pinned their hopes on Henry Tudor to be king instead of Richard III. Henry had already set sail from France.

Richard's response was typically ferocious. Sweeping down from the north, Richard and his loyal supporters easily put down the rebellion. Henry Tudor, sailing from France to take part in the rebellion, turned back. Richard showed no mercy to Buckingham. Without trial, Richard had him executed on 2 November 1483.

Why did Buckingham change sides? Maybe he thought Henry Tudor would be a better king. Maybe he wanted to be on the winning side. Maybe he had set his own sights on the crown. Maybe he suspected Richard had killed his two nephews. We do not know. So Richard won but Buckingham's rebellion had been a terrible shock. It proved to Richard that he had failed to inherit Edward IV's support and it had identified a new rival in the shape of Henry Tudor.

Did you know?

John Rous wrote *A History of the Kings of England*. He began writing it in Richard III's reign. During the reign of Henry VII, John Rous altered a lot of what he had written about Richard. He said that Richard had been in his mother's womb for two years instead of the usual nine months (medically impossible!) and that when he was born he had teeth in his mouth and hair down to his shoulders.

Did Richard III rule England well?

Richard ruled for only two years. These were his main actions.

- Richard's only Parliament passed measures to help the poor and make the courts fairer for them and justice more accessible to them.
- Richard set up the Council of the North in July 1484 under the control of his nephew, John de la Pole, Earl of Lincoln, to govern the north of England. This arrangement worked well, was popular and was continued for another 150 years.
- Edward IV had left the treasury almost empty. Richard made strenuous attempts to improve royal finances. However, Richard seems to have spent most of his brief reign trying desperately to ward off threats to his throne.
- Richard's first move, after Buckingham's rebellion, was to reward those who had shown him loyalty. He gave them powerful jobs and money.
- Northerners were generally more loyal to him than southerners, so he moved many northerners down to the south and put them in positions of power and influence. This caused a lot of resentment amongst the southern gentry, many of whom lost their jobs.
- He made sure that Elizabeth Woodville and her daughters lived comfortably and in a manner suitable to their rank. Maybe he was just being kind; more probably he was hoping to end the Woodville threats to his position.
- He needed too to make sure that when he died he had a son to succeed him. So he was frantic when his only child Edward died in April 1484. He named his nephew John de la Pole as his successor. But he also continued his efforts to have a son. His wife Anne was too old to have any more children. She died in March 1485 and there were rumours that she had been poisoned. Free to search for another wife, Richard reportedly wanted to marry his niece, Elizabeth Woodville.

Henry Tudor arrives in England

However, none of Richard's measures could deal with the one of most worrying threats of all to his throne – the Lancastrian claimant to the English throne – Henry Tudor. He had failed to land his small fleet in England during Buckingham's rebellion. But back in France he was building up a bigger army, with the help of the King of France and some soldiers and supplies from Scotland as well. In the summer of 1485 he decided that now was his moment to launch another bid to seize the throne from Richard. He landed on the west coast of Wales at Mill Bay (Milford Haven) and marched through Wales. Although the people of Wales had usually backed the House of York, Henry himself had Welsh ancestry and that helped him to gather soldiers as he marched. Eventually Henry arrived in England with an army of around 5,000 soldiers.

Task
Use these last four pages to add further evidence to your timeline.

Did you know?

We have several reports about the Battle of Bosworth which contradict each other and don't tell us clearly and exactly what happened. They even disagree as to where the battlefield was!

Did you know?

There were four categories of soldier. In order of pay:
- The **foot soldiers** who carried a spike and a hook with which they would try to attack the enemy and pull the knights off their horses.
- Skilled **archers** who would use the longbow to deadly effect.
- **Men-at-arms** wore heavy armour and carried deadly weapons including hammers, battleaxes and clubs.
- Cavalry – **knights** mounted on horses

The Battle of Bosworth Field

When Richard III and Henry Tudor faced each other on Bosworth Field on 22 August 1485, Richard seemed to have everything going for him. He was a king defending his own land and he had a fighting force three times greater than that of Henry Tudor. But it was not as simple as that.

Richard's forces included soldiers commanded by the Duke of Northumberland who could not be relied on. He was suspicious of Richard. Even more of a problem for Richard were the Stanleys. They had brought a large army but in the past they had changed sides more than once to suit their own purpose, and Henry was Thomas Stanley's stepson. So to make sure that Stanley stayed loyal, Richard had taken his son hostage. This was a high-risk strategy.

Henry's army was smaller but he had 3,000 professional French soldiers with him. He also had some loyal followers: while he had been waiting in France, a steady stream of English exiles had joined him. Henry had, too, picked up a following of about 200 men as he marched his troops from Milford Haven towards Nottingham. Henry's weakness was that he had very little experience as a military leader. Henry's luck was that Richard had made enemies and he couldn't even rely on his own supposed supporters.

Map ❶

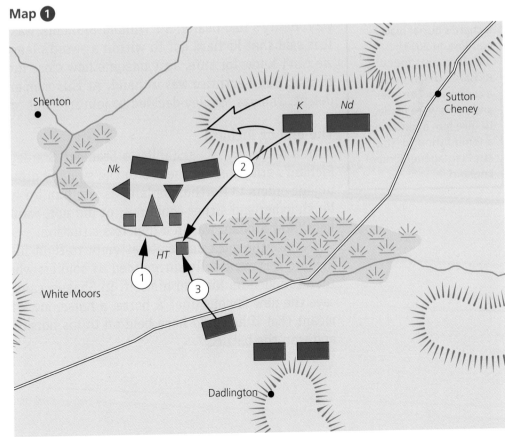

Key

- Royals (K=King Richard III, Nk=Norfolk, Nd=Northumberland)
- Rebels (HT=Henry Tudor)
- Stanleyites
- Swampy ground
- Hill

A map of the probable site of the Battle of Bosworth Field.

┌─ **Did you know?** ─┐

Richard was the last English king to die in battle. He is also the only English king who has no royal tomb. After Bosworth, Richard's body was taken to the Franciscan abbey in Leicester. On Henry VII's orders, Richard's body was on display so that anyone who wanted to make sure he was dead could go and have a look. Some years later Henry gave £10 for a coffin into which the Franciscans could put Richard's bones. When the friary of the Greyfriars was demolished after the dissolution of the monasteries in 1538, Richard's burial place was lost. In 2013, archaeologists found Richard's bones under a car-park in Leicester, and plans were made to give him a burial in a tomb fitting for the last Plantagenet king of England.

The battle begins

The first attack came from Henry's forces led by the Earl of Oxford (1 on the map, Map 1 on page 91). As their foot soldiers charged towards Richard's armies they were met by troops commanded by the Duke of Norfolk. The fighting for the next hour was bloody in the extreme. The foot soldiers, using any weapon at their disposal, stabbed, hit and slashed each other. An hour of such close hand-to-hand combat resulted in the death and injury of many of the soldiers. One casualty of the fighting was the Duke of Norfolk. It was noticeable that Stanley and Northumberland had not got involved. First blood to Henry.

Richard's charge

But all was not lost for Richard. He remained at the top of Ambion Hill away from the chaos that was happening down below. As the battle became ever more desperate, Richard spotted across the battlefield that Henry and his closest supporters had become cut off from the main body of their army. This was his chance to see off Henry once and for all. Richard rallied his cavalry of 1,500 knights and charged across the battlefield towards Henry's position (2).

It must have been a terrible sight for Henry. His faithful knights formed a protective guard around their leader and waited for the worst. Richard and his cavalry crashed across the battlefield, cutting down everything in their way. Henry's flag bearer, Sir William Brandon, was cut down to the ground. It is said that Richard got to within a sword's length of Henry, although we can't know for sure. Just imagine how close Richard was to keeping his throne. But a surprise was in hand. At this moment, seeing Henry close to defeat, Thomas Stanley decided to join in – but on Henry's side!

The end of Richard

With a battle-cry of, 'a Stanley, a Stanley!' Stanley's soldiers charged into Richard's army forcing them into the swampy ground (3). Richard sent urgent orders to Northumberland asking him for help. But none came. Northumberland either could not, or did not, want to come to Richard's help. Now Richard was in a hopeless situation.

Despite the most desperate attempt to fight his way out of trouble, Richard was eventually surrounded by soldiers who killed first his horse and then rounded on Richard himself. In Shakespeare's play *Richard III*, Richard says the now famous line: 'A horse, a horse, my kingdom for a horse!' which meant that if he could have held on to his horse, he might have escaped and won the battle.

Task

Every year, in some newspapers, a notice appears on 22 August in the *In Memoriam* section. It reads 'In memory of King Richard III, treacherously slain on Bosworth Field'.

1 Explain why someone might believe that Richard III was 'treacherously slain'.

2 Do you agree?

But there was no horse. Richard was cut to the ground. Even chroniclers hostile to him commented on his courage. Polydore Vergil reported: 'Alone, he was killed fighting manfully in the press of his enemies.' No fifteenth-century battle continued once the leader of one side was killed – so it was with Bosworth. With Richard dead the battle was over. Legend says that one of Henry's men found Richard's crown nestling in thorn bush, and Henry was crowned King of England, there on the battlefield by his stepfather Lord Stanley.

Richard's body was stripped, thrown onto a horse and taken from the battlefield. The last Plantagenet ruler left Bosworth as a naked corpse. Henry left it as King of England.

The rule of the Tudors had begun.

The mystery of the missing princes

One of the most damning accusations made against Richard III was that he murdered his two nephews, Prince Edward (Edward V) and his younger brother Prince Richard, while they were in his care in the Tower of London. For hundreds of years people have argued about the evidence and interpreted it in different ways. Now it is your chance to join the debate.

These are the facts on which everyone agrees.

- In May 1483 Prince Edward arrived in London and went to stay in the royal apartments in the Tower of London. This was the most important royal palace in London.
- Prince Edward was soon joined by his brother, Prince Richard. The boys were seen playing together in the Tower gardens.
- Arrangements were begun for Prince Edward's coronation as Edward V in June.
- Suddenly, it was declared that Edward had no right to become king because his parents were not legally married.
- Parliament declared that Richard, the boys' uncle, should be king in Prince Edward's place. He was crowned King Richard III on 6 July 1483.
- After Richard's coronation, the Princes were not seen again. Rumours began circulating that they had been murdered.
- Richard III was killed at the Battle of Bosworth in August 1485. When the victorious Henry Tudor rode into London, he took over the Tower. No mention was made of the two Princes.
- In 1502, Henry announced that as far back as 1483 Sir James Tyrell had confessed to murdering the Princes. Tyrell said he did it on Richard's orders.

Turn over for the source investigation and see what you think happened.

THE CASE OF KING RICHARD III AND THE MISSING PRINCES

The evidence against Richard

The first two pieces of evidence come from Dominic Mancini and the anonymous author of the continuation of the *Croyland Chronicle*. They were writing about Richard earlier than anyone else.

Source Ⓐ

After June 1483 Prince Edward's servants were kept from him. He and his brother Richard were taken to rooms further inside the Tower. They were seen behind the windows and window bars, but less and less often, until finally they were seen no more. I have seen men burst into tears at the mention of Prince Edward's name, for already some people suspected he had been done away with. I have not discovered if he has been killed, nor how he might have died.

From a book written by Dominic Mancini in 1483 called *How Richard III Made Himself King*. See page 80 for more information about Mancini.

Source Ⓑ

For a long time the two sons of King Edward remained under guard in the Tower. Finally, in September 1483, people in the south and west began to think of freeing them by force. The Duke of Buckingham, who deserted King Richard, was declared their leader. But then a rumour was spread that the Princes had died a violent death, but no one knew how.

From the anonymous author of the *Croyland Chronicle*, writing in 1486.

QUESTIONS

1 On what do **Sources A** and **B** agree?

2 Is there any **evidence** here that the Princes were murdered?

3 What does Thomas More say in **Source C** about Richard's motive for murder?

4 What proof does Thomas More give to show that his story is true?

5 Do you believe More's story? Why?

Source Ⓒ

After his coronation in July 1483, King Richard decided he must kill his nephews. This was because as long as they were alive, people would not think him the true king. He wrote to Sir Robert Brackenbury, the Constable of the Tower, asking him to put the children to death. Sir Robert refused. Then his page suggested Sir James Tyrell. Tyrell agreed and Richard sent him to Brackenbury with a letter commanding Sir Robert to deliver up the keys of the Tower to Tyrell for one night.

Tyrell decided that the Princes should be murdered in their beds the next night. He chose Miles Forest and John Dighton to do the job. Forest was one of the Princes' guards and had murdered others. The two men pressed feather beds and pillows on the children's faces until they stopped breathing. Tyrell had the Princes buried at the foot of the stairs, deep down under a pile of stones. But King Richard wanted them to have a better burial and so they were dug up and buried secretly in another place.

This story is well known to be true because when Sir James Tyrell was imprisoned in the Tower in 1502 for treason against King Henry VII, he and Dighton confessed that they had done the murder in the way I have described.

From a book written by Sir Thomas More in 1513 called *The History of King Richard III*. More was only five years old when Richard came to the throne. He got most of his information from John Morton. John Morton was an enemy of Richard's, who had invited Henry Tudor to invade England and become king in Richard's place.

What...?

ALDERMAN
A senior officer of a town council, next in importance to the mayor.

Source D

During the Mayor's year of October 1482–October 1483, the children of King Edward were seen playing in the garden of the Tower at various times. After Easter 1483 people began whispering that King Richard had put the Princes to death, but there were many opinions about how they died. Some say they were suffocated between two feather beds. Some said they were drowned in wine. Others said they were poisoned. Tyrell was reported to be their murderer, but others thought it was an old servant of King Richard's.

From *The Great Chronicle of London* written in 1513 by Robert Fabyan. He was a London draper 1483–85. During the reign of Henry VII he became an ALDERMAN in the City of London. He was interested in history but was not always very accurate.

QUESTIONS

6 In what ways is Robert Fabyan's story in **Source D** different from that of Thomas More?

7 Why do you think their stories are different? (Hint: think about whether they were in a position to know what they were writing about.)

The case for Richard's defence

QUESTIONS

8 How far do **Sources E and F** agree?

9 How likely do you think it would have been for Elizabeth Woodville to let her daughters go to Richard's court for Christmas if she believed he had murdered her two sons?

10 When does Philip Lindsay (**Source G**) think the Princes were murdered?

11 Why does Philip Lindsay blame King Henry VII for the Princes' death?

Source E

In 1484, after strong persuasion from Richard, Queen Elizabeth Woodville sent all her daughters to Richard's court at Westminster. Christmas Day that year was celebrated with great splendour in the Great Hall at Westminster. There was far too much dancing and fun. King Richard presented Queen Anne (his wife) and Lady Elizabeth (the Princes' sister) with a set of new and fashionable clothes each. This caused a lot of gossip.

From the anonymous author of the *Croyland Chronicle* writing in 1486.

Source F

Richard decided to try all he could to make his peace with Elizabeth Woodville. He sent messengers to her and after a time she forgot her troubles and sent her daughters to stay with Richard at court. After this she wrote secretly to the Marquis of Dorset advising him to forget Henry Tudor and return quickly to England where he would be sure to be treated well by King Richard.

From *The History of England* written by Polydore Vergil in 1517. Vergil was an Italian writer and churchman. He came to live in England in 1507. Henry VII gave him a good position in the Church and asked him to write a history of England.

Source G

I do not doubt for one moment that the Princes were alive when Henry VII came to London in August 1485. He issued a proclamation, giving all Richard's supposed crimes and this list did not include the killing of the Princes. That to my mind is definite proof that the Princes were not even missing. They must still have been in the Tower. Richard had no reason to kill them: Henry had every reason. If they lived, all he had fought for would be useless because Prince Edward had more right to be king than Henry Tudor. Henry was capable of such a crime, so the boys were quietly but efficiently murdered. Elizabeth Woodville, the boy's mother, was locked into a nunnery. Henry spread the word that Richard had done the killing. Henry Tudor, murderer and liar – it's time the truth was known!

In 1972 Philip Lindsay, a historical writer, wrote an article in the magazine *Argosy*. This is an extract.

QUESTIONS

12 When does Professor Kendall (**Source H**) think the Princes were murdered?

13 Why does Professor Kendall blame the Duke of Buckingham for the Princes' death?

Task

Use the sources and your answers to the small questions to answer the big one:

'Did King Richard III kill the Princes in the Tower?'

You have a choice of three verdicts: 'guilty', 'not guilty' or 'not proven'.

Remember to back up what you say with evidence from the sources or your own knowledge.

Source 🄷

There is no **proof** that Richard murdered the Princes. On what is the accusation based? It is based on rumours, on hearsay evidence and on statements from unreliable and inaccurate witnesses. The Duke of Buckingham had the same opportunity and stronger motive. As Constable of England he could get into the Tower and to the Princes. Remember he didn't go with Richard on his tour after the coronation in 1483. Instead he stayed behind in London and caught up with Richard at Gloucester. Then Buckingham went to Wales and began plotting to overthrow Richard. His motives for murdering the Princes were stronger than Richard's. They were in his way because he wanted to claim the Crown himself, or help Henry Tudor claim it. By murdering the boys and then spreading a rumour about their death he could blacken Richard's character. Looking at the facts, Buckingham appears much more likely to be their murderer than Richard.

From *Richard III* by Professor Paul Kendall, published in 1955.

Summary task

Over the past 19 pages you have been gathering evidence about Richard III. You are now going to use that evidence to help you draw conclusions: 'Was King Richard a wicked uncle or a loyal brother?' To help you focus you can use this outline.

Exam practice

Using **all** the sources and your own knowledge, was King Richard a loyal brother or a wicked uncle?

Paragraph 1

Explain the question in your own words.

Paragraph 2

Describe at least two of Richard's actions that show him to be treacherous, ruthless, evil or cowardly.

Paragraph 3

Describe at least two of Richard's actions that show him to be loyal, kind, good or brave.

Paragraph 4 (optional)

Explain the problem we have in using evidence from the time about Richard.

Paragraph 5

Your overall conclusion. Explain which way the balance falls for you – wicked Richard or loyal Richard? Include your strongest reason to support this view.

Exam practice

Using all the sources and your own knowledge, was King Richard a loyal brother or a wicked uncle?

Source Ⓐ

Richard wrote to the Council declaring that he had been loyal to his brother Edward at home and abroad, in peace and war, and would be, if only permitted, equally loyal to his brother's children. This letter had great effect on the minds of the people who now began to support him openly and aloud, so that it was commonly said by all that the Duke [Richard] deserved the government.

From Dominic Mancini *The Usurpation of the Realm of England by Richard III* written in December 1483. Here he is writing about the time Richard was made Lord Protector.

Source Ⓑ

The best guess must surely be that the Princes in the Tower had met a violent end by early October 1483 – an end authorised by their uncle as the final act of several months spent in ruthless pursuit of personal security and political power.

From Keith Dockray, *Richard III* published in 1997.

See page 185 for a practice evidence question on Richard III.

Source Ⓒ

A contemporary picture of King Richard and Queen Anne, dressed for their coronation on 6 July 1483.

Pulling it all together

Through Section 1 you have been compiling record sheets like this. Complete three more sheets now for the monarchs Richard II, Henry V and Richard III.

King:		
Top tasks for a king	**Score out of 5**	**Reason for score**
Win wars		
Gain territory/keep what you've got		
Get on well with barons		
Get on well with church leaders		
Keep law and order and peace in the country		
Spend money wisely		
Have healthy sons		
Be a good leader		
Have a good claim to the throne		
Average score		

Now it is time to draw some conclusions. Work in groups to compare your charts and decide between you:

a) Who was the best monarch and why?

b) Who was the worst monarch and why?

c) Who was it easiest to agree about and why?

d) Who provoked most disagreement and why?

e) Who would you most like to find out more about?

f) Which of the king's jobs on page 9 do you now think was the most important, that is, the one the king **had to get right** to be a success?

Religion in the Middle Ages

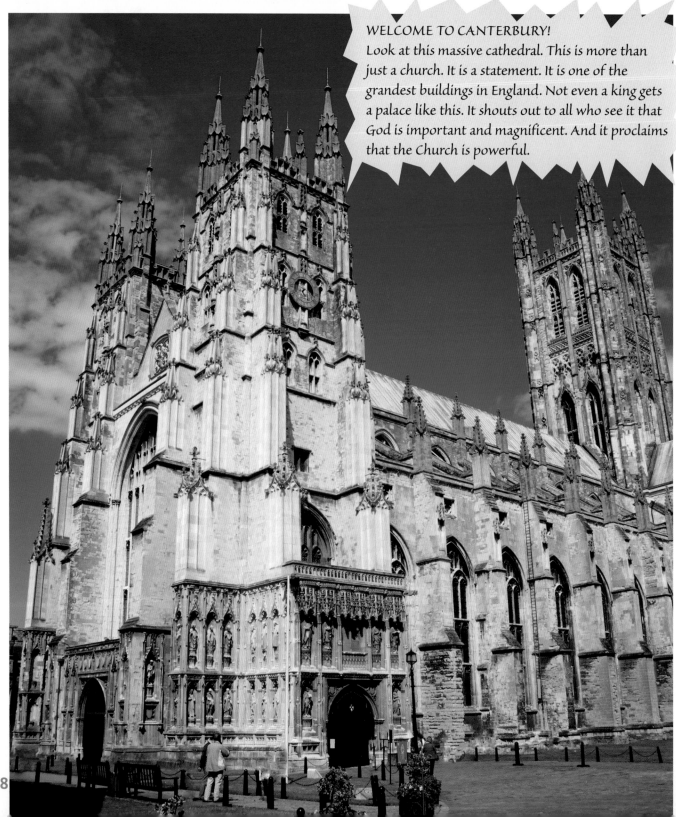

WELCOME TO CANTERBURY!
Look at this massive cathedral. This is more than just a church. It is a statement. It is one of the grandest buildings in England. Not even a king gets a palace like this. It shouts out to all who see it that God is important and magnificent. And it proclaims that the Church is powerful.

If you are going to understand the Middle Ages you have to understand the power and significance of the Christian religion. In our time religion is a matter of personal preference: some people are religious, others are not; some go to church, most do not. In the Middle Ages it was very different.

- Religion was a matter of life or death – for almost everyone.
- Religious leaders – the leaders of the Christian Church – were as powerful as kings.
- The leader of the Church – the Pope, who was based in Rome – was probably the most powerful individual in Europe.
- The Church was rich. It owned masses of land and earned a lot of money. Tens of thousands of people worked for the Church.
- Every village in England had its own outpost of the Christian religion – a parish church, with its own priest, where once a week all the people came for Mass, to be told how to live, and to take one more step – so they hoped – on their road to heaven.

Unlike the previous section which told a single story from the beginning of the Middle Ages to the end, this one is thematic. The stories here overlap each other and they overlap with the stories in Section 1. You will need to use the timeline on page 3 to keep your bearings. Each unit focuses on one topic or depth study which will add a particular dimension to your understanding of religion in the Middle Ages.

- In the previous section you will already have seen how important it was for a king to work well with Church leaders. Some of the most spectacular failures were the kings who fell out with the Pope or with the Church leaders. In **Unit 8** you are going to examine one of the most famous fallings-out between a king and the Church, which led to the murder of Archbishop Thomas Becket. You will consider what this tells you about the importance of religion in the Middle Ages.
- In **Unit 9** you will find out more about cathedrals – with a particular focus on Canterbury. You will find out what to look out for on your own site visit to a cathedral.
- In **Unit 10** you will investigate monasteries and convents – with a special focus on Fountains Abbey in Yorkshire. You will think about why so many people wanted to become monks or nuns and what life was like for them in the monastery or convent. You will also see how important the monasteries were by the end of the Middle Ages.
- In **Unit 11** you will study how religion affected the lives of ordinary people in villages – the peasant farmers, who formed the vast majority of the English population. You will join them as they try to get to heaven.
- Finally in **Unit 12** you will shift focus and scale entirely and look at the ways that religion helped to cause a series of wars between Christians and Muslims – known as the Crusades – that lasted for over 200 years. What do these chilling events tell us about religion in the Middle Ages?

Task

You won't need to study all these units, but whichever topics or depth studies you follow throughout the section, your challenge will be to create your own spider diagram or concept map to sum up what you have found about religion in the Middle Ages. See page 135 for ideas.

UNIT 8 Church and State: Henry versus Becket

What is this all about?

Henry II was King of England from 1154 to 1189. He was one of the most powerful and successful kings of the Middle Ages. His reign was one of peace and stability in England. He ruled a vast European empire known as the Angevin Empire that spread across France and the British Isles. He introduced a number of changes in how England was run so more money could be raised to pay for the upkeep of the empire.

You can see a suitably 'king-like' portrait of him on page 37. Yet Source 1 on this page shows him in a very different situation: humiliated, and at the mercy of the monks of Canterbury. In this unit you find out what this tells us about the struggle for power between king and Church in the Middle Ages.

Task

Source 1 is a stained glass window. Write the text for a plaque to go beneath this window explaining what it shows and what this event tells you about the power of the Church at this time. You have a limit of 200 words.

Thomas Becket was the son of a merchant. He did not come from a noble family. He worked as a clerk and archdeacon at Canterbury Cathedral. When Henry was looking for a new CHANCELLOR, Archbishop Theobald recommended Becket and in 1155, Henry appointed him. Soon they became close friends. In 1162 Henry needed a new Archbishop of Canterbury and he wanted Becket.

Control of the Church

Henry thought that, with Becket as Archbishop of Canterbury, he would have greater control over the Church. In particular, he would be able to get all the churchmen to swear an oath of allegiance to him rather than the Pope. However, as soon as Becket was appointed, it became clear that he was not going to do what Henry wanted. There was one issue above all others which was to prove to be a battleground between them.

Source ❶

Henry is whipped by monks at Becket's tomb.

Source ❷

A man of reddish, freckled complexion with a large round head, grey eyes which glowed fiercely and grew bloodshot in anger.

A writer at the time, Gerald of Wales, describing Henry II.

What...?

THE CHANCELLOR
Had to deal with the day-to-day government of the country as well as act as the king's AMBASSADOR. In 1158 Becket went to Paris for Henry with eight five-horse wagons and 24 changes of clothes. To impress his hosts he gave away all his gold and furs.

Did you know?

One hundred years before Becket, Anselm, the then Archbishop of Canterbury, spent roughly half his time in exile. This was because he believed he should obey the Pope over the king, much to the annoyance of William II. Becket's problem was not new.

What...?

PENANCE
Self-punishment for doing something wrong.

Did you know?

Before Becket's exile in 1164, he and Henry used to have huge rows. It was reported Becket once said to Henry: 'We ought to obey God rather than men.' To which Henry responded: 'I don't want a sermon from you. Are you not the son of one of my peasants?'

Henry did not like the fact that priests and members of religious orders were not being tried in the King's courts but in Church courts. Henry believed that this undermined the power of the King.

Constitutions of Clarendon, 1164

At the meeting of the Great Council at Clarendon in 1164 Henry demanded that Becket, the bishops and barons accept a king's rights to try priests. In short, Henry insisted that royal justice should rule. The agreement at the end of the meeting, known as the Constitutions of Clarendon, also gave the King the right to appoint archbishops and bishops. Becket initially agreed to the King's points but then refused to add his seal to the agreement.

Becket flees

Henry was now out to get Becket. In 1164 he put Becket on trial on a number of charges. Becket fled into exile in France. In 1169 he met Henry in France but they failed to resolve their differences. They met again in France in 1169, the outcome being that Becket agreed to return to England in December 1170. However, immediately on Becket's return rumours spread round Henry's court that Becket was bullying bishops and looking for revenge against Henry.

Becket is murdered

When these rumours reached Henry he exploded with rage. Four knights decided to teach Becket a lesson. They travelled to Canterbury Cathedral to find him. They first met him unarmed but an argument followed, the knights failed to arrest him and they stormed out. They returned fully armed and determined to arrest Becket. A struggle followed and Becket was murdered in the cathedral (see next page).

Becket the Martyr

When Becket's body was prepared for burial it was discovered that he was wearing underclothes made of horsehair, a sign of PENANCE. A number of people began to claim that miracles were taking place because of Becket. A blind woman called Britheva claimed to be able to see again after some of Becket's blood had been put on her eyes. Thousands travelled to Canterbury in hope of a miracle. A shrine was built for Becket and, in 1173, Becket was made a saint.

Henry's penance

Henry was forced to back down over Church courts and in 1174 he did penance at the shrine of Thomas Becket. This involved him walking barefoot into the cathedral, lying on the floor of Becket's tomb, being whipped by the monks and the bishops and sleeping on the ground by the tomb without food.

THE MURDER OF THOMAS BECKET

There are different accounts of Becket's murder. Here are four of them. See if you can work out from the sources what actually happened.

QUESTIONS

1 Some points of information are mentioned or shown in every source. Read through the sources and pick out three of these **common** points.

2 Some points are mentioned in only one source. Pick out one point from each source that is **unique** to that source.

┌─── **What...?** ───
│ MARTYR
│ A person who dies for
│ their cause.
└──────────────────

Source Ⓐ

The knights entered the cathedral with swords drawn, shouting in a rage:

'Where is Thomas Becket, traitor of the King and kingdom?'

No one responded and instantly they cried out more loudly,

'Where is the archbishop?'

Becket descended from the steps to which he had been taken by the monks who were fearful of the knights and said in an adequately audible voice:

'Here I am, not a traitor of the King but a priest.'

The MARTYR Becket sensed he would be killed and with his neck bent as if he were in prayer and with his joined hands he prayed to God, St Mary and St Denis. He had barely finished when one of the knights, fearing Thomas would be saved by the people and escape alive, suddenly set upon him and cut off the top of Becket's head. The lower arm of the writer [Edward Grim] was cut by the same blow. Indeed the writer stood by Becket, holding him in his arms – while all the other priests and monks fled. Becket was hit on the head again and with the third blow he bent his knees and elbows and fell.

The third knight then struck Becket; and with this blow he shattered the sword on the stone and his crown [the top of his head] separated from his head so that the blood turned white from the brain yet no less did the brain turn red from the blood. A clerk who came in with the knights placed his foot on the neck of the holy priest and precious martyr and (it is horrible to say) scattered the brains with the blood across the floor, exclaiming to the rest, 'We can leave this place, knights, he will not get up again.'

From Edward Grim, The Life of St Thomas, Archbishop of Canterbury. Edward Grim was a witness at the murder and is mentioned in a number of the stories.

Source Ⓑ

And these four knights came to Canterbury on the Tuesday in Christmas week. They came to Saint Thomas and said that the king commanded him to apologise for his mistakes and reverse the excommunication on the bishops. Thomas said that he could not do that. The knight Sir Reginald said that if he didn't do as he was told it would cost him his life.

Then one of the knights hit him on the head as he kneeled before the altar. Sir Edward Grim put his arm out with the cross to defend Becket. The sword hit the cross and nearly cut Grim's arm off. Grim then fled in fear as did all the other monks. The knights then each hit Becket, they cut off a great piece of the skull of his head, that his brain fell on the pavement. They were so cruel that one of them broke the point of his sword against the pavement. And when he was dead they stirred his brain and then stole his goods and horse.

The Golden Legend or Lives of the Saints, compiled by Jacobus de Voragine, Archbishop of Genoa, 1275.

Source C

Becket stood by the east wall. He might have easily fled or hidden himself but he refused. Realising the moment of death had come he bent forward to pray. After killing Becket, the knights hurried out of the cathedral and back into the archbishop's palace. There they stole anything of value including gold, silver, furniture, rings, books and clothes.

From John Guy, *Thomas Becket*, published in 2012.

Source D

QUESTIONS

3 How does **Source A** differ from **Source B** in its account of Grim's reaction? Why do you think there were these differences?

4 What impression does the historian in **Source C** give of Becket and and the knights?

5 What would make an historian think that the artist who drew **Source D** based his ideas on Edward Grim's account (**Source A**)?

6 Using **all** the sources and your own knowledge, write an accurate account of Becket's murder.

A contemporary picture of the murder of Becket from an English psalter.

Exam practice

See page 182 for a practice evidence question on Archbishop Becket.

UNIT 9 A visit to Canterbury Cathedral

What is this all about?

The most powerful person in the English medieval Church was the Archbishop of Canterbury. When William I conquered England he got rid of the Anglo-Saxon Stigand from this job and appointed his loyal friend and adviser Lanfranc. Archbishop Lanfranc appointed many other Normans to the key roles in the Church and together they began a huge programme of cathedral building. Many of these cathedrals are still standing today. In this unit you are going to visit one of them.

What...?

SECULAR
In medieval times, it meant not attached to an abbey. Now it means non-religious.

Did you know?

The builders of cathedrals were very keen to put them in places where they could be seen for miles around. In Durham the new cathedral was put on a hill next to the castle. Those cathedrals that were built in low-lying areas such as Salisbury Cathedral were built with very tall spires.

Did you know?

Cathedrals were built by large armies of labourers but they also needed hundreds of skilled craftsmen. Stonemasons carved the columns, windows and doorways. Glaziers designed amazing windows. When the building was completed, artists decorated the inside with beautiful pictures and designs.

What is a cathedral?

England was divided into areas called dioceses, each of which had a bishop. Each bishop had a throne. The word cathedral comes from the Latin word *cathedra* which means 'bishop's throne'. So a cathedral is simply a church with a bishop's throne in it.

So far it is quite simple. However there were two types of cathedral in England:

- Monastic cathedrals such as Canterbury or Winchester were run by monks. These cathedrals were really part of a monastery.
- SECULAR cathedrals such as York or Exeter were run by priests.

A cathedral had other functions too. It was like in administrative centre – a place from which to organise and run a diocese. It was also a symbol of the power of the Church just as a castle was a symbol of the power of the king or the barons. So it needed to be impressive.

In 1072 the King's Council at Windsor ordered that all cathedrals be placed in towns or cities. Some bishops were told to move; for example the Bishop of Dorchester moved to Lincoln and the Bishop of Selsey moved to Chichester.

Every diocese was divided into areas called archdeaconries and every archdeaconry divided into groups of parishes called deaneries. From now on, the Church was better organised.

Did you know?

LANFRANC
Born in Italy in around 1005, he taught as a monk at the monastery of Bec in France where he prepared young men for a life in the Church (including the future Pope Alexander II). He was well known for having an excellent understanding of the Bible. He became a loyal adviser to Duke William of Normandy. He served as Archbishop of Canterbury from 1071 until his death in 1089.

Task
The drawings below show you the styles of church windows and doors in the Middle Ages.
1 Which do you like the best?
2 Canterbury Cathedral has been added to over the years. Which of these styles best fits the photo on page 98?
3 Next time you visit a cathedral, see if you can tell, from the windows and doors alone, in which period it was probably built.

Canterbury Cathedral

Since the Archbishop of Canterbury had the most important job in the Church, the cathedral there was also the most important in the country. There had been a cathedral in Canterbury since Anglo-Saxon times. The Anglo-Saxon building had been badly damaged by a fire in December 1067. In 1070 Lanfranc ordered that Canterbury Cathedral be rebuilt from scratch in the Normans' favourite 'Romanesque' style and took a personal interest in the plans. From 1071 to 1077 the rebuilding of the cathedral took place at breakneck speed.

We have been left an account of the rebuilding of the cathedral by a monk, Eadmer. He tells of a number of problems that needed to be overcome before the cathedral could be rebuilt. One problem was that people were buried in the old cathedral. Eadmer tells us that the bodies in the east end of the cathedral were dug up and stored in the west end until the east end was rebuilt, then the bodies were reburied.

ROMANESQUE

Round windows and arches

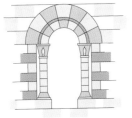

Most cathedrals and churches built between the tenth and twelfth centuries were built in this style. It is sometimes called Norman.
1066–1190

EARLY ENGLISH

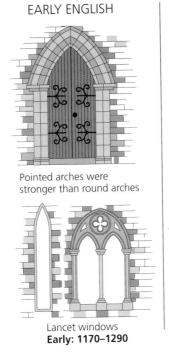

Pointed arches were stronger than round arches

Lancet windows
Early: 1170–1290

GOTHIC DECORATED

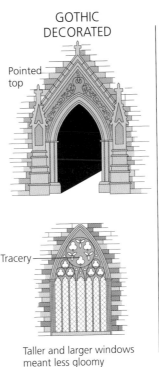

Pointed top

Tracery

Taller and larger windows meant less gloomy cathedrals and churches
Middle: 1250–1360

PERPENDICULAR

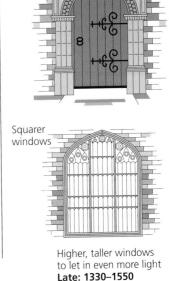

Flat top

Squarer windows

Higher, taller windows to let in even more light
Late: 1330–1550

Main features

This plan shows Canterbury Cathedral as it is today. Some of the features date back to the Normans. Some are more recent. Parts of the cathedral would be used for different things. All around were small chapels and shrines. The cathedral was also a monastery so many of the features relate to the daily life of the monks.

THE CLOISTER
The Cloister was the centre of daily life in the monastery. This was where the monks lived and where Lanfranc set up a school for local children. It was also where the monks were trained.

THE CHAPTER HOUSE
This was where the monks would meet to hear a Chapter of the Rule of St Benedict read to them. They would then deal with the business of the monastery.

MARTYRDOM
A small altar marks the spot where, on 29 December 1170, Archbishop Thomas Becket was murdered. It is called the Altar of the Sword's Point because it used to house the tip of Richard le Breton's sword which broke on the pavement as he attacked the Archbishop (see pages 102–103).

THE NAVE
The Nave is at the centre of the cathedral. The present Nave was finished in 1405 and is an example of Perpendicular architecture. It replaced the Nave built by Lanfranc.

Did you know?
The rebuilding of Canterbury Cathedral in 1071–1072 was done so quickly that a writer at the time called William of Malmesbury commented: 'You do not know which to admire more, the beauty or the speed.'

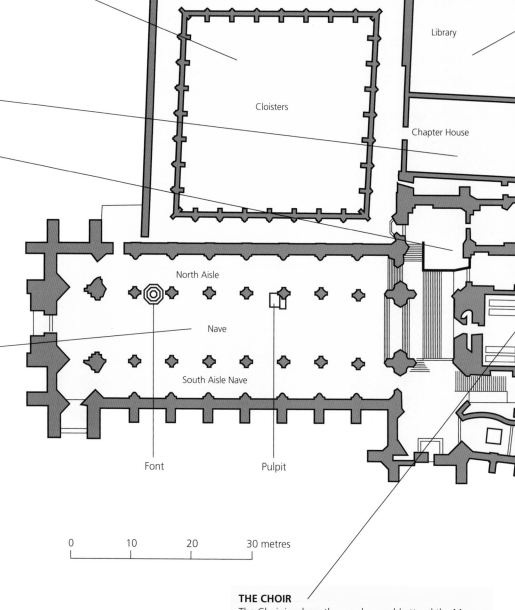

Library

Cloisters

Chapter House

North Aisle

Nave

South Aisle Nave

Font   Pulpit

0   10   20   30 metres

THE CHOIR
The Choir is where the monks would attend the Mass. The Choir is the longest of any English cathedral. It is also noted for its height. It was built in the Gothic style by William of Sens, and was finished by 1184.

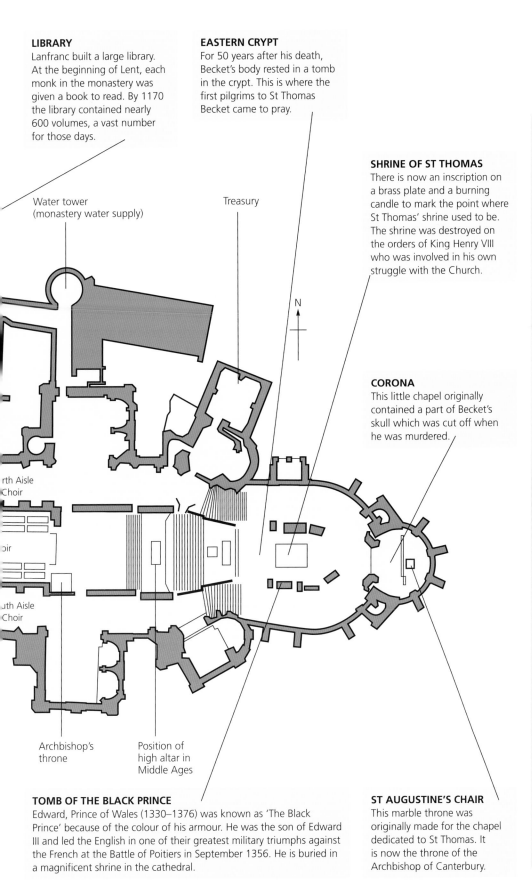

LIBRARY
Lanfranc built a large library. At the beginning of Lent, each monk in the monastery was given a book to read. By 1170 the library contained nearly 600 volumes, a vast number for those days.

Water tower (monastery water supply)

EASTERN CRYPT
For 50 years after his death, Becket's body rested in a tomb in the crypt. This is where the first pilgrims to St Thomas Becket came to pray.

Treasury

SHRINE OF ST THOMAS
There is now an inscription on a brass plate and a burning candle to mark the point where St Thomas' shrine used to be. The shrine was destroyed on the orders of King Henry VIII who was involved in his own struggle with the Church.

N

CORONA
This little chapel originally contained a part of Becket's skull which was cut off when he was murdered.

rth Aisle Choir

oir

uth Aisle Choir

Archbishop's throne

Position of high altar in Middle Ages

TOMB OF THE BLACK PRINCE
Edward, Prince of Wales (1330–1376) was known as 'The Black Prince' because of the colour of his armour. He was the son of Edward III and led the English in one of their greatest military triumphs against the French at the Battle of Poitiers in September 1356. He is buried in a magnificent shrine in the cathedral.

ST AUGUSTINE'S CHAIR
This marble throne was originally made for the chapel dedicated to St Thomas. It is now the throne of the Archbishop of Canterbury.

Summary task
Research project
If you are lucky enough to be taken on a trip to a cathedral, try to collect as much information as you can. This information might include the following:
• a booklet or leaflet about the cathedral's history
• postcards or pictures
• plan of the cathedral.

When you get home or back to school, write about the cathedral. Try to answer the following questions:
• When was the cathedral built and who by?
• What style is it built in?
• What has been changed in the cathedral since it was first built?
• Which individuals and stories are associated with the cathedral?

Then finally compare your cathedral with Canterbury.

UNIT 10 Monks and nuns: what did they do and why did they do it?

What is this all about?

Many men and women decided to dedicate their lives to the service of God. The men joined monasteries or abbeys and the women went to convents or nunneries. They separated themselves from ordinary people. They followed strict rules. They spent hours in prayer. This might sound a hard life but in the Middle Ages it was very popular. By the 1300s there were thousands of monks and nuns. What was the attraction and what was life really like for them?

What...?

MEDITATE
To think deeply and quietly about something.

FAST
To go without food.

The rule of St Benedict

The basic idea of separating yourself off from the world in order to focus on God came from early Christian times. Men would go off into the desert, on their own or in groups, to MEDITATE and to FAST. The idea gradually spread to western Europe, where the monks followed rules set down by St Benedict who lived 480–547.

All monks and nuns had to make three vows. They had to keep these solemn promises throughout their lives:

- **Poverty** No monk or nun could own anything at all. Whatever they owned when they joined a monastery or convent had to be given up to the community and used for the good of all.
- **Chastity** No monk or nun could get married or have sexual relations with anyone at all, ever. This showed that they put God first, above everything.
- **Obedience** Monks and nuns had to obey the head of their monastery or convent at all times and without question.

St Benedict built on these vows by writing a detailed set of rules. These rules were really a code of behaviour that covered all aspects of a monk's day. St Benedict's rules included what clothing the monks should wear, what the sleeping arrangements in dormitories should be, the sort of food that could be eaten, how guests were to be looked after and how the sick were to be cared for. Monks who followed the Rule of St Benedict were called Benedictines. Here are some extracts.

Source ❶

- Idleness is the enemy of the soul. The brothers should have set times for manual work and for reading prayers.
- A mattress, woollen blanket and pillow are enough for bedding.
- All monks should take turns to wait on each other so that no one is excused kitchen work.
- Above all, care must be taken of the sick.

The thinking behind this code was that if there were rules that had to be followed, monks could then focus their time on worshipping God and not on petty squabbles like what to wear.

Source ➋

Monks and nuns at prayer. Benedictine monks wore black HABITS with a cowl hood that they could pull over their heads if they wanted to. The nuns wore headgear called wimples that covered their hair and hid most of their faces. Both monks and nuns had girdles round their waists with three big knots tied in them to remind them of the three vows they had made.

What...?

HABIT
The garment a monk or nun wears.

Did you know?

At Canterbury, food was to be basic and only the very sick were allowed to eat meat. Only on certain occasions and times of the year were the monks allowed the luxury of eating lard. The abbot (who at Canterbury was also the archbishop) had to eat at the same table as his monks.

In the Middle Ages there was a great boom in the number of people wanting to dedicate themselves to God and enter monasteries and convents. It has been estimated that in 1066 there were around 1,000 monks in Britain; by the beginning of the 1300s this number had risen to 13,000. By this time, one man in every 200 was a monk. In addition, there were about 30,000 people who were connected to the life of monasteries because they worked there as servants. This meant that monasteries (and to a lesser extent, convents) had a tremendous impact on their local communities and on Britain itself.

┌─ Did you know? ─┐

LAY BROTHER
The Cistercian order had lay brothers who made vows and worked in and for monasteries, but were not full monks like the choir monks. They attended fewer church services and were allowed to mix with the outside world.

CHOIR MONK
A novice who made his vows and became a full monk, usually in the Cistercian order.

How did boys become monks?

In the early days, families sometimes gave a boy to a monastery to be trained as a monk. This was supposed to show that the family was deeply religious. We don't know what any of these boys thought about being given away like this, but some of them can't have been too impressed! By the 1100s this practice had died out, and all boys and young men going into a monastery did so voluntarily.

Task

In 1141, Orderic Vitalis wrote a book called *History of the Church*. In it he described how his parents sent him off to become a monk. Read what he wrote carefully (below), and try to work out whether Orderic's father sent him away because of his love for God or because of his love for Orderic.

Source ❸

When I was five years old I was sent to school in the town of Shrewsbury. There, Siward, a priest, taught me to read and write and instructed me in the psalms and hymns. Then, O glorious God, you inspired my father to put me under your rule. So, weeping, he gave me, a child of ten, into the care of the monk Reginald. My father sent me away for love of you and never saw me again, for he promised me in your name that if I became a monk I should go to heaven after my death.

Boys could go into a monastery from the age of ten. If they went in that young, they could change their minds and leave at any time before they took holy orders. However, most young men decided to take up the religious life when they were about fifteen. They were welcomed into monasteries as trainee monks, called novices. They would work alongside the monks learning how to do different jobs and singing in the choir. They would also be taught how to read and write. All the novices would be supervised by the Master of Novices for at least a year. He would watch them carefully and try to work out if they really were suited to the religious life and, if they were, when it would be appropriate for them to become fully fledged monks. To become a monk would mean taking the three vows of poverty, chastity and obedience. The novices would have to leave all their old life behind and become obedient to God and to the rules of the monastery. They wouldn't even be able to leave the monastery without the abbot's permission. This sort of life didn't suit everyone and some did leave after having a 'taster' as a novice.

Once a novice was ready, he took the three vows that committed him to the monastic life and was given a tonsure (a special haircut). Then the really serious learning would begin. The young monk would have to learn what was expected of him at the different services and at all the different stages of a monk's day. He would need to train, too, to be a useful member of the religious community as, for example, an illustrator or a cellarer (see page 116) or an infirmarian, who cared for the sick and dying. And he

┌─ Did you know? ─┐

A monk had the top of his head shaved so that he had a bald patch. This was called a tonsure. The ring of hair that was left was supposed to represent Christ's crown of thorns.

Did you know?

Some orders required their monks and nuns to take a vow of silence. So they developed sign language to ask for what they wanted. If, for example, a nun wanted some more fish for her dinner, she would wiggle her right hand sideways, like a fish moving through the water; if a monk wanted bread he would make a circle with both thumbs and the next two fingers.

What...?

TITHES
A system whereby a tenth of what everyone produced – barley, hay, flour, eggs, for example – had to be given to the Church.

would have to take his share of the everyday jobs that keep a community going. All this while being obedient, chaste and poor!

Was it the same for girls?

Not quite. There were far fewer convents than monasteries. Between 1250 and 1540, well over 100 convents were set up, but only four had more than 30 women in them and 63 had fewer than ten. By 1200 there were about 3,000 nuns in Britain compared to 13,000 monks. Why was this?

It is true that many nuns believed they had a calling to give up the world and enter a religious order. But there were others who saw entry into a convent as a sensible career move. It meant they were spared the necessity of getting married and would be educated and gain experience in living within and managing an organisation. But this applied only to girls from wealthy families. Convents had less money than monasteries, and families often had to pay to send their girls there. Poor families could not afford this, and, besides, their daughters had to work to bring in much needed cash.

Convents were separated from monasteries so that nuns and monks could not meet and be tempted into relationships. But convents still depended on monasteries. Local abbots and bishops usually gave them TITHES, and sometimes wealthy men and women would leave them money in their wills, but they did not attract the funding that monasteries did. Many convents took in paying guests – usually wealthy widows and wives – for short breaks from the stresses of life. This wasn't always a good thing as this sort of contact with the outside world made many nuns wish things were different for them.

Task

a) List the various reasons why someone might join a monastery or convent.
b) Highlight in different colours those that apply to just men, just women and both men and women.

Source 4
An historian writes

Once monks and nuns had taken their final vows they were bound to stay in their abbey for life. Some clearly regretted their decision because there are many records of runaways (known as apostates). Monasteries were often energetic in their pursuit of runaways and could use the law to enforce their return.

Tony McAleavy, *Life in a Medieval Abbey*, published in 1996.

Source ⑤

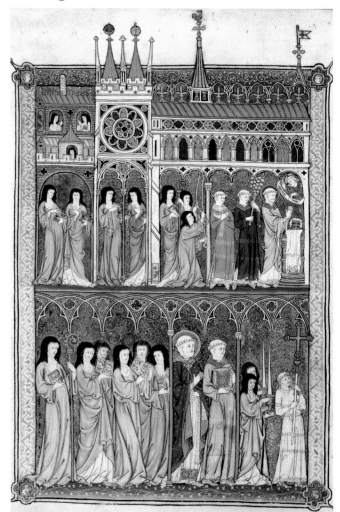

Source ⑥

Source ⑦

Source ⑧

Task
Work it out
Using the information on pages 108–111, work out what is happening in each of these four pictures. (For answers, see page 190.)

Did you know?

By the twelfth century, Lanfranc's rules were being ignored. The abbot started to eat separately from the monks and usually rather well. When Gerald of Wales visited Canterbury monastery in the late twelfth century he was served a sixteen-course meal with wine!

Different orders

The Rule of St Benedict was a hard Rule to follow. It wasn't surprising that, over the years, little by little, many monks and monasteries slid away from parts of it. Then, gradually, breakaway groups founded new religious orders, trying hard to get back to what they saw as the purity of St Benedict's Rule. More and more religious orders were founded, all of which adapted the Rule of St Benedict to meet their needs and beliefs. There were so many that, in 1215, the Pope banned any new orders. New monasteries had to adopt the rules of the existing ones.

Not all religious orders expected their members to spend all their time in isolation. Some went out into the world and taught ordinary people about Christianity. They were called friars.

Order	Where was the Order founded?	When did the Order arrive in Britain?	What were the aims of the Order?	Did you know?
Benedictine	In 525 by Benedict in Italy.	597. Led by Augustine who founded a monastery at Canterbury and became the first Archbishop of Canterbury.	To follow St Benedict's Rule that would enable them to lead a godly life.	Called the 'black monks' because of their black habits, which they wore over white gowns.
Cluniac	In 910 when William of Aquitaine gave land for a new monastery at Cluny in France.	1077. First monastery built at Lewes in Sussex.	To lead a strict and holy life.	Followed St Benedict's Rule but spent more time praying and in church services than the Benedictines.
Cistercian	1098 by Robert de Champagne at Cîteaux in France.	1131. First monastery built at Rievaulx in Yorkshire. Became the most popular Order in England.	To follow a strict interpretation of St Benedict's Rule.	Built monasteries in remote areas. Supported choir monks (full monks) and lay brothers who were not educated but who took vows and worked as labourers. Became skilled sheep farmers. Made their habits from the grey/white wool of their sheep and were called 'white monks'.
Carthusian	1084 by St Bruno at Chartreuse in France.	1178. First monastery built at Witham in Essex.	To lead a solitary life while keeping strictly to the Rule of St Benedict.	Lived in individual cells and hardly ever spoke. Ate one vegetarian meal a day. Strictest of all the Orders. Wore white habits.
Dominicans (Friars)	1216 by St Dominic in Spain.	1221.	To teach ordinary people about Christianity.	Better educated than most priests and very good teachers. Inspired by the ideas of St Francis.
Franciscans (Friars)	1209 by St Francis of Assisi in Italy.	1224.	To teach ordinary people about Christianity.	Travelled the country, without any possessions or money, teaching and preaching to ordinary people.

Did you know?

The monks at Fountains Abbey washed their feet every Saturday, had their heads shaved every three weeks and had a bath four times a year.

Did you know?

THE DOLE

Poor people waiting at the gates of Fountains Abbey for food were given the 'dole'. This was usually a 'mess of pottage' which was a mixture of peas and beans, a farthing loaf and a farthing's worth of beer (a farthing was a quarter of an old penny).

Task

Source 10 is written by Walter Map and comes from his book called *Courtier's Trifles*. It combines court gossip, fables, stories of extraordinary events (including some early 'vampire' stories). 'Concerning the origins of the Cistercians' is one story in the collection. So put Source 10 through the 5Ws test (see page 4) then explain how far you trust Walter Map's account of the Cistercians.

Case study: Fountains Abbey

Fountains Abbey was a large Cistercian monastery founded in North Yorkshire in 1132. It began when a breakaway group of Benedictine monks decided their life in York Abbey had become too soft. They wanted to get back to the strictness of the Rule of St Benedict and persuaded the archbishop to let them have some land in Skelldale, a remote corner of north Yorkshire. There they planned to build a monastery and join the new order of Cistercians.

One of these monks was Brother Hugh. In 1206 he remembered what he had been told of these beginnings, and he wrote about them in the *Fountains Chronicle*:

Source 9

The land was thick with thorns, lying between the slopes of mountains and among rocks jutting out on both sides. It was more suitable as the home of wild beasts than the home of human beings.

Here the holy men gathered to seek shelter, keeping off the harsh winter as best they could, with straw and grasses thrown over them. At night they usually sang psalms according to the Rule. By day they worked: some weaving mats, others using young trees to build a chapel and some cultivating gardens.

Before long, the monks had built a huge church from stone. Each year, they added new buildings and extended existing ones. They gradually extended the land they owned, too, until Fountains Abbey was the largest landowner in north Yorkshire. The lay brothers became highly successful sheep farmers and the Abbey itself ran many farms (called granges) scattered throughout northern England. Important churchmen, merchants and pilgrims visited Fountains and were entertained in the guest rooms. Fountains wool became famous, not just in the local markets but throughout England and northern Europe. The choir monks and lay brothers were good at what they did. Fountains Abbey became very rich and very powerful.

Not everyone approved of the Cistercians! At the end of the 1200s, Walter Map wrote:

Source 10

The Cistercians work so hard that they have become very rich, but they are mean and do not like to spend their wealth. They are happy to borrow farming equipment from others, but they will not lend anyone their ploughs. Their Rule does not allow them to work as parish priests, so when they are given new lands they destroy any villages there and throw out the people who live there.

Fountains Abbey, like all the English medieval monasteries, now lies in ruins. You can find lots of photos of what it looks like today on the internet, for example at www.nationaltrust.org.uk/Fountains-abbey. The artist Alan Sorrell drew the picture below. How could he have worked out what the abbey looked like?

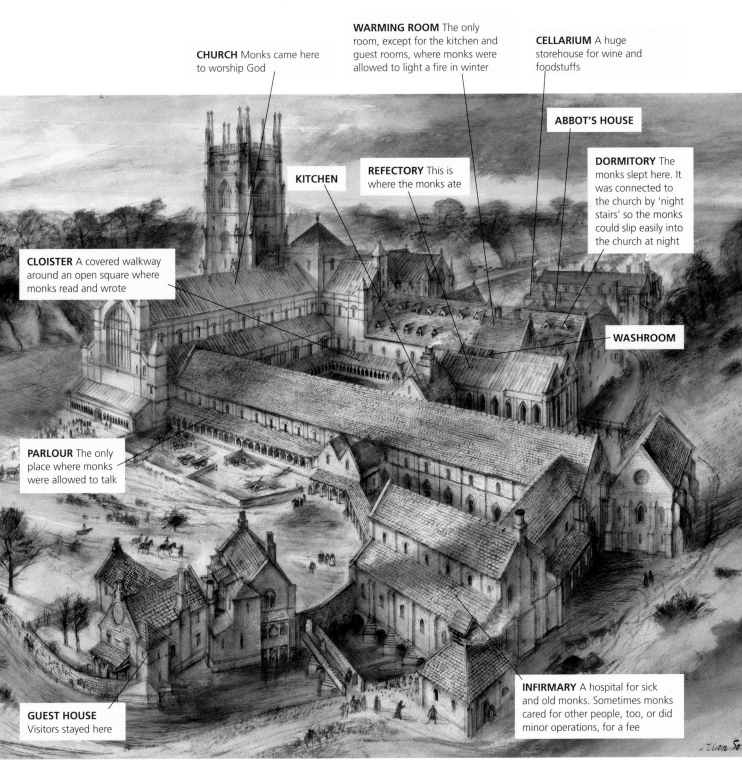

WARMING ROOM The only room, except for the kitchen and guest rooms, where monks were allowed to light a fire in winter

CELLARIUM A huge storehouse for wine and foodstuffs

CHURCH Monks came here to worship God

ABBOT'S HOUSE

KITCHEN

REFECTORY This is where the monks ate

DORMITORY The monks slept here. It was connected to the church by 'night stairs' so the monks could slip easily into the church at night

CLOISTER A covered walkway around an open square where monks read and wrote

WASHROOM

PARLOUR The only place where monks were allowed to talk

INFIRMARY A hospital for sick and old monks. Sometimes monks cared for other people, too, or did minor operations, for a fee

GUEST HOUSE Visitors stayed here

What did the monks do?

At its peak, Fountains Abbey probably housed about 50 choir monks and around 200 lay brothers. The Abbey was a highly organised unit.

I'm in charge here. I've entertained the King and many noblemen.

I'm responsible for the church services, the music, and the choir books. I teach the monks to sing and how to read aloud clearly.

I look after the valuable linen, the embroidered robes and banners and the gold and silver plate on the altar.

I'm responsible for all the goods stored in the cellarium. I deal with tradesmen from outside.

Abbot

Precentor

Sacristan

Cellarer

I'm in charge of the refectory and the serving of food. I have to make sure there are fresh rushes on the floor and that lamps are lit on dark days and in the evenings.

I look after all the clothes and bed linen. I have to make sure the fire in the warming room is well stoked and that there is enough hot water.

The young novices are my responsibility. I have to care for them, educate them and decide whether or not they're suited to life in the monastery.

I see to the distribution of food and clothing to the poor when they come to the monastery gates every morning.

Refectorian

Chamberlain

Novice master

Almoner

Daily schedule at Fountains Abbey	
When?	**What?**
0200 hrs	*Vigils* The night service, followed by reading and prayers until dawn
Dawn	*Lauds* A short service
0600 hrs	*Prime* A short service followed by Mass
0700 hrs	*Chapter* Monks listen to readings from the Rule of St Benedict, confess where they have broken the Rule and are disciplined, discuss the work for the day and sort out their duties The monks then worked in the workshops or gardens
0900 hrs	*Tierce* A short service
1000 hrs	Reading and writing
1200 hrs	*Sext* Short service after which the monks had a wash and then *Prandium*, the main meal of the day After the meal, another wash and a rest
1500 hrs	*Nones* A short service, then a drink and more work
1800 hrs	*Vespers* A short service followed by supper
1900 hrs	*Collation* Where one monk read aloud to the others
2000 hrs	*Compline* The last service of the day
2100 hrs	To bed

Daily schedule

The day at Fountains Abbey followed a set pattern, but the timings shifted slightly between summer and winter. The labels on page 115 tell you where these things would take place.

Impact on the community

Fountains Abbey provided:

- food and clothing for the poor
- employment for ordinary people
- health care for local people.

Monasteries were important for other reasons:

- Monks kept chronicles recording the events of the time.
- Monks copied out old books and saved old learning from being lost.
- Infirmarians who looked after the sick became expert in medicine and basic surgery.
- Monasteries were healthy places. They developed systems to supply hot water, drainage and sewage. Monks washed, used lavatories and cared for the sick in buildings away from the main body of the monastery.
- Some monasteries taught local children how to read and write.

Task

On page 116 are some of the different responsibilities monks had in Fountains Abbey.

List them in order of importance

a) to the smooth running of the monastery
b) to the community outside the monastery.
Now compare your lists with a partner. Where are they different? Where are they the same?

Discuss why and see if you can arrive at a list with which you both agree.

Summary task

What good did monasteries do, and for whom?

Write an essay explaining your answer.

WHAT WAS LIFE REALLY LIKE FOR MONKS AND NUNS?

Source Ⓐ

Before I came here I could never have kept silent for so long and given up the gossiping I loved so much. I used to do whatever I liked, laugh and chatter with my friends, go to rich feasts, drink much wine and sleep late in the mornings.

Now how different it is! My food is very little and my clothes are rough. I sleep on a hard mat, tired out with work. Just when sleep is sweetest, the sound of the bell wakes me up.

I can only talk to three men. I obey my master like an animal. Yet here there are no grumblings and quarrellings. Here everything is shared equally and 300 men cheerfully obey one master.

A novice monk in about 1200 wrote what he felt about his life at the monastery of Rievaulx, a big Cistercian monastery in Yorkshire.

Source Ⓑ

I am tormented and crushed by the length of the services at night. I am often overcome by the hard work I have to do with my hands. The food sticks to my mouth. The rough clothing cuts through my skin. I am always longing for the delights of the world and sigh for its pleasures.

In about 1200, another novice monk wrote what he felt about his life at the monastery of Rievaulx.

Source Ⓒ

A monk copying out a manuscript. Before the invention of printing, all books were made this way.

Source Ⓓ

Nuns caring for the sick at the Hôtel-Dieu in Paris.

118

Source E

A painting of a cellarer from a thirteenth-century illuminated manuscript made by monks.

Source F

Archbishops and bishops were shocked that nuns wore golden hairpins and silver belts, jewelled rings, laced shoes, slashed tunics, low-necked dresses, costly materials and furs. Bishops regarded pets as bad for discipline and tried to turn the nuns' animals out. The nuns just waited until the bishops went and whistled the dogs back again. Dogs were easily the favourite pets, but nuns also kept monkeys, squirrels, rabbits and birds. They sometimes took animals to church with them.

An extract from a book called *Medieval Women*, written by Eileen Power, published in 1975.

QUESTIONS

1   Study **Source A**.
    What does Source A tell you about this novice monk?

2   Study **Sources A** and **B**. These novices were living and working in the same monastery at roughly the same time.
    How far are their accounts similar and how are they different? Can you suggest reasons for this?

3   Study **Sources C, D** and **E**.
    What can you learn from these three pictures about the work of monks and nuns?

4   Study **Sources D** and **F** or **Sources A** and **E**.
    These sources give very different views of nuns/monks.
    Does this mean that one of them must be wrong? Explain your answer.

5   Study **Sources A, C** and **F**. Using these three sources and your own knowledge, how far do you agree with the view that monks and nuns led a comfortable life and did no good for anyone except themselves?

UNIT 11 Why was the Church so important to peasants?

What is this all about?

In the early Middle Ages most of the people in England were poor peasant farmers. They lived and worked in the same village most of the lives. They lived in simple homes, had simple lives, ate simple food. What did religion mean to them? In this unit you will explore how the Church affected the lives of ordinary men, women and children.

What...?

PARISH
Part of a diocese that has its own church and priest to whom tithes were paid.

BAPTISM
The ceremony by which people become part of the Christian Church, usually by being sprinkled with holy water.

CONSECRATED GROUND
Ground set apart by the Christian Church for holy purposes, such as the burial of the dead.

The parish church

The most important building in a medieval village was the church. It was usually built of stone and had a tall tower, or steeple, pointing skyward. It was a constant reminder to the peasants of the presence of God in their everyday lives. They heard the church clock strike the hours throughout the day and night when they were working in the fields or trying to get to sleep at home. At times of celebration, the church bells rang out joyfully.

The hub of village life

The church was more than a building and bells. Peasants went to the PARISH church for all the important events in their lives.

- They took their babies to church when they were only a few weeks old so that the parish priest could BAPTISE them. In medieval times many babies died before their first birthday, and a baby that wasn't baptised couldn't be buried in CONSECRATED GROUND and didn't stand a chance of getting to heaven.

Source ❶

A medieval parish church in Aylesford, Kent today. Notice how it towers over the houses in the village.

— Did you know? —

The Christian Church adapted some traditional festivals, for example, Lammas on 1 August. The ancient custom was to bury a loaf of bread in the first furrow to be ploughed after harvest. The Church turned this into a Christian festival where the priest celebrated Mass with the first loaf of bread made from the newly harvested corn.

Christmas, too, borrowed from and adapted far older festivals. No one really knew the date on which Jesus Christ was born and so the early Church decided, in about AD 300, to fix on 25 December close to the winter solstice, when days are at their shortest, which was an important time for many ancient religions.

- Men and women were married in the parish church or, more usually for villagers, in the church porch.
- It was in the parish graveyard surrounding the church that they were buried when they died.
- It was to the parish church that villagers went every Sunday and holy day for Mass.
- They went to confess their sins to the priest and to receive, through him, God's forgiveness for the wrongs they had done.

Parish churches were not just religious buildings. They were open to everyone throughout the week and were usually very busy places. They were like modern community centres. Without pews or any sort of fixed seating, church buildings were sound, weather-proof spaces where markets were held and people swapped information and news. Churches might be used as theatres where travelling actors performed plays and entertained the villagers with music and dancing. Feasts and fairs were held in churches and churchyards.

Feast days, festivals and fun

Religious festivals were also the focus of fun. The church reserved certain days as special feast days or festivals, called holy days. In theory no one worked on these days but there were over fifty a year. The lord would not like that so the Church chose a few specific festivals that would be holy days (holidays) for everyone.

Activities inside a medieval parish church. These would not normally all be happening at the same time. ❓▶ *How many can you name?*

The parish priest

The parish priest was the direct link between ordinary people and the vast and powerful organisation that was the Catholic Church (see diagram below). The parish priest was chosen by the lord of the manor and in the early Middle Ages the lord would choose someone from among the villagers.

Source ❷

A medieval parish priest conducting a burial.
❓ *What do you think is the message of the 'flying bones'?*

Diagram ❶

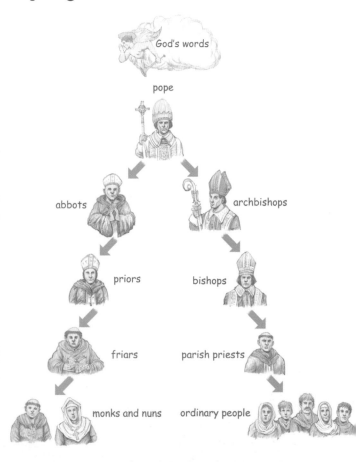

The structure of the medieval Catholic Church.

Spiritual duties

The central and most important work of the priest was to conduct services in the parish church on Sundays and other holy days. The most important of church services was the Mass. Here the priest read the service (which was in Latin) or, if he could not read, recited it from memory. Then he blessed some bread and wine and offered them to God. The Church taught that, at that moment, God miraculously changed the bread and wine into the body and blood of His son, Jesus Christ. This is called TRANSUBSTANTIATION. The priest would then drink the wine and eat the bread on behalf of the people, in the belief that this would bring them close to God. Peasants watching this familiar ceremony, week in and week out, would come to believe in the presence of God in their lives.

What...?

TRANSUBSTANTIATION
The belief that the bread and wine used in the Mass turn into the body and blood of Jesus.

What...?

TEMPORAL
This means here and now or of the time. So temporal duties were the priests' practical duties (as opposed to their spiritual duties dealing with people's souls).

ASUNDER
Separate or split into separate parts.

Priests also had to care for the sick, the troubled and the dying, hold church services and give spiritual advice to their parishioners. These were his spiritual duties.

Temporal duties

Through the Middle Ages the work of a parish priest became more and more complicated. He had to collect tithes, keep records of births, marriages and deaths in his parish, write wills, teach the children and sometimes check that feudal dues were being properly paid to the lord (his TEMPORAL duties). These duties demanded someone who was intelligent and educated. Increasingly the lord was likely to choose a man who could read and write and who had some understanding of the world beyond the parish. By about 1400 many priests were educated men from rich families.

Celibacy

Only men could be priests. In the early Middle Ages priests could be married and have families. By about 1400, nearly all priests were unmarried and were supposed to stay that way. The Church regarded them as being 'married' to their parish. They were supposed to treat everyone equally, which obviously they couldn't do if they were married.

Task

1 Try the 5Ws test on each one then consider: the 'good priest' source comes from a poem. The 'bad priest' source comes from an official church record. Which source do you think is most useful for telling us what parish priests were really like?

2 The text 'Temporal duties' describes how the role of the priest changed during the Middle Ages.
   How do you think those changes might affect the ordinary villagers?

Source 3

He truly knew Christ's gospel and would preach it
Devoutly to his parishioners.
He much disliked extorting tithe or fee,
Nay, rather he preferred beyond a doubt
Giving to poor parishioners round about
From his own goods and Easter offerings.
Wide was his parish, with houses far ASUNDER,
Yet he neglected not in rain or thunder,
In sickness or in grief, to pay a call
On the remotest, whether great or small.
His business was to show a fair behaviour
And draw men thus to heaven and their saviour.

In 1386, Geoffrey Chaucer wrote about a good parish priest in his *Canterbury Tales*. This is part of what he wrote.

Source 4

- The priest puts his horses and sheep to pasture in the churchyard.
- The priest was away for six weeks and made no arrangement for someone to take his place.
- The priest spends his time in taverns, and there his tongue is loosed to the great scandal of everyone. He is living with a woman called Margaret, and he cannot read or write so he cannot look after his parishioners' souls.

In 1397, the Bishop of Hereford collected evidence about bad priests in parishes under his control. These are some of the complaints.

Getting to heaven

Death was an everyday reality for medieval peasants. Many babies and children died young. Peasants would be considered old by 30 and many died before reaching 40. Plagues and famines, as well as ordinary diseases such as measles and flu, created havoc and, in times of epidemic, killed thousands of men, women and children. Death was ever present.

The Christian Church helped here too. The Church taught that after death there was eternal life. No matter how grim and short life was on Earth, eternal life in heaven was waiting. Or was it? Eternal life was waiting only for those who lived good lives, avoided sin and followed the teachings of the Catholic Church. And even then it wasn't that easy.

- Some people, those who never asked for forgiveness for their sins, went straight to hell.
- Everyone had sinned so no one was good enough to go straight to heaven. The souls of the 'maybes' went to purgatory. This was a pretty dreadful place, but not as grim as hell. Souls stayed there for possibly hundreds of years until their sins had been burned away and they could enter heaven. It was possible to speed up this process if friends and relatives said prayers for them, lit candles in church for them, visited holy places for them or bought pardons for them from travelling pardoners.

Medieval people were keenly aware of the terrors of hell and eternal damnation and the paradise of heaven, and the Church surrounded them with reminders. There were three main methods.

1 Sermons and stories

Some priests told stories to their peasant parishioners to try to get them to remember the teaching of the Church on various different matters. For example:

Source 5

There was once a worthy woman who hated a poor woman for more than seven years. When the worthy woman went to church, the priest told her to forgive her enemy. She said she had forgiven her. When the church service was over, the neighbours went to her house with presents to cheer her and to thank God. But then the woman said 'Do you think I forgave her with my heart as I did with my mouth? No!' Then the Devil came down and strangled her there in front of everybody. So make sure that when you make promises you make them with the heart, without any deceit.

Task

Which of the three methods of teaching – stories, paintings and stained glass – do you think would have most impact on the peasants? Explain your answer.

2 Paintings

Rich people could see the paintings in books, such as the prayer book (Source 6) below. However, most peasants could not read, so the walls of parish churches were decorated with large detailed paintings as well. Children would see them every time they went to church and eventually their message would become as familiar as breathing.

Source 6

Ⓐ

Ⓑ

These paintings are from the Queen Mary Psalter, c.1300. Paintings like this would be found on the walls of churches. In A, the righteous are being welcomed into heaven; in B, the wicked are being pitched into the fiery cauldron of hell.

Source 7

This window shows a Christian visiting prisoners, one of the 'acts of mercy' encouraged by the Church.

Map 1

A map of major pilgrimage sites in England.

3 Stained glass

The Church also got its message across through stained-glass windows. Many of the windows in parish churches were not made from plain glass, but were rich with colour and each one had a message. Some windows told part of the story of the life of Jesus Christ; others showed people what they should, or should not, do. See Source 7 for example.

Pilgrimage

A pilgrimage is a journey to a place believed to be holy. People went on pilgrimages for all kinds of reasons in the Middle Ages. They went to give thanks for something good that had happened to them, they went in hope of a cure for an illness, and they went to ask God for a special favour. They went, too, to show the world how holy they were.

● The most special place of all to go on a pilgrimage to was the Holy Land where Jesus lived and died.
● After that came Rome, where many saints were buried and where the Pope lived.

Such pilgrimages took time and money. They were out of the question for a poor person. So what could a peasant do if he or she wanted to make a pilgrimage?

Task

Map 1 shows sites of pilgrimage in England. Choose the one most local to you and use an internet search to find out:
a) when the saint lived
b) what made him or her famous
c) a story associated with that site.

Relics and shrines

The answer was, of course, to visit a local shrine or holy place. Relics of a saint – for example, hair, bones or toenails – would be kept in a special box. People believed that these shrines and relics had miraculous powers that could cure diseases.

People left offerings such as wax images of limbs at shrines as a 'thank you' to the saint for favours and miracles granted.

Source 8
An historian writes

Not all of those who visited a shrine were in need of a cure. Just as a pilgrimage could be used to make amends for past sins, so it could shorten a person's time in purgatory. If a person died between agreeing to go on a pilgrimage and actually performing it, the Church would allow a vicar to make the pilgrimage on their behalf. Many people took the precaution of leaving a sum of money in their wills for someone – a relative or a clergyman, for example, to make the pilgrimage on their behalf. It was not long before some people took this a step further, and, while they were still alive, paid people to make pilgrimages for them.

J. Sumption, *Pilgrimage: an Image of Medieval Religion*, published in 1975.

Attitudes

Running through the information on the past seven pages has been a common attitude; God was all powerful. People felt themselves to be in the hands of God. God made them ill or healthy. God made the weather good or bad. God also made them rich or poor.

Source 9

The head reliquary of St Oswald, who was King of Northumbria and died in 642. Reliquary means a container for relics. There is a head inside this casket. It is supposed to be St Oswald's.

Exam practice
How important were pilgrimages?

Summary task
Explain how significant the church was in the life of peasants.

(Hint: this is an essay question. You should look at different aspects of a peasant's life and at the involvement of the Church in them, then reach a balanced conclusion.)

UNIT 12 What do Crusades tell us about the power of religion in the Middle Ages?

What is this all about?

The Crusades is the name given to a series of wars that started in 1095 and that lasted for over two centuries. At the heart of these wars was the battle between Christian and Muslim armies for control of Jerusalem. However, that struggle was only one part of the story. The same fervour that drove Crusader knights also led thousands of young children to join the Children's Crusade, and yet others to murder Jews in Germany and England. It was a complex and strange time. We have focused on three stories. See what they suggest about the power of religion in the Middle Ages.

BACKGROUND EUROPE

Christianity was easily the most important religion in England. It was also the main religion in the rest of Europe. However, it was not the only one. In areas of southern Europe and the Middle East, Islam was much stronger.

For 300 years, Muslims and Christians mostly lived in peace with each other. From the middle of the eleventh century this began to change. Fearful of being completely overrun, the emperor of Byzantium, Alexius Comnenus, appealed in 1095 to Pope Urban II for help in defeating the Seljuk Turks. The Pope appealed to the Christian world to join the battle.

Map

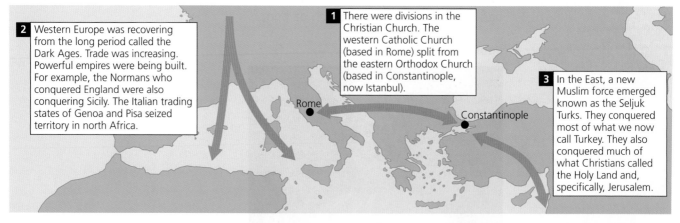

2 Western Europe was recovering from the long period called the Dark Ages. Trade was increasing. Powerful empires were being built. For example, the Normans who conquered England were also conquering Sicily. The Italian trading states of Genoa and Pisa seized territory in north Africa.

1 There were divisions in the Christian Church. The western Catholic Church (based in Rome) split from the eastern Orthodox Church (based in Constantinople, now Istanbul).

3 In the East, a new Muslim force emerged known as the Seljuk Turks. They conquered most of what we now call Turkey. They also conquered much of what Christians called the Holy Land and, specifically, Jerusalem.

The pressures building in Europe in the eleventh century.

BACKGROUND JERUSALEM

To Christians: The hill of Calvary in Jerusalem was the place where Jesus Christ was crucified. It was in Jerusalem that he was resurrected and went to heaven. From the fourth century Christian pilgrims from all over the world flocked to visit the holy sites of Jerusalem. In 1076 Jerusalem fell under the control of the Seljuk Turks who were less willing to allow Christian pilgrims into Jerusalem.

To Muslims: Jerusalem was the place where the Prophet Muhammad had ascended to heaven from the al-Aqsa stone in the centre of the city. The mosque that was built on the site became the third holiest place in the Muslim world.

Source ❶
A horrible race has violently invaded the lands of the Christians. They have destroyed the churches of God and even changed them into churches for their own religion. Jerusalem is now the prisoner of the enemies of Jesus Christ. These people don't even know how to pray to God. Everyone going to fight to free Jerusalem will be forgiven their sins.

Pope Urban II speaking in 1095.

Story 1: The First Crusade 1095–99

In 1095 Pope Urban II appealed to the Christian world to join a battle to drive back the Seljuk Turks (see Source 1).

In those days communication was not as easy as it is now. So Urban travelled around preaching this message many times and also sent other bishops, priests and travelling preachers round Europe to preach the same message. It worked. The response was overwhelming. Tens of thousands of men and women, rich and poor, young and old, peasants and professional soldiers flocked towards Constantinople.

In the so-called Peasants' Crusade, about 12,000 peasants led by Peter the Hermit and Walter the Penniless, were the first group to reach Seljuk territory. They were massacred on 21 October 1096.

But others followed. You can see their routes in Map 2 on page 130. Many of the crusaders were French including probably the most effective military leader, Bohemond of Taranto. Their journey to Constantinople was bloody. In Germany, Crusaders attacked and killed hundreds of Jews.

They had various **motives**. Many believed that if they fought and recaptured Jerusalem they would go to heaven. They were told that fighting in a holy war resulted in any sins that they had committed being forgiven. For some the Crusades were a chance to get rich. And Crusaders were excused taxes because, by taking part in a Crusade, they were officially pilgrims.

Source ❷

A Crusader knight.
❓ *What is he doing? What impression does this give you? Is he noble, peaceful or warlike?*

┌─ **Did you know?** ─┐

CRUSADES

Those who first
volunteered to go to the
Holy Lands on crusade
cut out red crosses and
sewed them onto their
tunics. The French word
for these crosses is
croisades which turned
into Crusades. Those who
'took the cross' were
blessed by a priest before
they departed for the
Holy Land. The Muslims
called the Crusades the
'Frankish Invasion'.

Map ❷

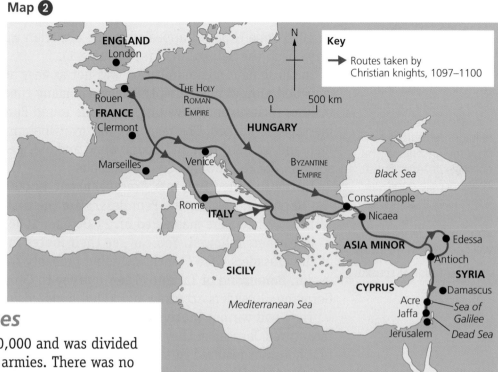

A map of the Crusaders' routes.

Crusader successes

The Crusader force was 30,000 and was divided
into a number of smaller armies. There was no
single leader and division was later to weaken
the Crusaders. But at this stage the Crusaders
were lucky because the Seljuk Turks had been
divided too since the death of their powerful
leader Malik Shah in 1092. In May 1097 the
Crusader and Byzantine armies captured the
important town of Nicaea and in June 1098
Antioch fell (Source 3). Now the Crusaders had
Jerusalem in their sights.

The fall of Jerusalem

The Crusader armies laid siege to Jerusalem.
Battering rams broke into the walls and gates
whilst siege towers were used to scale the walls.

The defenders attempted to use bales of straw
to soak up the impact of the battering rams but
these were easily set on fire. They also threw oil
and sulphur onto the attackers.

The Holy City fell to the Crusaders on 15 July
1099. The story of what happened next was told
in *Deeds of the Franks*, written by a Crusader who
was in Jerusalem (Source 4).

Source ❸

Crusaders on the First Crusade attack Antioch.
❓ *What weapons are being used by the attackers
and the defenders?*

Source ④

As soon as one of our knights, Lethold, climbed the wall of the city the defenders ran away. Our men chased them, killing as many as they could until they were up to their ankles in blood. When our men captured the Temple they killed whoever they wished. Soon our soldiers took the whole city and seized gold, silver and houses full of treasure.

Those Muslims who had survived were forced to collect bodies. The dead Muslims were piled up high outside the city and their bodies burned.

Source ⑤

The fall of Jerusalem, painted by Emile Signol in 1847.

Exam practice

Using all of the sources and your own knowledge, how far do you agree with the view the main aim of the Crusaders in 1099 was to occupy Jerusalem?

See page 181 for a practice evidence question on the First Crusade.

Perhaps as many as 70,000 Muslims were killed. The holy Muslim site of the Dome on the Rock was wrecked. The victorious Crusaders set up a Kingdom of Jerusalem and elected Godfrey of Bouillon as their first king.

The success of the First Crusade did not end the fighting. The objectives broadened. The Crusaders decided to press on to the capital of the Islamic world, Baghdad. It was a disaster. They were massacred.

However, thousands of Crusaders continued to arrive, particularly from France, and they settled down to live in the region. They built castles to protect their newly conquered lands.

Did you know?

THE TEUTONIC KNIGHTS
A number of soldiers from Frederick's army stayed on in the Holy Land to run a hospital at Acre. By 1198 they had turned themselves into the Teutonic Knights. For the next 200 years the Teutonic Knights were a formidable fighting force, conquering parts of eastern Europe.

Did you know?

Why have we missed out the Second Crusade? Well, there were at least fourteen Crusades so we cannot cover them all here. If you want to know more about the ones we have missed, use the internet to look up the Crusades on Wikipedia or a similar site.

Source ⑥

During a siege of one of the towns, one of the European women came to us asking to see Saladin. She said that her daughter had been taken by Muslims in the night. Tears came to Saladin's eyes and he sent a horseman to the local slave market to look for the girl. He returned soon after with the girl. The girl's mother threw herself to the floor with emotion.

Saladin had the reputation for being a kind man. Here is one example from a story written by Baha ad-Din Ibn Shaddad.

Story 2: The Third Crusade 1189–92

The rise of Saladin

In 1171 a new Muslim leader, Saladin, gained control of Egypt which he then united with Syria. In his next move, Saladin recaptured the southern part of Palestine, which was an important victory. Many Muslims in Egypt went through this region on pilgrimage to the holy cities of Mecca and Medina. Now their passage was assured. Saladin's next mission was to defeat the Crusaders and win back Jerusalem. In 1187 he defeated a Crusader army at the Battle of Hattin and on 2 October he captured Jerusalem. He still allowed Christian pilgrims into the city to visit holy sites but the reaction in the West was one of horror and fury.

Pope Gregory VIII appealed to the kings of Western Europe to send armies to recapture Jerusalem. The first to respond to his call was Frederick I Barbarossa who set off for the Holy Land in 1189. The Byzantine Emperor had made a secret treaty with Saladin so Frederick could expect no help from him as his army travelled across the Byzantine lands. They crossed as quickly as possible, and captured the Seljuk capital of Iconium on 18 May 1189. Then in June 1190, Frederick was drowned trying to cross a river; his forces split up and were easily defeated when they reached Syria.

In 1188, King Henry II of England and King Philip II of France imposed a tax called a Saladin Tithe on their subjects to pay for a new crusade. They even stopped the war that they were fighting between themselves. The rivalry did not stop. In 1189 Henry II died, to be replaced as king by his son Richard I (the Lionheart). In 1190 Richard and Philip set out for the Holy Land. They argued with each other when they met on the way in Sicily. Richard then took a detour and conquered Cyprus.

There is a sense of déjà vu here. The Third Crusade sounds just like a repeat of the First. However, the outcome was different.

Failure to take Jerusalem

The crusading armies eventually reached the Holy Land and laid siege to the strategically important city of Acre. By July 1191 the city had been captured. However, the rivalries between the Crusader leaders got worse.

- Philip made allies with the French noble, Conrad of Montferrat, who hoped to be made king of Jerusalem.
- Things were complicated further by the arrival of Leopold of Austria who wanted to be accepted as the equal of Richard and Philip.
- Richard would not accept this and took down Leopold's banner which was flying over the conquered Acre.
- Philip became so fed up with Richard that he went back to France in August 1191.

Task
List some similarities and differences between the First and Third Crusades.

What...?

TRUCE
An agreement to stop hostilities or fighting temporarily.

Source 7

The land where Christ was born has fallen into the hands of pagans [people who did not believe in the Christian God]. The bodies of saints have been fed to animals and our churches have been turned into stables. Those of you who join up to free the land of Christ's birth from the pagan will be granted a place in heaven by God.

Pope Celestine III in 1195 encouraging Christians to fight in the Holy Land.

What...?

PROPHET
Someone who is given special insight by God, so can explain what God wants people to do.

Truce

Richard did not manage to capture Jerusalem. He also acquired a bloodthirsty reputation. In August 1191 he ordered the execution of 3,000 Muslim prisoners because he said that Saladin had not kept to his side of the agreement that ended the siege of Acre. See the practice source exercise on page 181. Richard managed to capture the port of Jaffa, and he and his armies were victorious against Saladin's troops at Arsuf in September. But Saladin's armies were too large and although Richard twice came within sight of Jerusalem he never managed to set foot inside the Holy City. In the end Saladin and Richard agreed a TRUCE. The Crusaders could keep a strip of land which included Acre and unarmed Christian pilgrims could visit Jerusalem. But the city remained in Muslim hands. Richard left the Holy Land for home.

On his way home Richard was captured by Leopold of Austria (who he had offended in Acre). Leopold turned Richard over to the Emperor of the Holy Roman Empire, who demanded a huge ransom for Richard's release. The money was eventually raised and Richard was released.

Source 8

Jerusalem is our Holy City from where the Prophet Muhammed made his miraculous journey. On Judgement Day when we meet God our people will be united there. We do not want to give it up to the Frankish beasts who are only interested in conquering land and riches.

A Muslim writer in the twelfth century.

Story 3: The Children's Crusade 1212

This was not really a crusade but a movement that attracted children and young people from across Europe.

Stephen in France

The movement started with a peasant boy called Stephen who lived in a French village called Cloyes. Stephen's imagination had been stirred by stories of the Crusades. On 25 April 1212, he was further excited by calls made by the priest at his church for the recapture of Jerusalem. Stephen claimed he had a vision of Jesus commanding him to call the children of France to holy war, promising them that they would be successful. According to Stephen, the children would not need to be armed because Jesus had promised to look after them.

Stephen set off on the road to Paris, preaching on the way. Children across France from as young as eight started copying Stephen, claiming that they were PROPHETS and calling all children to war in the name of God. Groups of boys and girls formed and started walking to Paris. The king, Philip Augustus, ordered the children to go home but he was ignored as were the pleas of thousands of parents.

Nicholas in Germany

In a village near Cologne, a ten-year-old boy called Nicholas also started preaching that it was God's will for children to go on crusade. In response, thousands of children answered his call and met in the city of Cologne to start on their way to the Holy Land. The numbers of those involved soon fell because of the lack of food. Hundreds of children died on the roadside. But others pressed on.

Slavery

Some of the German children reached Rome, where the Pope, Innocent III, persuaded the children to go back to Germany. Another German group, after great hardship, walked all the way to Brindisi in southern Italy. There they waited for weeks for the sea to part (as they had been prophesied it would do) so they could walk to Jerusalem on dry land. But the sea did not part, and the children were rounded up and sold into slavery.

The French children met with a similar fate. After a tiring journey south they reached Marseilles. There they were tricked by two Christian slave merchants, Hugh Ferreus and William Porcus. Pretending to be ordinary merchants, they told the children that they would take them to the Holy Land. They packed the children onto seven ships and set sail for the slave markets of Alexandria in Egypt. Two of the ships sank, and the children that survived the journey were brought not to the Holy Land but to the slave markets of North Africa where they were sold to Muslim nobles and merchants.

Task

Read Source 9 carefully.

1 What reasons did the children give for going to the Holy Land?

2 What is the attitude towards the children of the person who wrote this chronicle?

Source ⑨

In this year occurred an outstanding thing and one much to be marvelled at, for it is unheard of throughout the ages. About the time of Easter and Pentecost, without anyone having preached or called for it and prompted by I know not what spirit, many thousands of boys, ranging in age from six years to full maturity, left the ploughs or carts which they were driving, the flocks which they were pasturing, and anything else which they were doing. This they did despite the wishes of their parents, relatives, and friends who tried to stop them going. Suddenly one ran after another to take the cross.

Thus, by groups of twenty, or fifty, or a hundred, they put up banners and began to journey to Jerusalem. They were asked by many people about who had told them to set out upon this path… especially since only a few years ago many kings, dukes and other powerful people had gone to the Holy Land but had returned with the business unfinished. The present groups, moreover, were still of tender years and were neither strong enough nor powerful enough to do anything.

Everyone, therefore, called them foolish for doing this. The children replied that they were doing God's will and that, whatever God might wish to do with them, they would accept it. They thus made some little progress on their journey. Some were turned back at Metz, others at Piacenza, and others even at Rome. Still others got to Marseilles, but whether they crossed to the Holy Land or what their end was is uncertain. One thing is sure: that of the many thousands who rose up, only very few returned.

Extract from a chronicle, the *Chronica Regiae Coloniensis*, written in 1213.

The impact of the Crusades

Before the time of the Crusades, Christians and Muslims coexisted fairly peacefully. The Crusades ushered in a new, less tolerant period. Further Crusades were launched against other countries and other religious groups. In Germany and England, for example, the Jews were viciously persecuted. Religious war became a fact of life for hundreds of years. The invasions sparked a call for jihad or holy war that in the end led to the invasion of Europe by the Ottoman Turks in the fourteenth century.

The focus of the struggle between the Christian and Islamic worlds shifted from the Middle East to Europe.

Although the Crusades changed relations between the Christian and Muslim world for the worse, there was greater contact between the two cultures.

- Trade in goods such as sugar, spices and lemons increased.
- European architecture, art and castle building were influenced by the east, such as the use of light and dark stone.
- The west learned mathematical and medical skills. They adopted the Arabic numbers, which made maths easier.
- New weapons of war (such as the trebuchet) were developed and new military tactics emerged.

Pulling it all together

Throughout Section 2 you have been studying different aspects of religion in the Middle Ages. You may have been building up a concept map like this. You are now going to pull all this together to answer one big question:

How do we know that religion was so important to ordinary people in the Middle Ages?

- You could present your findings as an essay, or as a poster, or as PowerPoint presentation.
- You could include ideas from your summary tasks for previous units, for example, what going on Crusades shows us about people's religious beliefs and attitudes.
- Use carefully selected examples and evidence from this section that show that religion was a powerful force in people lives.

Aim high

- If you wish you could also add some notes, or an extra paragraph, or an extra slide comparing the power of religion in the Middle Ages with the power of religion in the modern world. Do you think that religion has a less powerful, more powerful or equally powerful influence on events in the 21st-century world?

Summary task

Explain the consequences of the First Crusade. Make sure you consider both short term and long term.

SECTION 3

How did ordinary people live?

The medieval market place

If someone visiting the UK from another country said to you, 'I know all about your country because I have been to London', you would probably think, 'How stupid – there is more to the UK than London'. And you would be right.

So when you look back in time to the Middle Ages, avoid falling into the same trap. Remember that any period, and any country, is full of rich varieties. Even in the Middle Ages, life in villages was different from life in towns.

Life was different for the rich and the poor. Life was different for men and women. Life in 1500 was different from life in 1066.

In this section you are going to look at some of those variations as you study villages and towns (**Unit 13**), health and medicine (**Unit 14**), law and order (**Unit 15**) and the experiences of women (**Unit 16**). Your final task will be to prepare a medieval gallery of people you have found out about. Make them as varied as you can. What will they say about their lives?

Task
Can you spot anachronisms?
Another trap to avoid is thinking the past was just like today. Here is a picture of a market in the Middle Ages. There are at least 10 things in the picture that could not possibly have been there in medieval times. These are called 'anachronisms' – things that are in the wrong period of time. Can you spot them all?

1 Work with a partner to list as many as you can.
2 Underline anything in your list that you are completely sure about.
3 Put a circle round anything where you are not so sure.

UNIT 13 Villages and towns: how did they change and why?

What is this all about?

Nearly everyone in the Middle Ages lived in the countryside in small villages called manors, which had just a handful of houses each. In 1066 there were only eight towns in the whole of England that had more than 3,000 inhabitants. Through the Middle Ages, this gradually changed. Towns grew, slowly; villages changed, slowly. Find out how and why. At the end of this unit you will write an advertisement for a town or a village to attract people to live there.

13.1 Village life?

Task

Source 1 shows two illustrations from a Book of Hours, a medieval prayer book. They show people working in a medieval village. Look closely at them.

1 What jobs are the people doing?
2 Which job looks the hardest? Which looks the most pleasant?
3 What dangers are there?
4 What sources of food are there?
5 Which month of the year do you think each picture shows?
6 These pictures are painted in France and show a French countryside. Do you think that means they are useless for finding out about life in England at that time? Explain your reasons.

Source 1

Two illustrations from a Book of Hours (prayer book), made in France in 1412–16. There is a different picture for each month. You can see the entire sequence online. Simply search for Les Très Riches Heures du Duc de Berry.

Source ❷
An historian writes

Village life for men and women alike was busy, strenuous, unrelenting, much of it lived outdoors, with an element of danger that especially threatened children. Diet was poor, dress simple, housing primitive, sanitary arrangements almost non-existent. Yet there was love, sex, courtship and marriage, holidays, games and sports, and plenty of ale. Neighbours quarrelled and fought, suspected and lied, and took legal action against each other. But they also knew each other thoroughly and depended on each other to help with the ploughing and harvesting, to give evidence in court, and to respond when danger threatened.

Frances and Joseph Giles, *Life in a Medieval Village*, published in 1990.

What...?

HIERARCHY
A society with clear social ranks.

Task

Draw your own diagram to show this village hierarchy, in a similar style to page 122.

A village = a manor = a farm

It is best to think of a village or a manor as being a large farm or estate, not like a village today. The lord of the manor was granted the land by the king or by another baron. He controlled the land and decided what happened on it. The villagers were his workers or labourers. But it was more complicated than that.

Who's who in the village hierarchy?

- The **lord of the manor** was the most important person in the village, even though he might not have lived there and might have held several manors.
- The **priest** was the next most important person in the village. His land was called glebe land. It belonged to the Church and was usually worked by the peasants for the priest, who was busy doing other things.
- If the lord of the manor owned lots of land, a **bailiff** would work for him, keeping his accounts, making sure rents were properly collected, and generally overseeing the working of his estates.
- Every manor in England was run by a **reeve** on behalf of the lord. A reeve was usually a well-off peasant. He was responsible for seeing that the other peasants turned up on time to work the lord's land, that the right crops were planted at the correct time of year and that the lord's barns were kept in good repair.
- The **hayward** was responsible for the harvest.
- The **constable** made sure that wrong-doers were brought to the manor court, where their case would be judged by the lord, the bailiff and senior peasants.

At the bottom of the HIERARCHY were the peasants who were the labourers. However, there was also a hierarchy among the peasants.

- **Freemen** paid rent to the lord to work some of the lord's land.
- **Villeins**, instead of paying rent, gave the lord a certain number of days' work each week, plus extra work at harvest time. A villein's life was controlled by the lord. For example, in some villages they had to ask the lord's permission to leave the village or to get married.
- **Serfs** were similar to villeins but were virtually slaves. They could be sold with land and other goods. However, the lord had to look after them, for example, by taking care of orphaned children.
- **Cottars** were the poorest villagers who could not even farm any of the lord's land. They only had the garden around their cottage to feed them and their families.

Some of the villagers also had specialist trades or skills: **blacksmiths**, **carpenters** and **thatchers**, and **cowmen**, **pigmen** and **shepherds**. There would also be a mill run by a **miller**, where everyone took their grain to be ground, and a bakery run by a **baker**, where peasants took their bread to be baked.

Diagram ❶

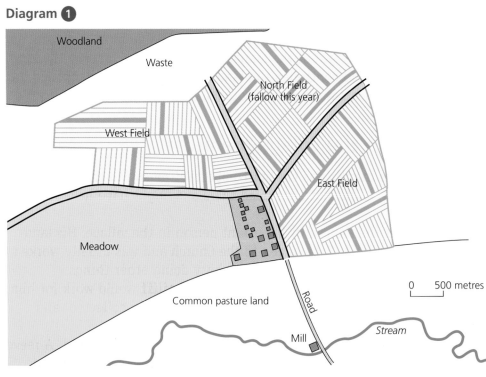

The strip system of medieval farming. One person's strips are shaded green.

How was the land worked?

The three-field system

Peasants would farm strips in each of three fields. Each year, one field would grow wheat, one would grow barley and the other would be left fallow, meaning for that year, nothing would be grown in it. Growing wheat or barley in a field takes a lot of goodness out of the soil. Leaving the field without a crop for the year allows the soil to recover its goodness.

Every year the crops would be rotated (changed around) so that each field had a chance to be fallow.

The lord's fields were called the DEMESNE. These were usually on the best land and the peasants worked for him as part of their feudal service.

Strips and furlongs

- Some of the land was divided into large open fields, which were subdivided into FURLONGS.
- Each furlong was divided up into long strips which were cultivated by ploughs pulled by oxen.
- The strips were deliberately long so that the plough teams did not have to be turned round too often.
- Which peasant got which strip depended on the feudal services owed to the lord of the manor. The strips would be scattered around the fields so that all villagers got some good and bad land (see Diagram 1).

Crops

The most important crops grown on the land in southern England and the Midlands were wheat for bread and barley for bread and brewing. The peasants had to agree which crops would be grown on their strips. They all had to grow the same.

Did you know?

The best form of fertiliser in the Middle Ages was animal manure. When a field was left fallow, animals were put into it to graze. What came out the other end was very good for the soil.

What...?

DEMESNE
Anglo-French word for 'domain'.

FURLONG
A furlong measures about 220 yards (just over 200 metres). Horse races are still measured in furlongs.

Did you know?

SUBSISTENCE FARMING
Everything that a village produces is used by the village, with no surplus.

Did you know?

There were possibly more sheep in England than people. Such was their importance, they were all counted for the Domesday Book in 1086. The Abbey of Ely alone had 13,400 sheep.

Task

Use the internet to find out more about the origins of the Lutrell Psalter. Try the 5Ws test (see page 4). Then consider how reliable it is for telling you about daily life in a medieval village. There are other pictures from the Luttrell Psalter on page 171.

Cottage gardens

Around each cottage was a garden. Peasants could grow what they wanted there and most grew vegetables and herbs. The poorest peasants, called cottars, couldn't afford to pay rent for strips of land and so they only had their cottage gardens from which to feed their families

Keeping animals

All peasants kept animals for food. They might keep goats, cows, ducks, pigs, hens or geese. Animals that could be eaten and which could produce eggs or milk when they were alive were specially prized. Sheep, for example, produced milk that could be drunk or turned into cheese, wool that could be spun into yarn and woven into cloth – and the sheep could also be eaten. Few animals were kept over winter because there was not enough food with which to feed them. The best were kept for breeding the following spring and the rest were killed and their meat salted or cured to keep it edible throughout the long, cold winter months. Everybody who lived in the village was allowed to graze their animals on common land. Each peasant was allowed to graze a certain number of animals according to their feudal rights. All the peasants could use the woodland, too. They gathered firewood there, and let their pigs run loose to root out acorns and other tasty morsels.

Fishing and hunting

The lord controlled hunting rights – who could catch wild animals – but fishing in the river or catching wild boar or birds was an important part of a peasant's food supply.

Source 3

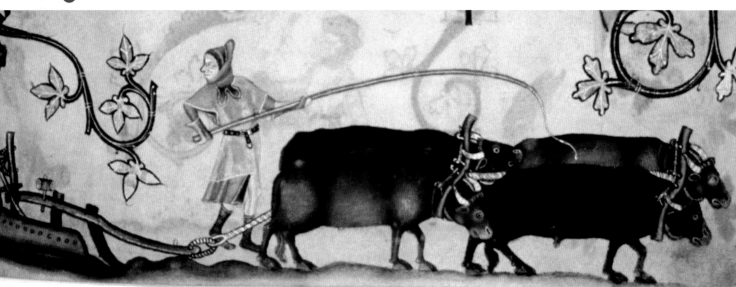

An illustration from the Luttrell Psalter. *The plough needed two people, one to goad the oxen, the other to guide the plough. This was a heavy piece of equipment and the oxen were hard to turn.* ❓ *How might this type of plough affect the way fields were divided up?*

How did villages change?

Task

The three pictures show an artist's impression of the same village in 1086 (at the time of the Domesday Book), in 1230 and in 1400.

1 Using all that you have so far found out about medieval villages, describe the features numbered 1–10 in the first picture. One has been done for you.

1 The manor house
Where the lord of the manor lived. He had the largest house – a big hall – and barns to keep his stores over the winter.

2 Compare each of these numbered features with the same feature in 1230 and in 1400. What has changed? What has not changed?

3 Now write a paragraph to summarise the main changes that you have observed. This does not mean just listing all the changes you have seen. It means picking out the biggest changes and writing in a more general way about the big changes.

1086

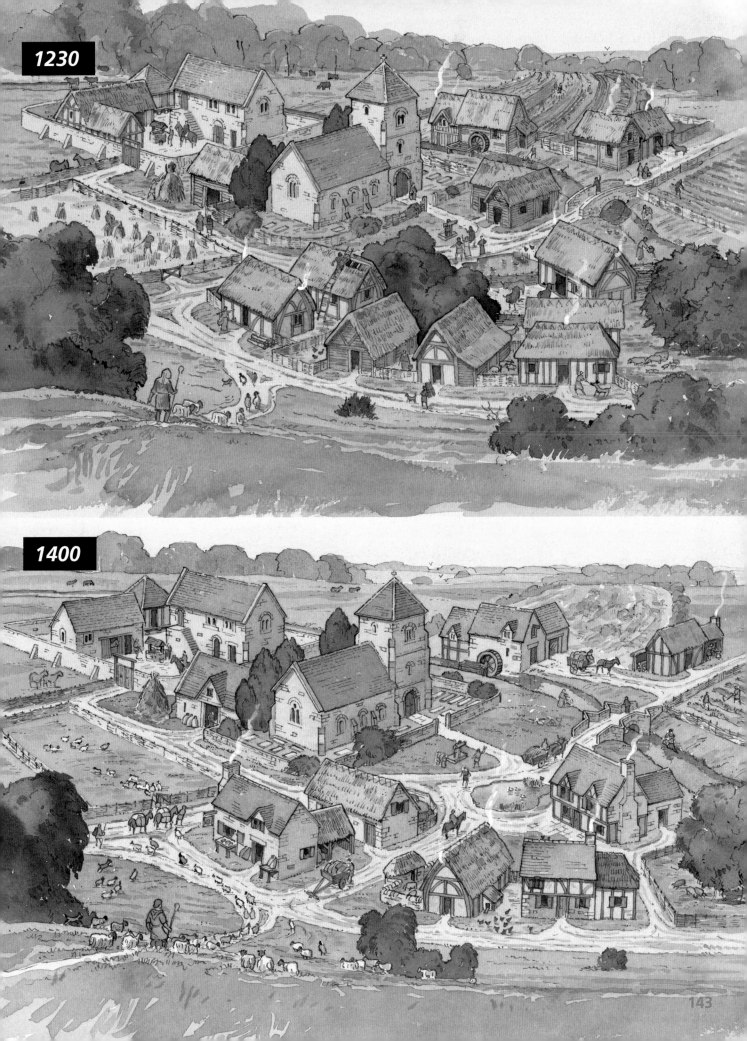

1230

1400

143

Why did villages change?

Population change

The population rose then fell over the period. At the time of the Domesday Book in 1086 the population stood at around 2.25 million. By 1230 it had risen to 5.7 million. It then plummeted in the late 1300s to around 3 million, mainly because of the Black Death (see opposite).

Woodland clearance

Wood was used to build houses and burnt for cooking and heating. As the population increased, so the demand for wood went up.

Wood was also used in the production of iron. As a result, roughly one third of English woodland was cleared between 1086 and the middle of the fourteenth century.

Land holding

As the population grew, so some peasants divided up their holdings of land between their children so that they all had land to work. Some lords of the manor made smallholdings out of their original demesne land. These plots of land were rented out to peasants in parcels of an ACRE or so. Eventually, some peasants were able to buy land and owned not only their own strips but also those worked by their neighbours.

> **What...?**
>
> ACRE
> A measure of land equivalent to approximately 4,047 square metres.

Source 4
An historian writes

The fifteenth century witnessed a return of prosperity – uneven, chequered with plenty of setbacks and slowdowns, but nevertheless a recovery for some villages. After the fall in population caused by the Black Death, individual land holdings grew in size, the fields that had grown cereal crops were turned over to grass and herds of livestock increased. Wealthy townsmen joined with the newly freed villagers by providing cash for their farming ventures in return for a share in their profits.

Peasant houses began to be constructed with masonry foundations and stronger frames, and many added rooms or even a second floor, with fireplace and chimney. Manor houses were enlarged and parish churches were rebuilt.

Not all villages shared in the prosperity, or even survived it. Many smaller villages were abandoned because they could not survive as economic units. Families packed up their belongings, drove their animals ahead of them, and departed the village.

Frances and Joseph Giles, *Life in a Medieval Village*, published in 1990.

Stone buildings

Village houses were made out of whatever local materials were available. In Suffolk, for example, they would be made from wooden frames and wattle and daub in-filling; in north Yorkshire they would be constructed from rough stone. Most houses in most villages, however, were built with a wooden frame and clay walls and floors. Houses were not large and often lasted only for a lifetime.

Later in the Middle Ages, when peasants became freer and relatively richer, people started to build from stone that lasted for many generations. Stone was an expensive building material for people who lived where it was not found naturally.

Improved technology

Better ploughs were developed that were not so heavy and were easier to turn around. This meant that fields did not have to be divided into such long strips.

Did you know?

After the Black Death, a frequent entry in the record held by the reeves was *Defectus per pestilentem* which is Latin for 'vacant due to the plague'.

The Black Death

Nothing changed village life as much as the Black Death (see pages 158–163). This first swept across England in 1348 and further outbreaks followed to the end of the century. It swept through rural villages, killing thousands. Some 1,300 villages were abandoned altogether in the years after 1350. The villages that survived experienced great changes.

- Many fields were permanently left fallow because there were not enough peasants left to work them.
- Lords turned to sheep farming as this needed fewer people to work on the land.
- Parish priests died along with their parishioners. Many villages, in the short term at least, were without a priest. The people could not use the church without a priest.
- The Black Death further changed the land holding. Farmers were able to rent more land and become 'tenant farmers'.
- The price of food went up and tenant farmers got more money for the crops they grew.

With workers in such short supply the villeins were able to sell their labour to the highest bidder and simply ignore the rule that they could not leave their village without the lord's permission. Now the peasants knew that a lord was desperate to have his land worked and, specifically, to get his harvest in. If the lord would not pay, then many peasants went to find a lord who would. The lords feared that this would cause chaos and, in 1351, persuaded the King to pass the Statute of Labourers. This said that:

- no peasant could be paid more than the wages paid in 1346
- no lord or master should offer higher wages than were paid in 1346
- no peasant could leave the village they belonged to without permission from the lord.

The tension that this statute created was an important cause of the Peasants' Revolt 30 years later (see Unit 5). In the end, however, the measure failed. Gradually, all villeins became freemen, who could work where they wanted.

Task

Look back to your paragraph describing the changes in medieval villages between 1086 and 1400. Add a second paragraph explaining **why** things changed so much. Again, don't just list the reasons. Pick the most important ones and explain them.

Put your two paragraphs together and you have an essay on 'How and why did village life in England change in the period 1086–1400?'

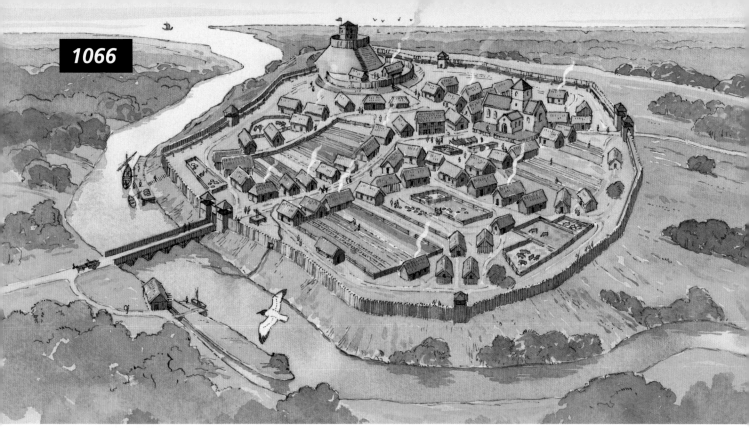

1066

Task
Study the two pictures carefully. Find as many changes as possible.

13.2 Town life

Just as village life changed from the twelfth to the fifteenth centuries, so the towns of 1500 were very different from those of 1100. Towns changed in size, in number and in what they offered. There were more of them. They grew bigger and more complex. In 1066, 5 per cent of the population lived in towns. By 1300 this had doubled to 10 per cent. Not only had existing towns such as London and York grown in size but also new towns such as Leeds, Liverpool and Hull had emerged.

1300

What were the typical features of a town?

A river crossing
Most major towns were built at a crossing point of a river, either a bridge, such as at Cambridge, or a ford such as at Oxford. Because the roads were poor, rivers carried most of the country's trade. Bridges were a meeting place for travellers and where cargo would be unloaded from boats.

Source 5

A painting of a shop in a medieval manuscript.
? *What do you think it is selling?* ? *Do you think this shows a shop in England? Give your reasons.*

A castle
The Normans built strong castles in the middle of existing towns. Some castles were built in open country where they needed to control a strategic piece of land. In some cases, Ludlow for example, the Normans built a new town around the castle. Castles were not only about military might. In many towns the castle became an important part of day-today life. For example, a town's law court and prison were often in the castle.

Gates and walls
Many towns had strong walls to protect their citizens. These were to keep intruders out not to keep citizens in. All travellers coming in and out of the town would have to pass through the town gates. These were defended with watchtowers. The watchman would question people to see why they wanted to enter the town. Carts, wagons and goods would be charged a toll at the gate.

Shops and markets
All towns held markets. Many held more than one. You needed the permission of the king to run a market so the right to run a market was both a status symbol and a source of wealth. The buying and selling of goods in the town was governed by detailed rules that were drawn up by the town's officials. Shops or stalls could only be set up in certain districts of the town, depending on what was being bought or sold. The names of streets often came from their shops or trades, for example Baker Street or Mill Lane. Stalls were set out neatly in the market square. Strangers who wanted to set up a new stall had to pay a tax called piccage.

Schools and universities
In villages, very few peasants learned to read. There was no need to. In towns there was more demand for reading. By 1500 many towns contained schools and some had universities; Oxford University was set up in 1167 and Cambridge University in 1209. As the wealth of towns grew, so did the demand for education from the wealthy. Schools and universities were usually provided by monasteries.

Did you know?

As part of their powers, the town officials could fix the prices charged in the market. A stallholder in Lincoln in the thirteenth century was not allowed to sell thrushes for more than 2d (pence).

Did you know?

One law recorded in Ludlow was clearly designed to keep the smell down:
'No one shall have any pig in the town, penalty 4d (pence) a pig.'

Who ran the towns?

In the eleventh and twelfth centuries, in major towns and cities such as London or Canterbury, the most important people were the king's and the Church's officials. The king or the Church was the lord. The citizens of the town had to pay taxes to their lord and ask him for permission for a range of things, from collecting tolls to holding a market.

Charters

As towns grew, so the wealthier townspeople wanted to run their own affairs. They could do this by asking the monarch to grant a Charter. In return for the Charter the monarch would be paid a sum of money every year. Those kings who needed money such as Richard I, or John, granted Charters to lots of towns. This meant that those who owned land in the town could become wealthier by charging rents and tolls. They were also free to introduce their own laws, for example, fines for selling bad meat in the market.

Burgesses

Important townspeople were known as burgesses. They would elect the officials of the town including the mayor and the aldermen. Under the town Charter, the burgesses would be granted certain rights and privileges (see Source 6). In return they had certain duties such as guarding the town.

Source 6

Know that I have granted to my burgesses of Bristol that they should be free of toll and every custom due throughout the whole of my land of England, Normandy and Wales, wherever they or their goods shall come. Wherefore I will and firmly command that they should have liberties and quittances and free customs fully and honourably as my free and faithful men.

Charter of Henry II in favour of Bristol (1155).

Freemen

One of the attractions of the town was freedom. In 1157, the Nottingham Charter stated very clearly that:

Source 7

If anyone from elsewhere lives for a year and a day in the borough of Nottingham, in time of peace, and without dispute, then no one afterwards except the King shall have rights over him.

He became a freeman.

Guilds

Guilds were organisations formed by craftspeople or merchants. These organisations made sure that the craft or trade was run properly, that those who needed help or support could get it and that standards were kept high.

Did you know?

When an apprentice was ready to become a master craftsman, he had to produce a 'master' piece which would be judged by members of the guild. This is the origin of the word 'masterpiece'.

This is an example from Bristol Weavers Guild in 1346:

Source
1. No cloth to be made unless it is six bondes in width. If anyone produces narrower cloth, let him be fined 40 pence.
2. If the threads of the cloth are too far apart; the cloth and the instrument on which it was made should be burned.
3. If any of the weavers works at night, let him be fined 5 shillings to the Mayor and 40 pence to the Alderman if he is found doing it a second time.

Within a guild, master craftsmen would train young people known as apprentices in their trade. An apprenticeship would last a long time, often for years.

Map ❶

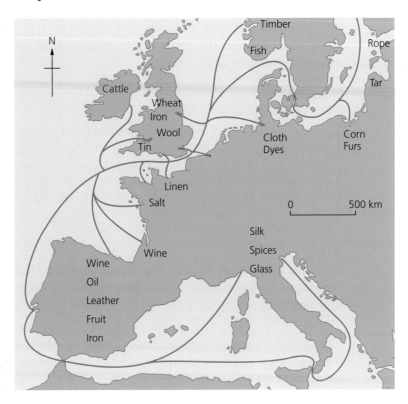

A map of medieval trade routes.

Trade

The most important reason medieval towns grew was the increase in trade. From the end of the eleventh century, trade with the rest of Europe increased dramatically. The single most important raw material produced in England was wool. Most English wool was exported to cities in the area of Flanders (now in Belgium), such as Bruges and Ghent. England was also a supplier of wheat to much of northern Europe. It exported iron from Gloucestershire and tin from Cornwall to the continent. In return, England imported goods such as leather from Cordoba, which would be sold at markets and fairs in towns but also at big annual fairs such as Boston and Stamford in Lincolnshire.

Did you know?

Leather workers were called cordwainers because they imported their leather from Cordoba. Many cordwainers made shoes.

The perils of town life

Town life was dangerous. Despite all of the riches that came from improved trade, towns were threatened by poor hygiene, fire and violence.

Hygiene

Towns stank. Animals were kept in the towns just as they were in the villages. Waste from houses and businesses, including butchers' shops, was thrown into the street or dumped in the river. The river often served as both the town's main sewer and the drinking water supply, as well as providing water for people to wash themselves, their pots and pans and their clothes.

Up to ten per cent of the population in 1316 died from diseases carried in the water, such as typhoid fever or dysentery. Other great killers included smallpox, measles and the plague, which could spread quickly in the cramped housing of the towns.

Source 9

For that so much dung and filth of garbage and entrails [internal organs of animals] be thrown away and put in ditches, rivers and other waters, so that the air there is grown greatly corrupt and infected, and many diseases do daily happen ... any people in London and other cities who do throw or put such annoyances as dung, garbages and entrails in ditches, rivers, waters, and other places, which means that they have to be avoided, and carried away, will have to pay a fine of £20.

An extract from a law passed for London, 1388.

Fire

Fire was a constant threat. Buildings were constructed very close together and were made of wood. Open fires would be used to heat buildings and it did not take much for a fire to start. Once it did it would spread rapidly. Between 1066 and 1230 there were eight fires that destroyed large parts of London. As a result, people were always on their guard and townspeople were all aware of their responsibilities. At CURFEW all fires had to be covered and raked. If there was a fire the chime of the church bells would ring backwards as a warning sign. All houses had barrels of water outside them just in case. Every house also had to keep hooked poles, which could be used to pull the thatched roofs off houses as a means of preventing the fire spreading.

Violence

Violence was part of everyday town life. Sometimes the violence in medieval towns and cities spiralled out of control, such as the riots of the Peasants' Revolt (see Unit 5) or the massacre of the Jews in 1190.

Did you know?

People knew that there was a connection between dirt and disease, but not what that connection was. That had to wait until the nineteenth century and the development of microscopes that could identify microbes, the minute organisms that cause disease.

What...?

CURFEW
A time at which everyone has to be inside their house. It was signalled in medieval times by the ringing of a church bell. The word curfew comes from the French *couvre feu* meaning 'cover fire', which is just what people did at that time.

Violence against Jews

Source 10
An historian writes

The complicated structure of town society could give rise to conflict as well as unity. Tensions sometimes arose between, for example, a town's ruling group and the main body of its inhabitants, between merchants and craftsmen and between masters and apprentices. There was conflict, too, between those who had invested financially in the town and those who were 'outsiders' or who were at least on its fringes: the poor, the foreigners, the strangers and the Jews.

Edward Miller and John Hatcher, *Medieval England: Towns, Commerce and Crafts 1086–1348*, published in 1995.

There were around 5,000 Jews in England in 1200, virtually all of them in towns such as London, York and Lincoln. The Jews usually lived together in what was known as a ghetto. In London the Jewish part of the city was called Old Jewry. Although they were allowed to practise their own religion, they were not free to do as they wished.

Because they were not Christians, the only job that Jews were permitted to do was lend money. This meant that, while they were useful, they were hated and despised by people who were dependent on their loans. It was too easy for a debtor (someone who owed money) to invent a grievance, start a pogrom (massacre of an ethnic group), have the Jews turned out and his debts revoked.

In London in 1189 many Jews were massacred after the coronation of the crusading King Richard I. A worse attack took place in York in 1190. A riot against the Jews led them to seek safety in Clifford's Tower, York Castle. The mob demanded that the Jews become Christians. Over 150 Jews committed suicide by setting light to the Tower rather than convert. Those who agreed to become Christians were butchered anyway.

In 1201, King John issued a charter confirming Jews' rights, but tolerance was not cheap. Jews were to be free from tolls and customs and were placed under royal protection. This meant, however, that they could be taxed whenever the King thought fit. By the late thirteenth century, the French and Italians had started lending money in England and people regarded the Jews as less useful. In 1272, hundreds of Jews were hanged in London and the rest thrown out of the city. Three years later, Edward I ordered that every Jew should wear a yellow armband so that he or she could be identified as a Jew. In 1290 every Jew was expelled from England.

Summary task

It is 1400. You have to compare the advantages and disadvantages of living in a town or a village.
1 Use a table to record as much detail as you can about each category.

	A village	A town
Work		
Freedom		
Wealth		
Dangers		

2 Once you have completed your table, work with a partner. One of you has to draw up an advertisement encouraging people to live in a village. Mention all the good things about it. The other person has to do an advert for a town.
3 Compare your adverts with others in the class and decide whether towns or villages win overall.

Exam practice

Choose EITHER towns OR villages. Explain how and why they changed during the Middle Ages.

What is this all about?

By today's standards the people of the Middle Ages had a very tough life. Average life expectancy was around 40 years for men and even less for women. Many babies and mothers died in childbirth. Deadly diseases were ever present and could rampage through villages or towns. People did their best to prevent these diseases spreading but they did not know what caused them, so it was often a losing battle. Even the weather could be a killer. In years when too much rain, or too little, ruined the harvest, tens of thousands could die of famine and malnutrition, much as they still do today in some countries around the world.

So keeping healthy was a challenge. This unit is all about how they responded to that challenge:

- In part 1 you will find out how people at this time treated the sick – and how effective these kinds of treatment were.
- In part 2 you will investigate one particular case study – the Black Death – a devastating epidemic of plague that killed millions of people in England. What does the spread of the Black Death and the people's response to it tell you about health and medicine in the Middle Ages?

Task
Make your own copy of this simple diagram then add to it as you work through the next five pages.

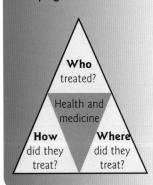

14.1 How were sick people treated?

Many medieval medical problems were similar to those today. People caught measles and chicken pox, mumps and scarlet fever, influenza and pneumonia. They broke their legs and smashed their skulls; they got appendicitis and blockages in their bowels.

Plant	Used to treat
Angelica	Coughs and colds
Broom	Bladder infections
Comfrey	Cuts and bruises
Dock	Skin rashes
Hyssop	Stomach complaints
Foxglove	Heart complaints
Marigold	Bee stings
Motherwort	Heavy monthly periods
Nettles	Nose bleeds
Parsley	Kidney problems
Thyme	Whooping cough

Herbal remedies

Most people, when they fell ill, were given herbal remedies. For ordinary, everyday problems like stomach ache and boils, the women in a family knew what to do. They knew which herbs to gather to make into a poultice to paste on the infected place, and which to make into a medicine that could be drunk (see Source 1 for example). Some women who became particularly skilled would also treat poor people outside their immediate family. The table (left) lists some

Source ❶

Take onion and garlic in equal amounts and pound well together; take wine and bull's gall, equal amounts of both, and mix with the onion and garlic. Put the mixture in a brass container and leave it to stand for nine nights. Then strain it well through a cloth. At night-time, use a feather to put some of the mixture onto the stye.

This treatment for a stye (a painful swelling on a person's eye) comes from an Anglo-Saxon book that was still being used in medieval times.

Source ❷

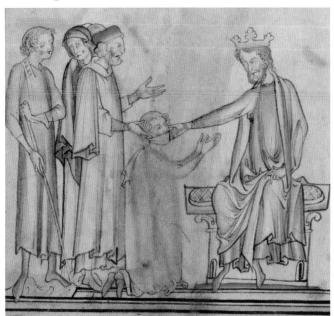

This drawing from the thirteenth century shows King Edward the Confessor (who died in 1066) touching people with the skin disease scrofula. The King's touch was supposed to make them better. This practice continued until the seventeenth century. It was called 'Touching for the king's evil'.

Source ❸

Write these words on the jaw of the patient. 'In the name of the Father, Son and Holy Ghost, Amen' the pain will stop at once, as I have often seen.

A fourteenth-century charm for curing toothache, used by John of Gaddesden, who was a leading doctor of the time.

of the plants and herbs they used. In towns, APOTHECARIES sold herbs and drugs that people could buy to make themselves or their families better – maybe! Even doctors, treating rich people, used herbs, and these might include more exotic ones from abroad. This was especially so after the 1200s, when public PHARMACIES in Italy began to export herbs and medicines.

Doctors came to believe that sugar was an effective medicine and by the 1400s it was imported in large quantities. Monks kept the best herb gardens. This was because monasteries were centres of care for the sick.

Healers copied treatments that their parents or ancestors had used. They also tried out new ideas to see what worked. By trial and error they arrived at some herbal remedies that worked. We now know that some natural ingredients of herbal remedies have the same properties as modern drugs. For example, many medieval remedies used PLANTAIN as an ingredient. Modern scientific analysis has shown that plantain has antibiotic properties so could combat an infection.

Supernatural treatments

Even today, many people rely on superstition and magic to explain what they do not understand. It is not surprising, therefore, that medieval people often looked to the supernatural for an explanation of why diseases happened and to find a cure.

The Christian Church taught that God was in control of the world. So it followed that God must also control who got ill and when, and who survived. So when someone got ill they would pray and ask God's help. Some believed that becoming ill was God's punishment for past sins so they might also confess their sins, try harder to please God or even punish themselves for their sins to try to get better. They would also seek the help of God's representatives on Earth. A priest might be called on to pray by the bedside of an ill person. For certain diseases the king (who people believed was chosen by God) would be asked to touch the sufferers (see Source 2).

Medieval people also believed in astrology: that the stars and planets had an influence on the world. If the planets and stars were in a 'favourable conjunction' good things would happen. If they were not then the disaster could follow. So surgeons would consult a chart like Source 4 (called a Zodiac man) to determine when was a favourable time to perform an operation. Astrologers would even study the state of the stars and planets at the time of a child's birth to determine whether it would be a dangerous birth and what would be the child's prospects in life.

Source 4

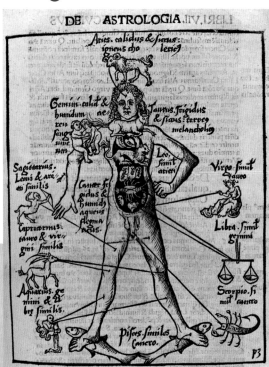

A Zodiac man.

Urine analysis

Most doctors used a urine chart to help diagnose illness. In Source 5, the writing around the chart describes the colour of the urine and whether it is cloudy or clear, the little drawings of urine bottles show the colour of the urine, and the writing in the middle groups the urine samples together according to what they tell the doctor about the patient's condition. Wealthy people might send their urine off for diagnosis every week.

Source 5

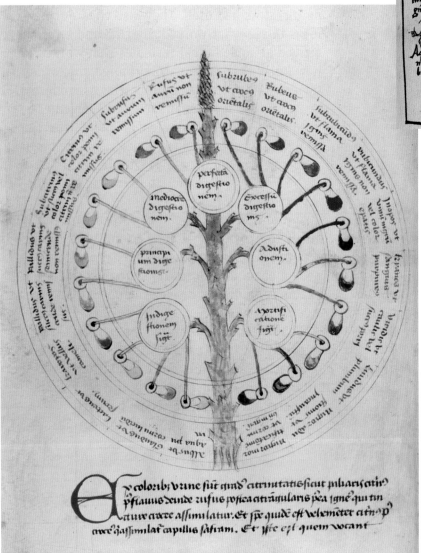

A medieval urine chart. ❓ *Can you work out which sample is a) most healthy; b) least healthy?*

Did you know?

The Theory of the Four humours may sound wrong to you but in the history of medicine it is important because Hippocrates was basing his ideas on scientific methods of observation and recording.

Bleeding

A doctor would open a vein, usually in the patient's arm, and drain some blood into a vessel called a bleeding cup. This may sound a strange treatment. The thinking behind it was the Theory of the Four Humours. Hippocrates, a Greek doctor in the fifth century BC, had suggested that illness arose when the four humours in a body (blood, phlegm, yellow bile and black bile) were not in balance with one another. So, to take blood out of a person would restore the balance of the four humours in his or her body. In fact, bleeding was highly dangerous. It could cause anaemia (not enough red blood cells) and septicaemia (blood poisoning). But it continued in use for 2000 years!

Surgery

Pain

Anaesthetics were not discovered until the nineteenth century. Operations had to be quick so as not to cause too much pain and shock to a person's system. However, even so, it was essential that a person wasn't fully conscious if an operation was to stand any chance of success. The most common method was to get a person drunk before operating on them. This recipe, used by surgeons in the Middle Ages, was a little more sophisticated but had the same effect.

Source ❻

To make a drink that men call dwale to make a man sleep while men carve him: take three spoonfuls of the gall of a boar, three spoonfuls of hemlock juice, three spoonfuls of wild nept, three spoonfuls of lettuce, three spoonfuls of poppy, three spoonfuls of henbane and three spoonfuls of vinegar and mix them all together and boil them a little. Put three spoonfuls of the mixture into half a gallon of good wine and mix it well together. Let him that shall be carved sit against a good fire and make him drink until he falls asleep. Then it is safe to carve him.

This mixture would certainly have had the desired effect and might even have put the patient to sleep for ever!

Infection and bleeding

Because of the problem of pain surgeons could only do short and quick operations such as amputations. Once the limb was cut off the next challenge for a surgeon was to stop the bleeding – they used a range of methods, including boiling oil to close up the severed veins and arteries. But the biggest problem of all was to follow – infection. Nowadays after an operation a patient is given antibiotics to fight infection and the wounds are covered with antiseptic dressings and ointments. In the Middle Ages they did not know about microbes and bacteria or how to prevent infection so they had to dress the wound and hope for the best. The patients with the strongest immune system and the cleanest wounds would survive. Many would die of blood poisoning and other infections.

Source ❼
An historian writes

Some improvements in medical practice did take place during the medieval period. These included new drugs, more hospitals and new surgical techniques, some of which were gained from Arabic doctors through trade or during the Crusades. However, dissection was discouraged by the Church and actually banned in 1300 by the Pope. This limited progress in understanding the working of the human body.

Judith Kidd and Linda Richards, *Power and the People 1066–1485*, published in 2002.

Source 8

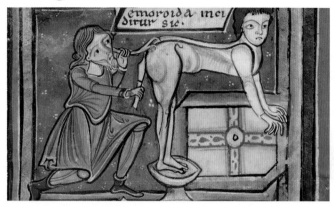

A medieval illustration of an operation on haemorrhoids, one of John of Ardennes' specialities.

Source 9

Care for the sick stands for all. You must help them, as would Christ, whom you really help in helping them. Also you must bear patiently with them as in this way you will gain greater merit with God. Let it be the chief concern of the Abbot that the sick shall not be neglected at any point.

One of the rules of St Benedict.

What...?

CONTAGIOUS
Describes a disease that can be passed on by touch.

Source 10

No lepers, lunatics, or persons having the falling sickness or other CONTAGIOUS disease, and no pregnant women, or suckling infants, and no intolerable persons, even though they be poor and infirm, are to be admitted in the house; and if any such be admitted by mistake, they are to be expelled as soon as possible.

The rules of the hospital of St John in Bridgwater, 1219.

John of Ardennes

Some surgeons worked carefully and used their skills of observation, and their knowledge of what had worked for other surgeons, to get things right. The best surgeons learned skills and techniques on the battlefield and passed these on to younger surgeons who were apprenticed to them. John of Ardennes was one of the most famous surgeons in medieval England. He started out as an army surgeon during the wars between England and France and, when the wars were over, returned to London to work there.

Childbirth

Having a baby was a dangerous business and many mothers and babies died in childbirth. Babies died because they were stressed by a long labour, starved of oxygen or because they were born feet or bottom first instead of head first. Mothers could bleed to death or die from an infection caught during or after the birth. Men usually kept out of the way and the dangerous and messy business of childbirth was left to the women.

Hospitals

The word 'hospital' comes from 'hospitality' and means a place to stay. It did not originally mean somewhere to be treated. Of the 1,200 hospitals in England and Wales in the Middle Ages, only 100 treated or cared for the sick. Nearly all the hospitals were set up or run by the Christian Church and based in monasteries. It was one of St Benedict's Rules that looking after the sick was a Christian duty (see Source 9). After 1066 the Church began to open hospitals away from monasteries, although they were still run by monks and nuns.

Most of the hospitals for the sick were opened in the 1100s and 1200s. In London, St Bartholomew's was founded in 1123, St Thomas's in 1170 and St Mary Spital in 1197. Some were very large – St Leonard's in York had over 200 beds – while others could only take half a dozen sick people.

There were some specialist hospitals. In thirteenth-century London there were at least four leper hospitals and six hospitals for the 'sick poor'. Richard Whittington, Lord Mayor of London, paid for an eight-bed extension to St Thomas's hospital for unmarried pregnant women. In Stamford a hospital cared for the blind, deaf and mute and the hospital of St Mary of Bethlehem looked after those who were mentally disturbed. Some hospitals made it very clear who they would, and would not, admit (see Source 10 for example).

Source ⑪

Source ⑫

Source ⑬

Source ⑭

Task

1 Here are four pictures of treatments from the Middle Ages. They all come from medieval manuscripts. Using the information from the past five pages work out what is going on in each picture and write a caption for each one. (For answers, see page 190.)

2 Put these four treatments into order on this scale. A scientific treatment is a treatment based on experiment and careful observation of patients. A non-scientific treatment is based on supernatural beliefs. Write some sentences to explain your order.

Least scientific ⟵⟶ Most scientific

3 Choose one treatment and write a short advert for the services of this medical specialist.

14.2 Case study: the Black Death, 1346–53

Now you know about the sort of treatments that were available to medieval people. How do you think these services would cope if a VIRULENT disease swept the country, striking without warning, killing within days and carrying off rich and poor alike?

The Black Death swept across most of Europe and Asia in the years 1346–53. It seemed that nothing could escape: millions of people died as well as animals and birds. Whole communities were destroyed. An Arab historian, who lived through it, wrote: 'A devastating PLAGUE struck East and West. Whole populations vanished. The entire world changed.'

What was the Black Death?

We now know that the Black Death was a combination of three diseases – all caused by the same bacillus (bacterium) – but with different symptoms and spread in different ways.

- **Bubonic plague** was caused by a bacillus that lived in the bloodstream of black rats. When the fleas that lived on the black rat bit the rat and sucked its blood, the bacillus was transferred to the fleas. Then, when the fleas from the black rat bit animals and people, the bacillus was transferred to them. Bubonic plague attacked the body's lymph nodes and caused them to swell (the swellings were known as buboes).
- **Pneumonic plague** involved the same bacillus but affected the lungs. It was spread directly from person to person in their saliva, by coughing or sneezing.
- Either of these two types of plague could in turn lead to **septicaemic plague**, where blood poisoning set in and death occurred before other symptoms could appear.

However, these true causes of such diseases were not discovered until the nineteenth century, and so for medieval people all this was unknown. All they knew was that they were faced with a deadly disease that spread relentlessly, hit without warning and wiped out families and whole communities.

Why did the Black Death spread so quickly?

The Black Death followed the trade routes of merchants, traders and travellers over land and sea. The Black Death was recorded in the eastern Mediterranean in mid-1347 and by the summer of 1348 hit England. It seems to have travelled throughout southern England in the summer as bubonic plague. It hit London in September 1348. Plague fleas die in winter and this would usually stop the spread of plague. But there was no respite in the winters of 1346–49 and this was probably because the bubonic plague changed into the pneumonic version, which could spread from person to

---

What...?

VIRULENT
Of exceptional severity.

PLAGUE
An infectious or contagious disease that spreads rapidly over a large area and has a huge death toll.

person without the help of any fleas. It spread to East Anglia in the new year, and by the spring of 1349 was devastating Wales and the Midlands. The summer of 1349 saw the plague in the north of England and Ireland.

A monk, William of Malmesbury recorded:

Source 15

In 1348, at about the feast of the Translation of St Thomas the Martyr [7 July] the cruel pestilence, hateful to all future ages, arrived from countries across the sea on the south coast of England at the port called Melcombe in Dorset. Travelling all over the south country it wretchedly killed innumerable people in Dorset, Devon and Somerset. Next it came to Bristol, where very few were left alive, and then travelled northwards, leaving not a city, a town, a village or even, except rarely, a house, without killing most or all of the people there so that over England as a whole, a fifth of the men, women and children were carried to burial.

At Ashwell, in Hertfordshire, these words were scratched on the wall of the parish church:

Source 16

'Death' strangling a victim of the Black Death.

Source 17

1349 the pestilence. 1350, pitiless, wild, violent, the dregs of the people live to tell the tale.

When the Black Death reached Ireland, John of Clyn, an Irish friar, fearing they all would die, recorded what had happened. He recorded how the Black Death came to Ireland and about the thousands who died agonising deaths. He ended:

Source 18

Man and wife with their children travelled the same road, the road of death. To stop these notable events from perishing with time and fading from memory, I have set them down in writing whilst waiting among the dead for the coming of death. And to stop the writing perishing with the writer, I leave this parchment for the work to be continued in case in future any human survivor should remain. *[Here the writing stops. It is followed by a note in different handwriting:]* Here, it seems, the author died.

The population of England in 1348, before the Black Death struck, was around 3.5 million people. In the outbreak of 1348–50 the Black Death killed 30–45 per cent of them. But it didn't kill evenly. In some villages 80 or even 90 per cent of the population died; in Kilkenny, where John of Clyn lived and worked, everyone died. Other villages were less severely affected, with just a handful of people succumbing. Children and young people were particularly badly affected. By the 1370s, the population of England had been halved.

What were the symptoms?

The symptoms of the Black Death were terrible and painful and made more dreadful by the mental distress of knowing you were very likely to die.

- A person with bubonic plague would first feel desperately cold and tired.
- Then boils, called buboes, erupted first in their groin and armpits and then all over their body.
- The buboes filled with pus and turned black. If they burst, they stank.
- At the same time the victim would be running a high fever, with migraine-like headaches.

The illness lasted five to ten days and although death was probable, people could and did recover.

A Welsh poet, Ieuan Gethin described at the time what it was like to find a buboe in the armpit. He called it a 'shilling', which is a large coin.

Source 19

We see death coming into our midst like a black smoke, a plague which cuts off the young, and has no mercy for the fair of face. Woe is me of the shilling in the armpit; it is seething, terrible, wherever it may come, a white lump that gives pain and causes a loud cry, a burden carried under the arms. It is of the form of an apple, like the head of an onion, a small boil that spares no one. Great is its seething, like a burning cinder.

Pneumonic plague attacked a person's lungs, which filled with fluid causing them to have chest pains. They had difficulty in breathing and coughed up blood and pus. The disease was fast-working; people usually died within two to three days.

Explanations: What did people at the time believe caused the Black Death?

There wasn't just one explanation for the plague, but many. Here are some of the theories people had about it at the time.

Source 20

Between Cathay and Persia there rained a vast rain of fire falling in flakes like snow and burning up mountains and plains and other lands. And then arose vast masses of smoke; and whosoever saw this, died within the space of half a day.

An Italian chronicler.

Source 21

The general cause [of the Black Death] was the close position of the three great planets, Saturn, Jupiter and Mars. This had taken place in 1345 on 24th March in the 14th degree of Aquarius. Such a coming together of planets is always a sign of wonderful, terrible or violent things to come.

Guy de Chauliac, a famous doctor of the 1300s.

Task

1 From the information in Sources 20–27, draw up a full list of what or who people in the Middle Ages thought caused the Black Death.
2 Which of these explanations is closest to the truth?

Did you know?

Other explanations included over-eating and children being disobedient.

Did you know?

The theory in Source 24 arose from prejudice against the Jews (anti-Semitism) but was fuelled by the fact that fewer Jews than other people caught the plague. In fact, this was because of the Jews' strict obedience to the rules of cleanliness laid down in the Book of Leviticus.

Task

3 For each of the explanations in your list from question 1, identify
   a) a preventative measure
   b) a treatment that you might expect a person to use if they believed this explanation.
4 Which of these measures or treatments do you think would be most effective? You can find out what they actually did on pages 162–163.

Source 22

Terrible is God toward the sons of men. He often allows plagues, miserable famines, conflicts, wars and other forms of suffering to arise, and uses them to terrify and torment men and so drive out their sins.

The Prior of the Abbey of Christchurch, Canterbury, wrote to the Bishop of London on 28 September 1348. This is part of his letter.

Source 23

Sometimes [the Black Death] comes from a privy [lavatory] next to a chamber that corrupts the air in substance and quality. Sometimes it comes from dead meat or the corruption of standing waters in ditches.

A Swedish bishop, writing in the 1400s and basing his views on a book written in the 1360s.

Source 24

Some say that it [the Black Death] was brought about by the corruption of the air; others that the Jews planned to wipe out all the Christians with poison and had poisoned wells and springs everywhere. And many Jews confessed as much under torture. Men say that bags full of poison were found in many wells and springs.

A German friar writing in 1348.

Source 25

Any person that touched the clothes of the sick, or anything that had been used by them, seemed thereby to catch the disease. The rags of a poor man who died of the disease were thrown into the street. Two pigs came hither and took the rags between their teeth and tossed them to and fro – whereupon almost immediately, they gave a few turns and fell down dead.

In 1349, the author Giovanni Boccaccio wrote about the Black Death in a story called *The Decameron*.

Source 26

This epidemic kills almost instantly. As soon as the airy spirit leaving the eyes of a sick man has struck the eye of a healthy bystander looking at him, the poisonous nature passes from one eye to the other.

A French doctor writing in 1349.

Source 27

The plague was carried by infected people who, by sight, or touch, or breathing on others, killed everyone. It was incurable. It could not be avoided.

By an Italian historian, who lived in Padua during the Black Death.

Remedies: how did people try to prevent the plague, and treat and cure victims?

The things people did to try to stop the Black Death spreading and to treat people when they caught it, depended very much on what they believed caused the disease in the first place.

A Quarantine
Some cities and towns tried to quarantine themselves by making rules about who could come in and out of the city gates; others refused to allow strangers to come in. This badly affected trade.

B Ring church bells
Many people thought that if they could keep the air moving, the plague wouldn't have time to settle. They rang the church bells to circulate the air.

C Burning
The clothes of victims were burned. This was in itself dangerous work because many believed that contact with victims' clothes would spread the Black Death. Those doing the burning dressed in protective clothing with long-nosed masks over their faces and elbow-length gloves. They must have looked terrifying!

D Mourning
Times at which funerals could be held were restricted so that infected bodies, and those who mourned them, were not on the streets at busy times. Some towns and cities limited the number of mourners who could attend a funeral.

F Cleaning
Laws were passed to keep the streets clean. Butchers, for example, were ordered to remove intestines and wash away blood.

E Praying
God-fearing people prayed, and the Church organised special prayers and processions, pleading with God to take the Black Death away from them.

H Whipping
Men called flagellants, up to 600 in a single group, travelled the country. They stripped to the waist (and sometimes stripped naked) and whipped themselves in public. Their whips had knots in them and sharp nails stuck through them and the men bled a lot.

G Herbs and bleeding
Men, women and children who were hit by the Black Death were treated with the usual range of 'cures' available to healers and doctors – if these people could be persuaded to enter a house where there was a plague victim. So plague victims were, for example, bled and given herbal medicines. Some tried putting softened bread mixed with herbs on the buboes to draw out the infection. Others thought a dried toad would be more effective.

Did you know?

Men, women and children followed flagellants around, mopping up their blood with cloths. People believed that this blood had miraculous powers and would protect them from a plague death.

I Diet

John of Burgundy wrote one of the first books about the plague. He gave this advice to people on what they should do:

First you should avoid too much eating and drinking and also avoid baths which open the pores, for the pores are doorways through which poisonous air can enter the body. In cold or rainy weather, you should light fires in your room, and in foggy or windy weather you should inhale perfumes every morning before leaving home. If, however, the plague occurs during hot weather, you must eat cold things rather than hot and also drink more than you eat. Make little use of hot substances such as pepper, garlic and onions.

J Run away

Many, terrified and desperate, simply ran away. An Italian historian, who lived in Padua during the Black Death, described what happened:

Wives fled their husbands, fathers their sons, brothers fled each other. Even the house or clothes of the victim could kill. One death in the house was followed by the death of all the rest, right down to the dogs. Doctors admitted that they had no cure for it. Indeed, the best of them died of it.

How did the Black Death change Britain?

As you have seen in earlier units, the Black Death had a significant impact on ordinary people's lives in Britain. It led to the dismantling of the feudal system (see page 62), and it changed farming and land ownership (see page 145).

It also helped to change medicine. In the short term it increased people's sense of powerlessness. There seemed to be little they could do and so they resorted to supernatural remedies. In the longer term however it encouraged people to challenge traditional explanations; in particular religious explanations were undermined because the disease seemed to hit the good and wicked equally. The theory of the four humours was undermined because the treatments based on this theory were no more effective than the supernatural ones. It encouraged people to look for different explanations such as the links between dirt and disease. It helped progress towards scientific understanding.

Exam practice

Using sources from this unit and your own knowledge, how far do you agree that the Black Death changed England for the better?

See page 184 for a practice evidence question on the Black Death.

Summary task

'Medieval people lived such short lives because they had no effective way of coping with disease.' How far do you agree with this statement? Make sure you back up your argument with evidence from this chapter.

What is this all about?

If you were transported back in time from now to the Middle Ages what do you think is the biggest change you would notice? What do you think would be the greatest similarity?

In this unit you are going to investigate an aspect of medieval life – crime and punishment – that in some ways is very similar to how it is today but in other ways can be very different. See which you think are the greater – the similarities or the differences.

Task

The person in Source 1 has been caught redhanded. Let's give him the benefit of the doubt and say it is a first offence.
1 How do you think this person would be punished today?
2 How do you think this person would have been punished in the Middle Ages?
Record your ideas and, once you have finished studying this unit, look back and see if you want to change them.

Source 1

An illustration from a medieval manuscript.
❓▶ *What crime do you think has been committed?*

What crimes did people commit?

The most common crime committed in the Middle Ages was theft. Records of crime in eight counties between 1300 and 1348 show that theft accounted for 74 per cent of all crimes. But far more serious crimes were regularly committed. In the same period, nearly a fifth of all criminals were tried for murder. Indeed, it seems that outbursts of violence were common in medieval society.

In London in 1244, a rather painful but clearly not uncommon incident was recorded:

Source 2

Roger struck Maud, Gilbert's wife, with a hammer between the shoulders and Moses struck her in the face with the hilt of his sword, breaking many of her teeth. She lingered until the feast of Mary Magdalen, and then died.

In London, riots and fights between gangs of apprentices were common. But violent gang crime also happened outside the capital. In some areas, gangs of criminals roamed the countryside attacking and plundering homes. The royal records tell of a gang in Leicestershire in the 1320s, led by Eustace de Folvill, that terrorised honest people. In one instance the gang attacked the home of: 'Joan, late the wife of Ralph Basset of Drayton, and carried away her goods and held the manor by armed force'.

The APPRENTICES of London were well known troublemakers. The court records of 1244 tell of an incident when watchmen had arrested a group of apprentice boys who had filled a barrel with large stones and then rolled it down Gracechurch Street towards the River Thames, terrorising those in its way.

And what do you make of this crime? In 1310 a Justice of the Peace in Colchester heard the case of Henry Fylbrigge, William Paccard, Thomas Causton and the servant of Thomas Whitmersh. They were accused of gambling: '... until the early morning, then stripping off their clothes they go home naked, to the scandal of the people'.

> **What...?**
>
> **APPRENTICES**
> Young boys who spent years learning a trade such as that of a silversmith or cooper (someone who makes barrels).

> **What...?**
>
> **SHERIFF**
> A person responsible for keeping law and order in each county.

Source ❸
An historian writes

Henry II took steps to ensure that the county law enforcement official, the SHERIFF, carried out his duties. Clear and standard written instructions (writs) were issued. These had to be returned to the king to show they had been carried out. He also established the Court of the King's Bench in London to deal with the most serious criminal cases.

Allan Todd, *Crime, Punishment and Protest*, published in 2002.

How were criminals caught in the Middle Ages?

Catching and bringing to court those who had broken the law was no easier in medieval times than it is today. However, in medieval times the responsibility for making sure that criminals were brought to justice lay with all the members of a community, whether it was a village or a town.

Hue and cry

If a crime was detected, then it was the responsibility of all who had witnessed it to raise the 'hue and cry'. They had to make a lot of noise to attract the attention of other people so that the wrongdoer was caught.

Constables

Some towns and even some villages had constables or watchmen who had the power to arrest wrongdoers.

In London, the watchmen were instructed to arrest anyone who was wearing a 'visor or false face' (a mask). In the Middle Ages, as now, masked people were thought to be potential criminals. If the watchmen suspected anyone of wrongdoing, they had the right to go to that person's house, take out the windows and remove the doors.

Curfew

As many crimes were committed after dark, most towns had a curfew at sundown. Those caught breaking the curfew could end up in court. One such person was Henry Derex, who was brought before a court in Colchester in 1310 accused of: 'Being found with a long knife after the ringing of the last bell [which is] against the custom of the town'.

Did you know?

COMMON LAW
The term is used to mean that the law was applied in the same way across England. The king best known for making sure that there was a Common Law was Henry II.

Sanctuary

A criminal who managed to take refuge in a church when on the run could claim sanctuary under the protection of the Church. If the criminal then confessed to the crime he or she would be allowed to 'abjure the realm' (leave the country) instead of being punished. All property left behind automatically belonged to the king. In Oxfordshire in 1241 it was recorded that: 'Alice of Kingham stole a tunic at Newton Purcell and fled to the church there. She admitted the theft and abjured the realm. She had no chattels [belongings]'.

In another case in London in 1244, it was reported that: 'Henry de Buk killed a certain Irishman, a tiler, with a knife in Fleet Bridge Street, and fled to the church of St Mary Southwark. He acknowledged the deed, and abjured the realm'.

Source 4

This fifteenth-century illustration shows the Court of King Henry's Bench which was based in Westminster. It was set up by Henry II and became one of the most important royal courts. ❓ *Can you find: the judges, the jury, the accused waiting for their cases to be heard?*

Trials

Most court cases were heard at a local court.

In **villages** in the countryside these courts were known as manor courts. They were presided over by the local lord or his representative known as the steward or bailiff. Often these courts dealt with local disputes over day-to-day issues such as people ploughing someone else's land. Most of the villagers would attend the court and witnesses would often be called on to give evidence.

In **towns**, the mayor would sit in judgement at the mayor's court. Disturbances of the peace and petty crimes were either dealt with in the local courts, or were passed to the shire or county court that was presided over by the local Justice of the Peace.

Royal courts

Royal courts tried people under Common Law for crimes ranging from poaching game in royal forests to murder.

Eyre courts

Many cases ended up in a royal court known as the eyre court. The monarch appointed travelling judges. These men visited all the counties of England on a regular basis, and heard cases that were thought to be too difficult for the local courts to sort out, usually property disputes and questions of land ownership. For example:

Case study:
Joan Arsic loses her land

More often than not, the courts were called upon to make judgements on the ownership of land and belongings. The law about who owned what was quite complicated. That is why most monarchs tried very hard to uphold the idea of Common Law. The case below from 1241 is a good example of the kind of things that the royal courts had to deal with. In this case, the judge wanted to make sure that the king got his feudal rights.

- If someone held land directly from the king he or she was called a 'tenant in chief'.
- If an unmarried woman became a tenant in chief she was known as being 'in the king's gift'. This meant that it was up to the king who she married.
- If she got married without asking for the king's permission, as here, she lost her right to the land.

Source ❺

The jury say that Joan Arsic, daughter of Robert Arsic, holds £7-worth of land in Somerton of the king in chief, and she is in the king's gift. Evidence is given that Joan has married Stephen Simeon without the king's permission. So the sheriff is ordered to take all the land she holds off the king in chief and place it into the king's hand.

Judges were not always as honest as they should be. Indeed, in 1178 Henry II reduced the number of eyre court judges from eighteen to five because of the complaints about them.

Most cases at the eyre court lasted less than half an hour.

- Firstly, the evidence against the accused would be put to the court.
- The accused then had the right to defend him or herself.
- Sometimes witnesses would be called to give evidence on behalf of the prosecution or the accused.
- The judge would listen to each side, perhaps

asking a few questions.
- The cases would be heard in front of juries of twelve local men.
- The judge did not always ask the jury for their verdict but when he did, they did not leave the courtroom but would talk about it amongst themselves and then announce their decision. The juries would often make up their minds based on what they knew about the character of the accused.

However, there is evidence that, on other occasions, the jury did have to listen to the evidence as well as make a decision based on the personalities of the people involved.

Source ❻

Emma, wife of Walter of Elsfield, claims that, on the Thursday after Epiphany [6 January] 1238, Roger Mock came to her in her house and hit her with a pair of tongs in the eye so that she lost her right eye. Roger comes [to court] and denies everything, and it is shown that Emma did not mention this until now, and this event happened 3 years ago. The judge lets an enquiry be made by jury. The jurors say that Roger is not guilty, so he is ACQUITTED, but they say that Walter of Elsfield, Emma's husband, hit her so that she lost her eye, so he is sent to GAOL.

Another case from 1241.

What...?

ACQUIT
To release without charge, to clear an accusation.

GAOL
Jail, a prison.

Task

Study Source 6. How is the role of the jury different from the role of a jury today?

You may need to do some research. Use a good library or an Internet search engine to find out.

Church courts

Alongside these courts there was a separate system of Church courts. Ever since the reign of William I, cases involving members of the priesthood or religious orders could only be tried in a Church court. Such was the case of Richard Mansel who, in 1241, was charged with being an ACCOMPLICE to murder. He was brought in front of the eyre court but once the judge found out that he was a CLERK, he handed him over to the Church court of the Bishop of Lincoln. It was well known that Church courts were often more lenient, which means that they gave out less harsh punishments. Therefore, some accused would try to claim that they were in some way a member of the Church and should be tried in the Church court, not the King's court.

What...?

ACCOMPLICE
Someone who helps another person to commit a crime.

CLERK
An official in a cathedral, church or chapel.

Trial by ordeal

In the early Middle Ages, if a jury was unable to come to a verdict, they could ask that the accused stand trial by ordeal. Many of the ordeals took place in a church. The accused was put in a potentially dangerous position as his or her fate had to be decided by God. There was a range of ordeals that the accused might be put through including:

Ordeal by hot water The accused had to pick a stone out of a cauldron of boiling water. If their burns healed in a few days they were believed to be innocent. If a burn got infected or blistered the judges would rule that person guilty.

Ordeal by cold water The accused man or woman was tied up in a crouching position and thrown into water. If he or she sank, the verdict was innocent. If the accused floated, it was thought that the water had rejected him or her, and the verdict was guilty.

Ordeal by iron The accused had to carry a red-hot iron bar for a certain distance. The distance and the weight of the bar differed according to the seriousness of the crime. If the burnt hand healed in a few days, the person was regarded as innocent. If the blisters got infected, the person was guilty.

In 1215 Pope Innocent III banned trial by ordeal.

Trial by battle

This was a way to find out who was right and who was wrong in a dispute between two nobles. The Normans liked this method. The two people in dispute, or people chosen as representatives, would fight each other. The victor was assumed to be in the right because it was thought that he had won because he had God's protection. This practice had more or less died out by the later Middle Ages.

What...?

DETERRENT
Something to discourage an attack, a means of stopping something bad happening.

PILLORY
Also known as stocks, these were wooden frames into which the feet and/or hands of criminals were locked.

Source 7
An historian writes:

Medieval crimes were divided according to how serious they were thought to be. There are some surprises. Stealing was put in the same group of serious crimes as murder and rape. This was because medieval society was set up with different groups of people having a place in it above, or below, other groups. Those with most money and property wanted to protect it from those who had less, so they hanged thieves who threatened those who owned more.

Allan Todd and Martyn Whittock, *Crime and Protest*, published in 2009.

Punishments

The severity of the punishments handed down by the courts depended on the nature of the offence. Those convicted of a first offence of stealing apples might have got away with paying a fine. Most cases in the manor courts ended in a fine.

Humiliation

Certain kinds of crime were thought to deserve a public humiliation. This served as a DETERRENT to others.

In London in 1244, a certain baker called John Mundy was placed in a pillory for selling 'false bread' (which was bread of poor quality); the same punishment was handed out to Agnes Deynte because she sold 'false mangled butter' (poor quality butter). Those placed in the PILLORY or stocks were humiliated in front of their families, friends and neighbours. They also had to put up with the abuse of passers-by. In some cases rotten food would be thrown at them. The more unfortunate criminal might be pelted with sticks and stones.

Those convicted of sexual offences often had their heads shaved and were paraded through town before being placed in the pillory. The parade to the pillory was part of the humiliation. The London court records tell of a priest in the thirteenth century who was caught in bed with a woman. He was paraded through the streets with his trousers down, his priest's robes carried before him. Often those paraded through the streets would be accompanied by a minstrel who would make up songs about the criminal's wrongdoings to the amusement of the watching crowds. When the criminal arrived at the pillory, the show usually continued. Those accused of cheating people by selling them poor standard goods might have these goods burned in front of (or even underneath) them.

There were hardly any prisons in the Middle Ages. They were used simply to hold someone before their trial. They were not used as punishment.

Execution

Murder was almost always punished by hanging, unless the accused was a woman and could prove that she was pregnant. Every town and city had an execution site. In London it was at Tyburn. The first person to be executed at Tyburn was a man named William Longbeard who died in 1196. Those condemned to death would be led through the streets to their death. There are records in the fourteenth century of a man riding through the streets on the back of a horse dressed 'in a striped coat and white shoes' being accompanied by the hangman with the hanging rope in his hands for all to see. Some would escape justice by fleeing. They were then branded as outlaws, as in this case of a woman who had been accused of murder: 'Rose, widow of Robert King, and Maud her sister killed Robert and fled. So they were called to trial and outlawed. They had no belongings. No one else is suspected.'

Source ⑧
An historian writes

The big change in this period was the improved legal system. Medieval kings tried to deal more effectively with criminals who were caught. The system of trials became steadily more complex and was respected by the people. Juries, judges and sheriffs carried on doing their tasks for hundreds of years without major changes, which suggests that people thought that the system worked.

Ian Dawson, *Crime and Punishment through Time*, published in 1999.

The most common way to avoid execution was to claim 'benefit of clergy' because Church courts would never condemn anyone to death. To prove you were a churchman, you had to read out loud a verse from the Bible. Many criminals memorised the verse so that they could claim benefit of clergy. The verse was Psalm 51, verse 1: 'Oh loving and kind God, have mercy. Have pity upon my transgressions.' It was called the neck verse because it saved many criminals from the hangman's noose.

The ultimate punishment

The most serious charge anyone could face was that of treason, which was a crime against the king. Those accused of treason usually had led rebellions against the monarch and they were tried in the monarch's court. When the leaders of the Peasants' Revolt were put on trial in 1381 they were condemned to death by the young king, Richard II, and the mayor of London. Rebels and traitors were tortured and executed in public to act as a deterrent to others.

To combine execution with humiliation, many traitors were hanged, drawn and quartered. This involved the hanging of the condemned person and splitting his body open whilst he was still alive. The head of the traitor was then boiled and placed on a pole on London Bridge. The rest of the body was then hacked into four quarters and sent to different parts of the country. This was the fate of the Scottish rebel, William Wallace, who was found guilty of treason in 1305 (see pages 50–52).

Summary tasks

A. Recap

Now it is over to you to write a newspaper report on a medieval trial.

In this unit there have been brief descriptions of court cases and punishments and acquittals of real people. You can either choose one of these real cases or invent another case of your own. If you invent one, you must make sure it follows the patterns of crime, policing, trial and punishment described in this unit. Make your report as close to medieval reality as possible. Your report will need the following:

- A crime
- The capture of the criminal
- A court case, perhaps in an eyre court
- The verdict of the jury and the sentence.

If guilty:

- The parade to the punishment
- The punishment.

B. Analysis

How far do you agree that the Middle Ages was lawless and violent?

This is an essay question. You could try the following approach.

1   Choose examples from this Unit that:
    - support the view that the Middle Ages were lawless and violent, and write a paragraph or two about them
    - support the view that the Middle Ages were not lawless and violent, and write a paragraph or two about them
2   Then write a final paragraph, weighing the evidence, to explain how far you agree that the Middle Ages were lawless and violent.

UNIT 16 What about the women?

What is this all about?

A woman in medieval England was generally regarded as belonging to a man. She was one of his possessions. So men could, more or less, do what they liked with women but they were also responsible for them. Men were expected to control 'their' women folk. For example, fathers and husbands spoke for their wives and daughters in court and were responsible for their punishment afterwards. The Church taught that women should obey their husbands.

Men also wrote the medieval chronicles, and most of the time the affairs of women were ignored. Women were simply background, their stories seldom recorded or described; indeed hardly even mentioned. A bit of a shame for half of the population!

In this final unit we redress this balance as we focus on a few particular women. For some we know not much more than a mention in a court record. For a precious few we have their letters.

For your final task you will decide which of these five women most deserves to have a whole book written about her.

Task

Look at pictures 1–4 on this page.

1 Which of the pictures show women? What jobs are they doing?

2 Choose one of the pictures of women and put yourself in her place. Describe to a man why the job you're doing is important, for you, your family and the village.

What...?

FLAX
Plant from which linen is made.

Source ❶

The poorest folk are the widows with children. The landlords keep putting their rent up. The money they make by spinning has to be spent on rent, or on milk and oatmeal for the hungry children. The women are often miserable with hunger and cold. They get up before dawn to card and comb the wool, to wash and scrub and mend, and wind yarn.

In 1370, William Langland wrote a story called *Piers Plowman*. This is part of what he said about peasant women.

Source ❷
An historian writes:

A lord has power over whom his peasants might marry. If a widow has not remarried within a few months of her first husband's death, then the lord's land is in danger of being neglected. She will be ordered to choose a capable husband. If she does not, then the bailiff or reeve will choose one for her.

Ian Mortimer, *The Time Traveller's Guide to Medieval England*, published in 2008.

A peasant woman: Alice de Attwood

In Unit 13 you found out what life was like for peasants in English villages. Women worked in the fields, sowing seeds, weeding, harvesting and threshing the grain; they fed animals, milked cows and collected eggs. They brewed beer. They spun wool and FLAX and wove cloth. At home, they cooked, washed, scrubbed, and looked after babies and young children. Very few medieval women lived beyond the age of 30. Childbirth was a particularly dangerous time for women.

We can find out a little about the lives of ordinary women in the Middle Ages through court records. For example, this extract is taken from the Court Rolls of the village of Halesowen between 1270 and 1307. This is all we know about this particular woman, Alice de Attwood.

Source ❸

Ralf de Attwood has five daughters. The third, Alice, has married without the lord's permission. For this, Ralf is fined 2s. If this happens again, his goods are to be confiscated.

A mystic: Margery Kempe

One of the ways that ordinary women could find some degree of independence was through the Church. Here is someone who became a holy woman who worked independently of any nunnery.

Margery Kempe had a breakdown after the birth of her first child and then went on to have thirteen more children. She set up and ran two business enterprises, both of which collapsed. She then began to evaluate her life. It seemed to her that all she had wanted was profit and pleasure. Now she changed direction. She gave up sex, went on pilgrimages to Rome and the Holy Land and became a visionary, a holy woman. She gave away her money and visited the sick. She had fits of loud weeping at intense moments. These impressed some but irritated others, especially priests who had their sermons interrupted by her loud sobbing. However, Julian of Norwich supported and encouraged her. The Archbishop of Canterbury allowed her to take communion every Sunday (once a year was usual for ordinary people) and she was admitted to the Guild of the Holy Trinity, a powerful religious club. In 1438 she finished her book *The Book of Margery Kempe*, extracts of which were printed. Margery Kempe shows what a determined fifteenth-century woman could do – provided she was born rich.

Source ❹

[She] many times met with men of that district who said to her, 'Woman, give up this life that you lead and go and spin, and card wool, as other women do, and do not suffer so much shame and so much unhappiness. We would not suffer so much for any money on earth.'

Then she said to them, 'I do not suffer as much sorrow as I would do for our Lord's love, for I only suffer cutting words, and our merciful Lord Christ Jesus… suffered hard strokes, bitter scourgings, and shameful death at the last, for me and for all mankind, blessed may he be.'

Extract from the *Book of Margery Kempe*, published in the fifteenth century.

What...?

FEMME SOLE
A legally independent woman, married or single, who had the right to trade on her own account.

Source 5
An historian writes

Most women from the upper classes led very busy, active, and sometimes dangerous lives, running manors, farms and castles single-handed. This was because wealthy men spent most of their time away from home – travelling to and from their many estates, attending the king's court and fighting against neighbouring lords or in wars abroad. While they were away their wives took charge and ran the estates. Often they lived in isolated places and had no-one to rely on but themselves. There was no strong central government as today, and landowning families had great power over the local people. The lady of the manor was an influential person who had to deal with the management of acres of land, crops, animals and property; hundreds of employees and their homes; legal arguments, fights, riots and even armed attacks. She certainly had to be strong and very capable.

Adams, Bartley, Bourdillon and Loxton, *From Workshop to Warfare: the lives of medieval women*, published in 1983.

A merchant: Dame Claramunda

On pages 148–149 you read about the restrictions that different trades put on who could practise their trade and how. Trade guilds were particularly keen to control the entry of women into business. Only a few women were able to become merchants or traders, and here's one of them.

In the thirteenth century, Dame Claramunda was a well-known and successful Southampton wine merchant. We know she was successful because in 1258 she won an important contract to supply King Henry III with wine from France. We know, too, that she had been widowed twice and that she had been given permission to trade in Southampton as a FEMME SOLE. Dame Claramunda had combined two successful businesses and made them even more profitable. Widows in towns were often given permission to carry on with their dead husband's businesses, and this is one way in which town women managed to lead independent lives.

We know from town plans and from Southampton's taxation records that Dame Claramunda lived in one of the large merchants' houses on the quay. We know, too, that she owned property elsewhere in the town that she let out to tenants. Dame Claramunda had no children to whom she could leave her business. When she died, therefore, she left her wooden chest full of jewels and silver jugs and plates, together with her houses, to various churches and monasteries in and around Southampton. Many rich people left money to the Church in the hope it would speed their journey to heaven.

A landowner: Margaret Paston

Women in rich families usually lived longer than peasants because they were better fed, usually lived in warm, dry houses and had decent clothes to wear. However, even though they had time for leisure activities like dancing and music, they were expected to supervise the management of their household – and little else. Here is one of the best-known landowning women from the Middle Ages.

Margaret Paston was a great letter writer, and it is because of her letters that we know a great deal about everyday life in England in the fifteenth century. We also know a great deal about Margaret Paston herself, because of what she unwittingly reveals. She was certainly not a submissive wife!

Margaret started life in the Norfolk village of Mauntby, where her father was a wealthy landowner. On his death she inherited his lands and, in 1440, entered an arranged marriage with a neighbouring landowner, John Paston. This meant that John had to administer a very large estate indeed. Or did he? He was a lawyer and spent a lot of time away from Norfolk.

Task

1 What different things enabled Dame Claramunda and Margaret Paston to behave as independent women?

2 How independent of her husband do you think Margaret Paston really was? Explain your answer.

A queen: Eleanor of Aquitaine

The whole of Section 1 of this book was about the actions of kings. Nearly all of these kings had queens. Here we focus on one of those queens, Eleanor of Aquitaine. You read a little about Eleanor on pages 39–40. She was a lot more than just the wife of King Henry II or the mother of King John!

Eleanor was determined, arrogant, forceful and free-thinking. She started out in life as the very wealthy daughter and heiress of Duke William X of Aquitaine. Her lands and wealth made her very marriageable and when she was just fifteen, she was married off to King Louis VII of France. Once she had become Queen of France, Eleanor turned her attention to the old-fashioned, fusty French court. She encouraged poets and TROUBADOURS (many of whom were half in love with her), dancing and good manners, turning the French court into something of a trend-setter in medieval Europe.

Sitting at home and encouraging COURTLY LOVE wasn't enough for Eleanor. When Europe was gearing itself up for the Second Crusade, she was determined to join in. Appearing before the startled Abbé Bernard of Clairvaux, dressed as an Amazon (a mythical female warrior), Eleanor offered him thousands of her fighting men. Delighted to accept her troops, the Church must have been considerably less delighted when it became clear that Eleanor intended to go on the Crusade herself, planning to 'tend the wounded' along with about 300 of her ladies.

But money talked, then as now. Eleanor, her ladies and their servants, along with countless wagon-loads of supplies, set off for the Holy Land. Reaching Antioch, where her uncle, Raymond, was in charge, Eleanor agreed with him that the best plan would be for the Crusaders to make the recapture of Odessa their first objective. But King Louis disagreed. He was fixed on reaching Jerusalem and demanded that Eleanor fulfil her marriage vows and follow him there. Furious, she announced to the world that their marriage was not all that it should be – and in any case they should not have married at all because of some distant family connection. Louis asserted himself as her husband and insisted she rode with him to Jerusalem. She did. The expedition failed and Louis and Eleanor returned to France in separate ships.

Maybe Eleanor did try to be a dutiful wife. Back in France, she produced two daughters for him. But all was not well and when she was 29, the marriage was annulled (declared invalid). Eleanor left her two daughters to be brought up in the French court and the vast estates of Aquitaine came back under her control.

Not one to linger, within a year Eleanor threw herself into a new marriage to Henry Plantagenet, Duke of Anjou, eleven years her junior. They were well-matched in wealth and in temperament; this marriage was to be a stormy one. In 1154 Henry became King of England as Henry II.

What...?

TROUBADOURS
Travelling players.

COURTLY LOVE
A very formal type of behaviour at a royal court involving poems, songs, music, singing and dancing where men and women acted out the 'proper' ways of approaching each other.

Did you know?

When plans began for the Third Crusade, the Pope announced that no women whatsoever, rich or poor, were to be allowed to join in. All the Christian kings of Europe, including Louis of France, agreed. However, plenty of women still went.

Task

1 What do you find most surprising about Eleanor's life?

2 Compare Eleanor's career with that of
   a) Matilda (see Unit 2). She was Eleanor's mother-in-law.
   b) Elizabeth Woodville (see page 84), the wife of Edward IV.

   In what ways was Eleanor similar to, and in what ways was she different from, these other two queens?

Eleanor was pregnant for much of the next thirteen years, giving birth to five sons (William, Henry, Richard, Geoffrey and John) and three daughters (Matilda, Eleanor and Joan). Over a number of years, through tough bargaining, clever alliances and some fighting, Eleanor and Henry created a strong and powerful kingdom, stretching from the Pyrenees to the Scottish borders. But Eleanor wasn't satisfied with this. Exasperated by Henry's string of affairs (he wasn't unusual here: most medieval kings had mistresses and illegitimate children), strongly disagreeing with many of his decisions and weary of having to share the ruling of Aquitaine with him, she joined with two of her sons, Richard and John, in rebelling against Henry. The rebellion was soon put down, and Eleanor was imprisoned by Henry for the next fifteen years.

She was released when Richard succeeded to the throne in 1189, but she wasn't ready for retirement even though, at 67, she was a very old lady by medieval standards. She repeatedly intervened to defend Richard's land when he was away fighting in the Holy Land, and raised vast sums of money with which to pay his ransom when he was captured. Travelling constantly throughout Europe, she managed her army and her estates, supported English subjects and even found the time to search out a bride for Richard.

She died aged 82 at Fontevrault, her favourite religious community, where older aristocratic women went to find spiritual comfort.

Summary task

Which of these five women from pages 171–175 do you think most deserves to have a book written about her? Choose one and write a letter to a publisher suggesting a new book. Explain:
a) why the woman is so interesting
b) what else you would like to find out about her
c) what this woman's life can reveal about the roles and lives of women in the Middle Ages.

Pulling it all together

You have now met a lot of medieval people and discovered many things about their lives. Prepare a medieval gallery of the five that interest you the most. Start with a picture of each, either draw them or find them on the internet. Then write a speech or interview that explains what each person does for a living or what they have achieved in their lifetime.

Answering questions on a Common Entrance Paper

The Common Entrance History examination is set by the Independent Schools Examination Board (ISEB) but is marked at the senior school to which you have applied. ISEB sends a mark scheme to all schools to guide them as they mark the papers, although each school will have its own rules, too. So, while these pages can't tell you everything or guarantee you success, they can help you know what your marker should be looking for in your answers.

The history paper is divided into two sections: Section A contains evidence questions and Section B contains essay questions. They test different kinds of history skills and require different kinds of answers.

You will have to answer one question from each section. You can answer questions from Medieval Realms 1066–1485, The Making of the United Kingdom 1485–1750, or Britain and Empire 1750–1900. However, as this book is about Medieval Realms, all the examples here are drawn from medieval topics. But in your exam you can choose to answer questions from any topic wherever your knowledge is strongest.

Top Tips – The essentials

- Plan your time: You have 60 minutes for the whole exam. Sixty minutes is a short time! Match the time you spend to the marks available. Evidence questions are worth 20 marks. Essay questions are worth 30 marks. ISEB advise that you spend 5 minutes reading through the paper, 20 minutes on the evidence question and 35 minutes on the essay question.
- Check your work: You won't have time to revise your whole answer but it is worthwhile having a quick read through to check for obvious mistakes.
- Use good English: whoever is marking your paper will want all your work to be neat (easy to read) and clear, with a good use of English. It is always worth working hard at that.

Section 1 Evidence questions

There will be one question on Medieval Realms worth 20 marks. You will be told the topics in advance, drawn from one of the six topics on pages 180–185.

There will be **three** sources:

- a contemporary source (i.e. a source from the time – sometimes called a primary source)
- a more modern source (written after the event, usually by an historian – sometimes called a secondary source)
- a pictorial source.

There will only be **one** question on these sources. It will begin 'Using **all** the sources and your own knowledge…'. The questions will carry on by asking how far you agree with a particular opinion. So, for example:

- Using all the sources and your own knowledge, how far is it true to say that Harold stood no chance of winning the Battle of Hastings?
- Using all the sources and your own knowledge, how far do you agree that King John was a bad monarch?

At first glance, that might seem to be a bit scary. You will have to combine your source evaluation skills with your own knowledge of the topic, all in one answer. Let's go through what you will have to do.

Read the two written sources and look carefully at the picture source. Check out how they link to the question.

The sources will probably 'pull' in different directions. One will support the opinion in the question, one will give a different viewpoint and one will be somewhere in between. Make sure you sort out which is which before you begin, because to get a really good mark you will need to explore the evidence the sources give you for and against the opinion in the question.

What are the examiners expecting you to do?

The markers expect you to:

- show that you understand the sources and that you can make links between them
- work out how useful they are as evidence for or against the opinion stated in the question
- make a judgement about the opinion in the question that is supported by what you have said in your answer.

To do all this really effectively you will have to use your own knowledge as well.

How will you do it?

1 Introduction

This is where you show that you understand that what you have been given is an opinion about, for example, the Battle of Hastings, or King John, or the Black Death. Write a few sentences of information about the topic from your own knowledge, and then explain that there are different opinions about this issue.

Top tip

- Don't be tempted to write all you know about the topic! Write just enough to show that you understand what happened and that there are different views about it.

2 Compare the sources

You will compare the sources in different ways:

- content – the information in them
- tone – the style and kind of language the authors of the written sources use
- inference – what you can infer, or deduce, from the source but isn't actually said directly in it.

Start with the source that most agrees with the opinion and then move to the one that most disagrees, before bringing in the final score.

Top tips

- Use phrases that show you are linking the sources: 'However, Source Y disagrees…'; 'On the other hand the writer of…'.
- Use your own knowledge to help you compare the sources.

3 Evaluate the sources

You will then move on to evaluate the sources. Remember that 'evaluate' means to weigh up how far a source can be used as evidence for or against the opinion you have been given.

To evaluate the sources you need to consider:

- reliability – do you trust the source to tell the truth?
- utility – all sources are useful for something, but how useful are these sources for the specific question you are answering?

Top tips

- Use the 5W test: Who, When, Where, What and Why? (See page 4.)
- Read the caption provided which will give you information about the provenance.
- Your knowledge about the topic will help you evaluate the sources. For example, your knowledge may make you doubt whether a source was accurate.

4 Conclusion

This is where you pull it all together. You must reach a judgement about how far you agree with the opinion given in the question. The judgement you reach must be backed by the evidence you have found in the sources and by your own knowledge.

Top tips

- Don't go back over everything you have written. Just draw out the key evidence to support the judgement you are making.
- Remember that there is no right answer to the sort of question you are being asked. The examiners will want to see how you are using the sources and your own knowledge and understanding to reach a judgement.

Now use this advice to have a go at the practice questions on pages 180–185. There is one question on each of the nominated topics for Common Entrance Medieval Realms.

Section 2 Essay questions

The essay questions are worth 30 marks. There will be TEN essay questions on the Common Entrance History paper. You will need to choose one.

There will be questions on each of the main Medieval topics:

- War
- Rebellions
- Government and Parliament
- Religion
- Social history
- General Topics (including local history).

The questions might ask you to choose events, or issues or people or places. See examples on opposite page.

Top tips: How to choose the right question

1 Read all of the questions
You will know your strong topics and the questions you are hoping for. However, even though it may take you a couple of minutes, do read through all the questions before you make your final choice. You would kick yourself if you missed out on a really good question.

2 Make your choice
Choose the one you feel most confident about.

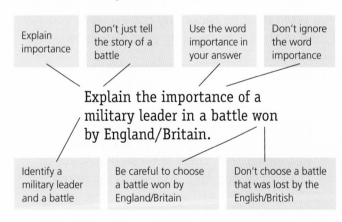

| Explain importance | Don't just tell the story of a battle | Use the word importance in your answer | Don't ignore the word importance |

Explain the importance of a military leader in a battle won by England/Britain.

| Identify a military leader and a battle | Be careful to choose a battle won by England/Britain | Don't choose a battle that was lost by the English/British |

3 Rewrite the questions inserting your chosen content
So, for example:
> 'Explain the importance of (a military leader) in (a battle won by England/Britain).'

becomes
> 'Explain the importance of Henry V in the Battle of Agincourt.'

Do you still feel you can answer it?

What are the examiners expecting you to do?
The examiners expect you to answer the question. They will also expect you to consider a number of factors or issues. You will get some marks for telling a story. However, you will get even more marks for linking your points into argument which is backed up with your own knowledge.

How will you do it?
You have got 35 minutes to plan and then write the essay.

1 Plan
You should spent two or three minutes planning your essay. In your plan you should quickly write down:

- three points that you are going to make
- your paragraph running order
- important facts that you might use.

2 Introduction
Do not write too much for your introduction, just two or three short sentences.

3 Main part of the essay
In the main part of the essay you will develop your argument. If you want top marks, you will need to structure your work. The best way to do this is to tackle each paragraph in the same way. Here is the advice we gave you on page 7, a good way that you can do it.

- **Point** At the start of the paragraph you should make your point.
- **Explain** your point further in a sentence or two.
- **Evidence** Provide evidence (facts) to back up your point.
- **Reiterate** Mention your point one more time.

For example, this paragraph comes from an answer to the question 'Choose a monarch you have studied. How far were they successful?' The candidate chose William the Conqueror.

This is the point of argument

These are the points of explanation

On one hand William's reign was successful because he gained control the country. This was down to the building of motte and bailey castles. The castles housed soldiers as well as the Norman rulers. They were very difficult to attack. After his campaigns in the North and West of England between 1067 to 1071, William built castles in towns including Exeter, Warwick and York. Castles were built in the border region between England and Wales. The failure of the 1075 rebellion was because the rebels were not able to take control of William's castles in Herefordshire. So building castles helped William control England and become successful.

This is the evidence

This is the point mentioned one last time

Top Tips

- Always write in paragraphs not bullet points or lists.
- Start each paragraph with a phrase that will help your argument develop (although try to avoid using the same phrase over and over again).

4 Conclusion

In your conclusion, go over the main points of your essay one last time. Remember the burger. You need a bottom bun too – otherwise everything falls out. Make it brief and to the point; just two or three sentences.

Essay questions – some examples

Here are some examples of the type of essay questions you might have to answer.

War and Rebellion

1 Explain, the most important consequences of a battle you have studied.
2 Choose a military leader or leader of a rebellion you have studied and explain why he or she is remembered.

Government and Parliament

3 Choose an event in the development of Parliament and explain why it was important.
4 Choose a king or queen you have studied and assess whether he or she was successful.

Religion

5 Choose an important religious event or religious development you have studied and explain its significance.
6 Explain the impact of an important figure involved with religion in the period you have studied.

Social history

7 Choose an event which changed the lives of people in the period you have studied and explain its consequences.
8 Was living in a town a good or bad experience in the period you have studied?

General Topics

9 Explain the significance of one woman's life in the period you have studied.
10 Describe an historical site you have visited. Why is it important in history?

1 The Norman Conquest 1066

Read the introduction and the sources and answer the question which follows:

Introduction

All the sources are about the invasion of England by Duke William of Normandy in 1066 and the Battle of Hastings that followed it. The battle was fought in October 1066 between the Normans, led by Duke William, and the Saxons, led by King Harold of England. King Harold was killed defending his country against the invaders.

SOURCE A: William's preparations for invasion as recorded in the Bayeux Tapestry.

SOURCE B: adapted from an account of the Battle of Hastings, written by William of Poitiers between 1071 and 1077. It comes from his *Gesta Willelmi*, which was a chronicle of the Norman Conquest of England. William of Poitiers had been trained as a knight and worked as a chaplain in Duke William's household.

Harold's large army was ready and lined up in close formation. Realising that they could not attack such an army without taking big losses, the Normans and their allies pretended to run away. The barbarians... thinking they were winning, shouted with triumph... and chased the Normans, who they thought were running away. But the Normans suddenly turned their horses round, surrounded Harold's men and cut them all down so that not one was left alive. The Normans played this trick twice with great success.

SOURCE C: an extract from a modern history book written in 2004.

Facing a double invasion was an enormous challenge for Harold. In the north, he defeated Hardrada in a lightning strike, waging a brilliant campaign. But then Harold played into William's hands. Although at Hastings his army was equal in size to William's, Harold's men were severely weakened in number and spirit by the two battles in the north. Furthermore, they did not have a chance to rest before fighting William. Edwin and Morcar, Harold's loyal brothers-in-law, were still marching south when Harold was at Hastings and Harold did not wait for them. Harold had perhaps planned on trapping William on the coast, and taking revenge for the damage done to his lands in Wessex. But William had already moved inland. Harold, not William, was taken by surprise.

QUESTION

Using **all** the sources and your own knowledge, how far do you agree that Harold lost the Battle of Hastings because he was a poor military leader?

2 The First Crusade 1096–1099

Read the introduction and the sources and answer the question which follows:

Introduction

All the sources are about the First Crusade, which began in about 1096 to free the city of Jerusalem from the control of the Seljuk Turks. They wanted total control of the region. They made it very difficult for Christian pilgrims to visit Jerusalem. In 1095, Pope Urban II made an important speech calling for a religious war against the Muslims.

SOURCE A: from *Alexiad* by Anna Comnena. Anna was the daughter of the Byzantine Emperor Alexus I. She started writing *Alexiad* in 1138. Throughout the work she shows her dislike for the Crusaders.

A Frank [Frenchman] called Peter had gone on a pilgrimage to Jerusalem but had been forced by the Turks and Saracens to turn back to France without reaching his destination. Peter was angry at having failed to get to Jerusalem and he was determined to succeed next time around. However, Peter realised that it would be difficult to reach Jerusalem on his own and that he would need company. So he came up with a cunning plan. He preached across Europe that God had told him to raise an army to relieve Jerusalem. His plan really succeeded. For after inspiring the souls of all he assembled a large army that filled every highroad. And those Frankish soldiers were accompanied by an unarmed crowd more numerous than the sand or the stars, carrying palms and crosses on their shoulders; women and children, too, came away from their countries.

SOURCE B: from a history book written in 1991.

In 1085 the Seljuk Turks seized Jerusalem and attacked the Byzantine Empire. The Byzantines were Christians. They appealed to the Pope for help. At a meeting in France in the year 1095 Pope Urban II urged the knights and princes of Europe to fight a crusade. Pope Urban's speech was so effective that kings and knights at once made plans to sail to the Holy Land. They wore a cross on the front of their armour as they went.

SOURCE C: a picture of Peter the Hermit leading the Crusaders. The picture was drawn in France in the beginning of the fourteenth century.

QUESTION

Using **all** the sources and your own knowledge, how far do you agree that people went on the First Crusade only because they were inspired by Pope Urban II's speech?

3 Archbishop Becket 1162–1170

Read the introduction and the sources and answer the question which follows:

Introduction

All the sources are about the quarrel between King Henry II and the Archbishop of Canterbury, Thomas Becket. The Church was very powerful at this time. Archbishops and bishops had so much influence over England's laws and land that some monarchs saw the church as a rival to their power in England. King Henry II was one of these monarchs.

SOURCE A: a picture from a medieval book about Thomas Becket. It was drawn in about 1235, and shows Henry and Becket quarrelling.

SOURCE B: an extract from a modern history book, written in 2008.

When Henry became king in 1154, he made Becket his chancellor. The two men worked well together to make the country strong and prosperous. They became good friends. One of the important things they did together was to set up a system of justice. This meant that the king's justice was the same everywhere and was respected throughout the land. But there was a parallel system of justice that Henry couldn't touch: the Church system. Monks, priests and anyone who worked for the Church could be tried in Church courts, which often gave more lenient verdicts than the king's courts. Henry wanted to stop this. Then Henry had a good idea: he would make Becket Archbishop of Canterbury. Becket would bring the church courts into line with the royal ones. And that is where the trouble began.

SOURCE C: an extract from *The Life of Becket* written by Roger of Pontigny in 1176. Roger was a French monk who knew Becket when he was in exile in France.

The King then said to the Archbishop: 'Have I not raised you from a poor and lowly position to high honour and rank? How is it then that so many proofs of my love for you have so soon been wiped from your mind? Why are you not only ungrateful, but oppose me in everything?' The archbishop replied, 'Far be it from me to show myself ungrateful or to act against your will in anything, so long as it agrees with the will of God. For kings should be obeyed, but not if this goes against God's will. Remember St Peter said "We ought to obey God rather than men."'

QUESTION

Using **all** the sources and your own knowledge, how far do you agree that Henry made the wrong decision in making Thomas Becket archbishop of Canterbury?

4 King John
1199–1216

Read the introduction and the sources and answer the question which follows:

Introduction

All the sources are about King John's strengths and weaknesses as king. He ruled England between 1199 and 1216. During his reign he lost almost all of England's lands abroad. He raised taxes in England. He quarrelled with the Pope. In 1215, the barons rebelled and forced John to give up some of his powers by signing the Magna Carta.

SOURCE A: a medieval drawing of King John.

SOURCE B: an extract from the *Greater Chronicle* written by Matthew Paris in 1235. He was born in about 1200, and as a young man became a monk in the St Alban's monastery. St Albans is situated on the road north from London, and many travellers stopped there overnight. Matthew wrote down a lot of what he heard from them.

John was a tyrant, not a king. He was a destroyer, instead of a governor, crushing his own people and favouring foreigners. He was a lion to his own people, but a lamb to foreigners and rebels. He lost the territory of Normandy and many other territories through laziness. As for Christianity, he was unstable and unfaithful. Foul as it is, Hell itself is defiled by the fouler presence of King John.

SOURCE C: an extract from a book written by two historians in 1986.

John made sure that justice was being done in his courts. He ordered that Jews were not to be ill-treated. He also made sure that mercy was given to widows, and poor people who had done wrong.

QUESTION

Using **all** the sources and your own knowledge, do you agree that John was a bad king?

5 The Black Death
1348–1350

Read the introduction and the sources and answer the question which follows:

Introduction

All the sources are about the Black Death. The Black Death appeared in England in 1348, and quickly spread across the whole of the country. People had no idea what to do when confronted by the disease, and the plague had a huge effect upon England in all sorts of ways.

SOURCE B: a painting from the fourteenth century. It shows flagellants whipping themselves to prevent the Black Death.

SOURCE A: from a letter from King Edward III of England to the Lord Mayor of London, 1349.

To the Lord Mayor of London
An order: to cause the human waste and other filth lying in the streets and lanes in the city and its suburbs to be removed with all speed. Also to cause the city and suburbs to be kept clean, as it used to be in the time of the previous mayors. This is so that no greater cause of death may arise from such smells. The King has learned that the city and suburbs are so full with the filth from out of the houses by day and night that the air is infected and the city poisoned. This is a danger to men, especially by the contagious sickness which increases daily.

SOURCE C: an extract from a book by modern historians, published in 2008.

Most historians think that the Black Death was bubonic plague. It was carried by fleas that lived on black rats, but which could be passed on to other animal and human fleas. Once an infected flea bit a person, that person would become infected. They became very tired and developed black swellings (called buboes) in their groin and armpits. Sometimes these swellings were the size of an apple. Sometimes they burst, splattering stinking pus over the person's body. The illness lasted between five and ten days. Although it was possible to recover, most people who caught the Black Death died.

QUESTION

Using **all** the sources and your own knowledge, how far do you agree that attempts to stop the Black Death were ineffective?

6 King Richard III 1483–1485

Read the introduction and the sources and answer the question which follows:

Introduction

All the sources are about the disappearance of the Princes Edward and Richard, and whether their uncle, King Richard III, had them killed. Richard declared that the boys were illegitimate, so they could not inherit the throne. A group of nobles asked Richard to be king. His coronation was held on 6 July 1483. The princes were never seen again.

SOURCE A: a picture called 'The Princes in the Tower' painted by Theodore Hildebrant, a German painter, in the nineteenth century.

SOURCE B: an extract from *The History of King Richard III* written in 1513 by Thomas More. More was five years old when Richard came to the throne in 1483. He got most of his information from John Morton, who hated King Richard. Morton was one of the people who had invited Henry Tudor to invade England and become king in Richard's place.

After his coronation in July 1483, King Richard decided he must kill his nephews. This was because as long as they were alive, people would not think him the true king. He wrote to Sir Robert Brackenbury, the Constable of the Tower, asking him to put the children to death. Sir Robert refused. Then his page suggested Sir James Tyrell. Tyrell agreed, and Richard sent him to Brackenbury with a letter commanding Sir Robert to deliver up the keys of the Tower to Tyrell for one night. Tyrell decided that the Princes should be murdered in their beds the next night. He chose Miles Forest and John Dighton to do the job. Forest was one of the princes' guards and had murdered others. The two men pressed feather beds and pillows on the children's faces until they stopped breathing.

SOURCE C: an extract from a book by a modern historian, written in 1972.

I do not doubt for one moment that the Princes were alive when Henry VII came to London in August 1485. He issued a proclamation, giving all Richard's supposed crimes and this list did not include the killing of the Princes. That to my mind is definite proof that the Princes were not even missing. They must still have been in the Tower. Richard had no reason to kill them: Henry had every reason. If they lived, all he had fought for would be useless because Prince Edward had more right to be king than Henry Tudor.

QUESTION

Using **all** the sources and your own knowledge, how likely was it that King Richard III ordered the killing of the Princes in the Tower?

GLOSSARY

ABDICATE   Give up the throne

ACCOMPLICE   Someone who helps another person to commit a crime

ACQUIT   To release without charge, to clear an accusation

ACRE   A measure of land equivalent to approximately 4,047 square metres

ALDERMAN   A senior officer of a town council, next in importance to the mayor

ALLIES   People with whom you have a friendly relationship

AMBASSADOR   A person chosen to represent their government/kingdom diplomatically

APOTHECARY   A person who prepares and sells drugs and other medicinal cures

APPRENTICES   Young boys who spent years learning a trade such as that of a silversmith or cooper (someone who makes barrels)

ASUNDER   Separate or split into separate parts

BAILEY   A compound

BAPTISM   The ceremony by which people become part of the Christian Church, usually by being sprinkled with holy water

BURGESS   An important person in a town

CAVALRY   Troops who fight on horseback

CHANCELLOR   A royal official who had to deal with the day-to-day government of the country as well as act as the king's ambassador

CHRONICLER   Someone, usually a monk, who wrote down what he thought were the most important events. The accounts were called chronicles

CIVIL WAR   A war between citizens of the same country

CLERK   An official in a cathedral, church or chapel

CONCENTRIC   Of circles, sharing the same centre

CONSECRATED GROUND   Ground set apart by the Christian Church for holy purposes, such as the burial of the dead

CONTAGIOUS   Describes a disease that can be passed on by touch

CORRUPT   Using dishonest means to achieve power or financial advantage

COURTLY LOVE   A very formal type of behaviour at a royal court involving poems, songs, music, singing and dancing where men and women acted out the 'proper' ways of approaching each other

CRUSADE   A military expedition, often religious in nature

CURFEW   A time at which everyone has to be inside their house. It was signalled in medieval times by the ringing of a church bell

DAUPHIN   The eldest son of the King of France

DEMESNE   Anglo-French word for 'domain'

DETERRENT   Something to discourage an attack, a means of stopping something bad happening

DYSENTERY   Severe infection and inflammation of the intestines

ESTEEM   High regard

EXCOMMUNICATION   Banishment from the Church: the most serious punishment that any Pope could hand out

FAST   To go without food

FEMME SOLE   A legally independent woman, married or single, who had the right to trade on her own account

FENS   Wet marshlands in the east of England. They have now been drained but in the eleventh century you needed a boat and local knowledge to get around

FEUDAL   Relating to the social system whereby poorer people held land belonging to a richer person in exchange for allegiance and service

FLAX   Plant from which linen is made

FURLONG   A furlong measures about 220 yards (just over 200 metres)

GAOL   Jail, a prison

HABIT   The garment a monk or nun wears

HARRYING   The act of raiding or attacking

HIDE   A measure of land area

HIERARCHY   A society with clear social ranks

HOMAGE   Honour and allegiance shown to a lord/king

HOUSECARL   A member of the king's bodyguard

JUSTICIAR   One of the most important officials at court in the Middle Ages. He looked after all of the king's business

KEEP   A strong and central tower of a castle

KINSMAN   A person related by blood or marriage, a relation

LEGITIMATE   Means 'legal'. A king's legitimate children were his children by the woman he was married to

LOLLARD   The name 'Lollard' comes from the middle Dutch word 'lollaerd' which means 'mumbler'

MAGNA CARTA   Translated into English means Great Charter

MARK   A weight of gold or silver equal to 8 ounces or 226.8 grams

MARTYR   A person who dies for their cause

MEDITATE   To think deeply and quietly about something

MEN-AT-ARMS   Servants who are also bodyguards

MONARCH   A king or queen who rules a country

MOTTE   A mound or hill

NOBLES   People of high rank in society

OATH   A formal promise, often sacred in nature

OUTLAW   Someone who has broken the law but is still free (has not been caught and punished)

OVERLORD   A powerful feudal ruler

PARISH   Part of a diocese that has its own church and priest to whom tithes were paid

PATRONAGE   Giving support or protection to someone, usually by putting them into positions of influence

PENANCE   Self-punishment for doing something wrong

PHARMACY   The place where an apothecary works

PHYSICIAN   Doctor

PILGRIM   A person who makes a journey to a holy place

PILLORY   Also known as stocks, these were wooden frames into which the feet and/or hands of criminals were locked

PLAGUE   An infectious or contagious disease that spreads rapidly over a large area and has a huge death toll

PLANTAIN   A type of plant

POITEVINS   People from Poitou in west central France

PROPAGANDA   The spreading of selected information and rumour in order to support a particular idea or viewpoint

PROPHET   Someone who is given special insight by God so can explain what God wants people to do

PROTECTOR   Someone who rules for a monarch when he/she is too young to rule by him/herself

RETINUE   People in the service of an important person who usually accompanied that person on his or her travels

SECULAR   In medieval times, it meant not attached to an abbey. Now it means non-religious

SEDITION   Activity or speech encouraging people to rebel

SHERIFF   A person responsible for keeping law and order in each county

STONEMASON   Someone who carries or carves stones

SUCCESSION   The process by which the Crown passes from one person to the next

TEMPORAL   This means here and now or of the time

TITHES   A system whereby a tenth of what everyone produced – barley, hay, flour, eggs, for example – had to be given to the Church

TRANSUBSTANTIATION   The belief that the bread and wine used in communion services turn into the body and blood of Jesus

TROUBADORS   Travelling players

TRUCE   An agreement to stop hostilities or fighting temporarily

USURP   To take power illegally or unlawfully seize another person's position of authority

VILLEIN   A peasant who was entirely subject to his lord and kept on the lord's manor

VIRULENT   Of exceptional severity

Photo credits

p.2 *t* © Dea Picture Library/Getty Images, *c* © The British Library Board (MS Yates Thompson 11 f.6v), *b* © The British Library Board (MS Add. 42130 f.171); **p.8** © The British Library Board (MS Royal 2 A. XXII f.219v); **p.9** © The British Library Board (MS Royal 14 C. VII f.8v); **p.12** The Body of Edward the Confessor (c.1003–66) is carried to the Church of St. Peter the Apostle, detail from the Bayeux Tapestry, before 1082 (wool embroidery on linen), French School, (11th century)/Musee de la Tapisserie, Bayeux, France/With special authorisation of the city of Bayeux/The Bridgeman Art Library; **p.13** © The Art Archive/Alamy; **p.16** *l* © The Art Archive/Alamy, *r* © The Art Gallery Collection/Alamy; **p.20** *t* © Image Asset Management Ltd./Alamy, *b* © French School/The Bridgeman Art Library/Getty Images; **p.22** © Dmitry Naumov/iStock/Thinkstock; **p.28** © Hulton Archive/Getty Images; **p.30** © Michael Freeman/Corbis; **p.33** © The British Library Board (MS Royal 20 A. II f.6v); **p.35** *l* © National Portrait Gallery, London (NPG 4980-3), *r* © The British Library Board (MS Cotton Nero D. VII f.7); **p.37** *t* © British Library/HIP/TopFoto, *b* © Anthony Baggett/iStock/Thinkstock; **p.41** © British Library Board/Robana/TopFoto; **p.43** Signing of the Magna Carta, 1215, Sims, Charles (1873–1928)/Houses of Parliament, Westminster, London, UK/The Bridgeman Art Library; **p.44** © The British Library Board (MS Royal 14 C. VII f.9); **p.47** *t* © The British Library Board (MS Royal 14 C. VII f.9), *b* © The British Library Board (MS Cotton Claudius D. VI f.9v); **p.48** © Chapter of York: Reproduced by kind permission; **p.52** *t* © 2005 TopFoto/Houghton, *b* © DeAgostini/SuperStock; **p.54** © Jupiterimages/Thinkstock; **p.55** © The Photolibrary Wales/Alamy; **p.56** © bpk/Kupferstichkabinett, SMB/Jörg P. Anders; **p.57** © Crown copyright (2014) Visit Wales (Painting by Ivan Lapper); **p.60** *t* © Mary Evans Picture Library/Alamy, *b* © 2004 Woodmansterne/TopFoto; **p.61** © The Granger Collection, NYC/TopFoto; **p.62** © Dea Picture Library/Getty Images; **p.68** © The British Library Board (MS Royal 18 E. I f.165v); **p.69** © The British Library Board (MS Royal 18 E. I f.172); **p.72** © Everett Collection/Rex Features; **p.75** © The Granger Collection, NYC/TopFoto; **p.76** © 2004 Woodmansterne/TopFoto; **p.77** © The British Library Board (MS Royal 20 E. VI f.9v); **p.80** Richard III (1452–85) (oil on panel), English School, (16th century)/Society of Antiquaries of London, UK/The Bridgeman Art Library; **p.82** © Commission Air/Alamy; **p.86** © Sonia Halliday Photographs; **p.88** © 2004 TopFoto; **p.97** © 2004 TopFoto; **p.98** © Fyle – Fotolia; **p.100** © 2004 Woodmansterne/TopFoto; **p.103** © The British Library Board (MS Harley 5102 f.32); **p.109** *l* © The British Library Board (MS Cotton Domitian A. XVII f.122v), *r* © The British Library Board (MS Cotton Domitian A. XVII f.177v); **p.112** *l* © The British Library Board (MS Yates Thompson 11 f.6v), *tr* © British Library Board/Robana/TopFoto, *cr* © 2000 Topham Picturepoint/TopFoto, *br* © The Bodleian Library, University of Oxford (MS Bodley 264 f.22r); **p.115** © English Heritage/Mary Evans Picture Library (drawing by Alan Sorrell); **p.118** *l* © Universal History Archive/Getty Images, *r* Patients and nuns at the Hospital of Hotel Dieu in Paris, from 'Le Livre de Vie Active de l'Hotel Dieu' by Jean Henry, c.1482 (vellum), French School, (15th century)/Musee de l'Assistance Publique, Hopitaux de Paris, France/Archives Charmet/The Bridgeman Art Library; **p.119** © The British Library Board (MS Sloane 2435 f.44v); **p.120** © The Travel Library/Rex Features; **p.122** © Sonia Halliday Photographs/Alamy; **p.125** *t & b* © The British Library Board (Royal 2 B. VII, f.303); **p.126** © Sonia Halliday Photographs/Alamy; **p.127** © akg-images; **p.129** © The British Library Board (MS Royal 2 A. XXII f.220); **p.130** Ms 828 f.33r Siege of Antioch, from the Estoire d'Outremer (vellum), William of Tyre (c.1130–85)/Bibliotheque Municipale de Lyon, France/The Bridgeman Art Library; **p.131** © Bridgeman Art Library, London/SuperStock; **p.138** *l & r* © Image Asset Management Ltd./Alamy; **p.141** © 2000 Topham Picturepoint/TopFoto; **p.147** © Alinari via Getty Images; **p.153** By permission of the Syndics of Cambridge University Library (MS Ee.3.59 f.21v); **p.154** *t* © Wellcome Library, London, *b* Ms Lat 11229 fol.19r Table for urine analysis, from ‹Petit Traite d›hygiene et Medecine› (vellum), French School, (13th century)/Bibliotheque Nationale, Paris, France/Archives Charmet/The Bridgeman Art Library; **p.156** © The British Library Board (MS Sloane 1975 f.93); **p.157** *tl* © British Library/Robana/Rex Features, *tc* © Wellcome Library, London. Wellcome Images, *tr* © The British Library Board (MS Sloane 1975 f.93), *b* © The British Library Board (MS Royal 6 E. VI f.301); **p.159** © Heritage Image Partnership Ltd /Alamy; **p.164** © Leemage/UIG via Getty Images; **p.166** © The Art Gallery Collection/Alamy; **p.171** *tl* © The British Library Board (MS Add. 42130 f.166v), *tr* © The British Library Board (MS Add. 47682 f.31), *bl* © The British Library Board (MS Add. 42130 f.172v), *br* © The British Library Board (MS Add. 42130 f.158); **p.180** © The Art Archive/Alamy; **p.181** © De Agostini/The British Library Board (MS Egerton 1500 f.45v); **p.182** f.2v Thomas a Becket departs from King Henry II of England and Louis VII of France, following the breakdown of negotiations at Montmirail and joins the common people, from the Becket Leaves, c.1220–40 (vellum), English School, (13th century)/British Library, London, UK/The Bridgeman Art Library; **p.183** © British Library Board/Robana/TopFoto; **p.184** © Henry Guttmann/Getty Images); **p.185** © bpk/Rainer Maria Schopp.

Answers to tasks

p.112
Source 5 – nuns attending mass with priests; Source 6 – a novice monk having a tonsure cut; Source 7 – a friar preaching in the open air; Source 8 – drunken nuns being taken home in a cart.

p.157
Source 11 – a doctor bleeding a patient; Source 12 – men consult the stars (astrology) while women attend to the practicalities of childbirth; Source 13 – a surgeon performing an eye operation; Source 14 – monks suffering from the plague are blessed by a priest.